LINCOLN CHRISTIAN COLLEGE AND SEMINARY

P9-DDW-425

NEW DAY BEGUN

THE PUBLIC INFLUENCES

OF AFRICAN AMERICAN CHURCHES,

VOLUME I

NEW DAY BEGUN

AFRICAN AMERICAN CHURCHES

AND CIVIC CULTURE IN

POST-CIVIL RIGHTS

AMERICA

EDITED BY R. DREW SMITH

DUKE UNIVERSITY PRESS

Durham and London

2003

© 2003 *Duke University Press*

All rights reserved

Printed in the United States of America on

acid-free paper ∞ Designed by Amy Ruth Buchanan

Typeset in Minion by Tseng Information Systems, Inc.

Library of Congress Cataloging-in-Publication Data

appear on the last printed page of this book.

An earlier version of chapter 6 was published

in *Women and Politics* 20 (3) 1999.

A PROJECT OF THE LEADERSHIP CENTER

AT MOREHOUSE COLLEGE. FUNDED BY

THE PEW CHARITABLE TRUSTS.

Facing the rising sun of our new day begun,
Let us march on till victory is won.

JAMES WELDON JOHNSON
"Lift Every Voice and Sing"

1737*

108199

CONTENTS

PREFACE

This volume is the first of two volumes to be published by Duke University Press featuring research developed as part of The Public Influences of African-American Churches Project (PIAAC). The aim of this research initiative, which is based at the Leadership Center at Morehouse College, is to examine the relationship of African American churches to American political life since the civil rights movement. The focus on the period after the civil rights movement is recognition of the fact that American politics in general, and African American politics in particular, have changed dramatically since the 1960s. This point will be made in a number of ways by chapters in the two volumes.

Moreover, the focus here on the latter-twentieth century context of black politics, and of black church involvement in politics, acknowledges not only new configurations of the political landscape but a troubling lack of research on recent black church involvements within that context. Although there is a substantial body of scholarship on black church activism during the civil rights movement, scholarly publications on contemporary political involvements by black churches have been limited, with only a few exceptions, to an occasional journal article or chapter. Consequently, a primary objective of the PIAAC Project has been to increase scholarly research in this subject area—working specifically with thirty scholars over a three-year period toward the development of a new generation of scholarship on black church public involvements. The volumes contain chapters contributed by many of these scholars.

The first volume focuses on relationships between ecclesiastical and civic culture and, specifically, on ways that black churches draw on civil religious ideas, black nationalist concerns, and community and economic development objectives. Chapters in this first volume also explore ways that the political dispositions of black churches are shaped by theological, gender, and other cultural considerations. The second volume analyzes black church activism on national public policy issues such as affirmative action, health

care, welfare reform, and public education. The volumes also provide analysis of data from 1,956 black churches surveyed by the PIAAC Project. The
churches surveyed were located in nineteen major cities across the country
and in twenty-six small rural counties in the South. Almost 90 percent of
the respondents were pastors. The vast majority of the churches were urban.
(Please see Appendix for detailed information about the sampling procedure
and database characteristics.)

The hope is that our interdisciplinary focus on black churches and politics
since the 1960s will fill in a few of the historical and analytical gaps within the
scholarship on this topic. To the extent that the volumes achieve those ends,
there are many who helped to make that possible. I extend thanks to each of
the project scholars I had the good fortune to work with during this project.
I am also grateful to the numerous church leaders across the country who
participated in our national survey and in interviews and discussions with
researchers connected with this project. I am extremely appreciative of The
Pew Charitable Trusts' commitments to research on religion and American
public life, and certainly appreciative of their generous funding of our three-
year project. Thanks go out, in particular, to Luis Lugo, who invited me to
develop a national project on black churches and public life, and to Kimon
Sargeant, who has been supportive of this project in numerous ways. I am
indebted to Raphael Allen at Duke University Press and to the manuscript
review team for their many helpful suggestions about ways to strengthen
the organization of the volumes and arguments within individual chapters.
I cannot offer enough thanks to my colleagues at the Leadership Center at
Morehouse College—especially Walter Fluker, whose vision and trust have
facilitated countless opportunities for ministerial and professional collaboration between the two of us, and Alexis Simmons, who has worked tirelessly
to insure the success of the Public Influences Project. Also, to Belinda White,
Sharon Hall-Jones, and Marci Stiger, your efforts on behalf of the project were
greatly appreciated. I am thankful, as well, for the important contributions
our data team made to this project, especially Mark and Robin Nichols at
Spectrum Data Link and our lead survey research assistant, Jerriline Smith.
Finally, to Angelique Walker-Smith, I will be forever grateful for your coun-
sel, commitment, and partnership throughout this process.

R. Drew Smith, Director
The Public Influences of African American Churches Project

INTRODUCTION

BLACK CHURCHES WITHIN A CHANGING

CIVIC CULTURE IN AMERICA

R. Drew Smith

In their widely read analysis of civic life within modern democracies, Gabriel Almond and Sidney Verba focus attention on the significance of a society's *political culture*—by which they mean "the political system as internalized in the cognitions, feelings, and evaluations of its population."[1] Like much analysis of democratic systems, the study by Almond and Verba makes clear that the vitality of democracy has as much to do with how the populace is disposed toward the political system as it does with the formal structures and mechanisms of the system itself. If the populace does not share an emphasis, for example, on "a pluralistic culture based on communication and persuasion," say Almond and Verba, democratic governance is jeopardized within that society.[2]

At the time Almond and Verba were writing these words (the early 1960s), a significant portion of the American population was supporting racial discrimination as a matter of law and practice. What was required to change this patently nondemocratic feature of the world's largest democracy was a democratic reform movement emanating from an unlikely standard-bearer of democratic ideals—namely, African American churches. And at least with respect to an emphasis on civil rights, this vanguard of activist black churches embodied a political culture more consistent with democracy than many within the American context. But as significant as the commitment to civil rights by African American churches has been, the political culture within African American churches has had many sides—some of which have enhanced the broader democratic culture, and some of which have not.

The impact that churches and other civil society institutions have had on American political culture has been a matter of ongoing debate. Noticeable

attention has been paid recently to the cultural aspects of democratic governance and the civil society sector, partly in response to the writings of political scientist Robert Putnam. Putnam points out that while "the performance
of government and other social institutions is powerfully influenced by citizen engagement in community affairs," the dilemma within the American
context (and elsewhere) is that citizen participation in activities such as voting and civic organizational life has declined, along with the "social trust"
that is a "strong correlate" of civic engagement.[3] According to Putnam, this
"social trust" and willingness by citizens to participate alongside others in
the social process is the "social capital" on which a healthy democracy, and
the fulfillment of the respective political interests of groups of citizens, depends. Putnam, and political analysts who share his concerns, place many of
their democratic hopes on the existence of a strong civil society sector that
will "enable participants to act together more effectively to pursue shared
objectives."[4]

Civil society institutions are commonly discussed as a "third sector," or
as "mediating structures or networks" where citizens are provided with a
terrain independent from governmental and business sectors for negotiat-
ing political and economic life.[5] By privileging the role of this "third sector,"
however, Putnam, and others, run into difficulty with critics who believe that
the role of the governmental sector should not be minimized as a facilitator of citizens' political objectives or the society's broader democratic ideals.
Marion Orr points out, for example, that the "danger of accepting Putnam's
model of social capital as a guide to making policy is that government—and
government officials whose decisions help cause anomie and social disinte-
gration—is let off the hook."[6] Moreover, the usefulness to African American
communities of Putnam's emphasis on civil society institutions is not entirely obvious given that, historically, this "third sector" has been the sector
of first resort for African Americans—due largely to constricted black access
to governmental and business sectors.

Not only has the importance of civil society institutions within African
American social life been well established but concerns have been voiced
about the possibility that African Americans may rely too heavily on these
institutions—and especially on voluntary and religious organizations. In his
1944 publication *An American Dilemma,* Gunnar Myrdal comments on what
he considers to be a disproportionately large number of voluntary associa-

tions in African American communities. He views their numerousness as evidence of a "pathological" social situation, in that "the great number of Negro voluntary associations . . . accomplish so little in comparison to what their members set out to achieve by means of them."[7] Others too have questioned (though in less condescending ways than Myrdal) black political approaches that have assigned a strategic priority to the civil society sector. For example, Preston Smith argues that, since the 1970s, responses to black social concerns have been increasingly influenced by an emphasis on "private over public action, on voluntarism over politics, [and] on decentralization over public investment."[8] One of the ways that this has manifested itself, says Smith (particularly in the political strategizing of conservative leaders and policy-makers), has been to "[divest] the public of its authority in order to transfer authority to traditional private sources within the black community."[9] Whether African Americans have relied too heavily, or not heavily enough, on the civil society sector, or the governmental sector, will continue to be debated. What is made clear by persons on both sides, however, is that black civil society is institutionally and culturally robust — and that black churches are a conspicuous presence within black civil society.

The Context of Black Church Civic Activism:
Shifts and Constants

The civic involvements of African American churches have generally reflected the contextual limitations and opportunities operative within their specific historical settings. With the enactment of the 1964 Civil Rights Act and the 1965 Voting Rights Act, a significantly different context of black church civic involvement emerged, characterized by, among other things, unprecedented black access to the mechanisms and structures of American politics and a heightened sense of empowerment and allegiance to procedural politics within black communities. Evidence of this historical shift is that the prevailing tactical paradigm within black politics in 1965 was direct-action protest and just over one hundred African Americans held elective offices; whereas, by the year 2000, there were more than 8,000 black elected officials and protest-oriented black activism had largely receded into the background.

Black churches have impacted and have been impacted by this reconfiguration of black politics. Their impact has been felt, primarily, in their logistical and voting support for black political candidates, including a number of black clergy who have been candidates for political office. With respect to the latter, six black clergy have been elected to the U.S. Congress since 1970 and a much larger number have been elected to state and local offices.[10] Also, during this period at least five black clergy have run unsuccessfully for congressional seats and two black clergy have run for President — including Jesse Jackson, whose 1984 and 1988 presidential campaigns drew particular attention to the voting clout of black churches.[11] Black churches were viewed as having played a significant part, for example, in successful black voter registration efforts prior to the 1984 elections and in the large 1984 black voter turnout, which exceeded the 1980 election turnout by two million. One analyst remarked that not only were churches internally organized to the point of functioning as precincts but "evidence of the church base of this infusion [of voters was that] the increase was particularly notable among women."[12]

The electoral potential of black churches has been drawn on heavily by Democratic candidates in most elections throughout the 1990s and during the 2000 presidential elections. Organizations such as the NAACP, the Southern Christian Leadership Conference, and even the Democratic National Committee have collaborated closely with black churches on voter mobilization efforts, particularly in the South and in targeted cities and states. These collaborations were viewed as responsible for substantial increases in black voter turnout throughout the 1990s in states such as Michigan and Georgia and in specific cities such as New York, Philadelphia, and Atlanta.[13] During the presidential elections in 2000, similar collaborations involving black churches were credited with producing record black voter turnouts in Florida and in Pennsylvania.[14]

Despite the instrumental value of black churches to black electoral progress, the religious content black churches contributed to civil rights movement politics has been less welcomed within post–civil rights movement politics. As Adolph Reed Jr. points out, this has been due in part to an increased black political emphasis on democratic proceduralism rather than on a politics of resistance and moral defiance, and an increased political emphasis on black elected officials rather than on black clergy as public spokespersons.[15] Reed argues that both of these preferences stem, on one level, from a "territorial defensiveness" on the part of black political officeholders.[16] However, the resistance to clergy political leadership may also be connected to the "classic liberal" underpinnings of American life—liberal underpinnings that have potentially influenced black political elites as much as other American political elites. Classic liberalism pertains to ideas tracing back to James Madison and Thomas Jefferson in the U.S. context that stress, among other things, equal rights, individual liberties, and protection of individuals from "intrusions by government or other groups"—such as religious groups.[17] With black liberal commitments to equal rights having finally gained legal reinforcement through successful civil rights movement activism, black political leaders could more confidently pursue other liberal instincts, including American liberalism's historical conviction that the nation's formal political affairs should be guided by secular reasoning and not by religious reasoning. Stephen Carter addresses the enduring liberal wariness of religious influences on American public life, pointing out that contemporary liberals persistently focus on ways to reiterate the unacceptability of religion-based moral logic as part of the formal public conversation. He also discusses the dilemma that this attitude toward religion created for liberals during the civil rights movement—given that the movement was overtly religious, on the one hand, but dedicated to achieving liberal goals of equal rights, on the other hand.[18] Carter's argument focuses on American liberalism, in general, but the argument undoubtedly applies as well to black liberals as a subset of American liberalism—notwithstanding higher levels of religiosity among blacks than among other Americans.[19]

With a secular black politics rapidly consolidating during the 1970s, the religious dimension (though thought to be reined in politically) was reasserted, with its substance and spokespersons emanating from multiple religious directions. First the Nation of Islam, a group with a discernible impact on black social life during the 1960s, was revived in the mid-1970s under the leadership of Louis Farrakhan. Although the Nation of Islam has generally maintained a separatist approach to American political life, Farrakhan established himself as an outspoken public critic of various policies and practices impacting African Americans. As Farrakhan was energizing his share of religiously oriented, grassroots supporters, Jesse Jackson was also building a public presence, and a support base particularly among black churchpersons, that propelled him toward his 1984 and 1988 presidential candidacies. Jackson's candidacies (which represented for many a kind of protest politics by different means) provided an important catalyst, not only for reestablishing mass activism on the part of conventional black Christians but also for bridging countercultural religious groups such as the Nation of Islam into more concrete involvements within the formal political arena. For example, Farrakhan mobilized Nation of Islam members around Jackson's 1984 campaign—even deploying a number of members to serve as Jackson's security detail during the early part of the campaign. Moreover, during the late 1980s and early 1990s, a number of Nation of Islam members ran for various electoral offices—encouraged no doubt by the protest connotations of Jackson's candidacies.

By the 1990s, a black religious influence on political life was being felt from a much different direction. Black Pentecostal and Charismatic churches, operating parallel to and sometimes in conjunction with a burgeoning white evangelical political mobilization, began to affirm the need for their own participation in politics as a way of advancing their theological and moral imperatives. By defining the problem as essentially one of a religious decentering of American public life, the issue for a number of black Pentecostal and Charismatic activists became the need for greater attention to the "faith factor" in responding to individual and aggregate social conditions. These black religious leaders became increasingly convinced that the "faith factor" was crucial to: (1) redeeming the educational prospects of inner-city youth; (2) rebuilding economically distressed neighborhoods; and (3) responding to the social service needs of people at the social margins.

These were not entirely new propositions within the context of African American church life. After all, social service and community development collaborations between black churches and government dated back to at least Reconstruction—expanding significantly during the late 1960s and early 1970s with the enlargement of federal antipoverty monies. But what differentiated these black Pentecostal and Charismatic initiatives from previous black church social activism was that the Pentecostal and Charismatic initiatives were aligned with broader political efforts to hold the government less accountable, rather than more, for social support for disadvantaged populations. Those promoting this approach have tended to argue that the nongovernmental sector rather than the governmental sector is better positioned to facilitate the social empowerment of disadvantaged populations because: (1) the remaining obstacles to social progress among disadvantaged populations are more attitudinal than structural and are remedied by normative adjustments rather than by public policy;[20] and (2) nongovernmental organizations, and especially churches, have more direct interaction with and, therefore, impact on disadvantaged populations.[21]

These perspectives gained support by the mid-1990s from legislative initiatives designed to expand the use of religious organizations as conduits for government social service monies — the Charitable Choice provision of the Personal Responsibility and Work Opportunity Act of 1996 and President George W. Bush's faith-based initiative. These legislative initiatives have provoked concerns, however, among some religious and governmental leaders, who have expressed concerns about: (1) potential religious infringements on politics and political infringements on religion; and (2) underlying declines in governmental antipoverty allocations accompanying these initiatives. Nevertheless, the combined effect of assertive promotion of these initiatives by government officials sympathetic to governmental collaborations with faith groups, and governmental readiness for trying new approaches to intractable social problems, has created attractive political opportunities for segments of black religious leaders that were heretofore largely inactive politically. Representative J. C. Watts (R-Oklahoma), who is also an ordained clergyman, has been one of the leading governmental proponents of these initiatives, and a number of prominent clergy within the Church of God in Christ (the largest black Pentecostal denomination) and within the National Center for Faith-Based Initiative (a consortium of Charismatic and Pentecostal church bodies) have been on the inside of discussions about the implementation of these policies.[22]

One objective of the present volume is to assess the contextual factors — both ecclesiastical and social — that have helped to shape black church responses to American civic life. The first section of the volume pursues this objective, exploring context in the sense of both the institutional parameters of black churches and in the sense of the broader social setting in which these institutions operate. The section opens with a chapter by Lewis Baldwin that lifts up historical antecedents of contemporary black church civic activism. Beginning with the abolitionist period and ending with the civil rights movement, Baldwin examines religious and social motives of this activism from one period to another, tying the earlier activism at points to some of the recent activism discussed in various chapters within the volume. Allison Calhoun-Brown also looks historically at black church activism but focuses on the relationship between socialization factors internal to churches (e.g., the development of certain "civic skills") and the positioning of black churches as civic actors within American society. In chapter 3, Corwin Smidt and I examine connections between black church civic activism and specific congregational characteristics including size, income, and the pastor's educational level, noting the relationship between congregational capacity and congregational willingness to navigate the contemporary political arena.

The second section of the volume explores theological and social assessments of the American political and ecclesiastical context. David Howard-Pitney's chapter on black civil religion utilizes a framework of "theistic, progressive, and prophetic" in interpreting the way contemporary religious leaders such as Jesse Jackson and Alan Keyes attach significance to American politics and to participation by themselves and others in those politics. The close relationship between theological and civic concerns within American civil religion generally raises nettlesome questions about the trade-offs between these two dimensions. Howard-Pitney explores quite a few such questions relating to the extent to which black churches intermingle theological and civic ideas, the reasons why they do so, and with what results. Walter Fluker's chapter on civility pursues a number of these questions as well. He delineates black church "traditions of civility" — based as they are on "allegiance to democratic idealism" — and shows the connections between these traditions and African American pursuits of "recognition, respectability, and loyalty."

The next three chapters in this section explore priorities and claims of constituencies that have not necessarily been central to the social agenda of activist black churches. Allison Calhoun-Brown's chapter outlines womanist and feminist critiques of black church responsiveness to women's rights and explores these critiques in light of survey data on black church practices. She specifically uses the survey data to examine the correlation between key measurements of black church activism (such as frequency of political discussion within worship services) and the promotion of issues related to gender equity. David Daniels focuses on black Holiness and Pentecostal activists and on the subtle connections between their theological emphasis on social justice and divine agency and their political emphasis on race and poverty issues. Daniels's chapter raises a distinction that receives fuller coverage in the chapter by C. R. D. Halisi—the contrast between liberal and black nationalist political orientations. Halisi examines black nationalist instincts within African American life dating back to the 1800s (particularly the importance assigned to collective political identity and to group independence), noting conjunctions between these principles in the activism of various contemporary black church activists. The chapters by Daniels and Halisi also draw attention to theological currents within black churches that often run counter to the more mainstream theological (and social) orientations stressed in the chapters by Howard-Pitney and Fluker.

The final section of the volume assesses economic development and social service collaborations between black churches, government, and other community sectors. Michael Owens's chapter outlines factors in recent years that have encouraged the creation of a growing number of church-based community economic development corporations and of broader economic development collaborations involving black churches. While Owens sees promise in many of these economic development collaborations, David Ryden and Samuel Roberts identify certain perils in black church social service collaborations with the government. Ryden cautions against these collaborations primarily in light of "constitutional constraints" on interactions between the government and religious groups, while Roberts raises theological concerns about the potential loss of church autonomy and of the church's critical voice.

In providing these accounts of black church political involvement, the Public Influences of African-American Churches Project (of which this volume is a part) has encouraged interdisciplinary analysis and a reliance on evidence drawn as directly as possible from black churches. The interdisciplinary emphasis was intended to insure that the analysis benefited from insights brought by disciplines that understand political life well and by disciplines that understand religious life well. In order to bring these various perspectives into dialogue with one another, seminars and conferences were convened between the religionists, theologians, and social scientists who were contributors to the Project volumes. In writing their chapters, many of the contributors drew on evidence from direct observations and from interviews with black religious leaders.

Another source of direct evidence generated within the Project (and highlighted in chapter 3 of this volume) was the 1999–2000 Black Churches and Politics Survey, which yielded survey data from 1,956 black church leaders across the country. The survey was conducted in nineteen metropolitan areas and in twenty-six predominantly black rural counties in the Southeast. The respondents were representative of the denominational distribution of African American churches (with the majority coming from the historically black Baptist conventions and the rest from black Methodist denominations, black Pentecostal denominations, and predominantly white denominations). Eighty-one percent of the respondents were pastors and the rest were mostly associate or assistant pastors. (See the appendix for further details about the survey characteristics and methodology.)

Nevertheless, for all the insights into the public involvements of black churches that we hope this volume (and this Project) provides, we are also aware of some of the limitations of the research. For example, critical issues that were not covered here (despite efforts to insure such coverage) include: (1) black church responses to politically disaffected youth; (2) black church facilitation of civic leadership among church-based youth; and (3) civic agency among black Christian women as expressed through church-related and non-church-related structures and organizations. These issues come immediately to mind, and there are others, no doubt, that deserve systematic, interdisciplinary research and analysis. We hope that our undertaking encourages further research on issues covered here and on those that were not covered, and that it stimulates interest in further analysis of the BCAP survey database.

Notes

1   Gabriel Almond and Sidney Verba, *The Civic Culture: Political Attitudes and Democracy in Five Nations* (Boston: Little, Brown, 1965), 13.

2   Ibid., 6.

3   Robert Putnam, "Tuning In, Tuning Out: The Strange Disappearance of Social Capital in America," *PS: Political Science and Politics* (December): 664–65.

4   Ibid., 665.

5   E. J. Dionne, ed., *Community Works: The Revival of Civil Society in America* (Washington, D.C.: Brookings Institution, 1998), 3.

6   Marion Orr, *Black Social Capital: The Politics of School Reform in Baltimore, 1986–1998* (Lawrence: University Press of Kansas, 1999), 6

7   Gunnar Myrdal, *An American Dilemma: The Negro Problem and Modern Democracy* (New York: Public Affairs Committee, Inc., 1944), 953

8   Preston Smith, " 'Self-Help,' Black Conservatives, and the Reemergence of Black Pri-
vatism," in Adolph Reed Jr., ed., *Without Justice for All: The New Liberalism and Our
Retreat from Racial Equality* (Boulder: Westview Press, 1999), 288.

9   Ibid., 282.

10 The six black clergymen who have served in the U.S. Congress since 1965 are: Walter Fauntroy, Andrew Young, William Gray III, Floyd Flake, John Lewis, and J. C.
Watts. For additional information on black clergy who have served in state and
local offices see R. Drew Smith, "Black Clergy, Electoral Participation, and Interest
Representation," *Humanity and Society* 18, no. 4 (November 1994): 35–46.

11 The five black clergy who ran unsuccessfully for Congress were Nicholas Hood III
from Detroit, Michigan (1980); Arthur Jones from Newark, New Jersey (1984);
Hosea Williams from Atlanta, Georgia (1984); Maurice Dawkins from Arlington,
Virginia (1988); and Al Sharpton from Brooklyn, New York (1992). With respect to
presidential races, a New York clergyman named Frederick Douglass Kirkpatrick
was the National Black Political Assembly's presidential candidate in the 1976 election and Jesse Jackson ran very substantial presidential campaigns in 1984 and 1988.

12 Allen Hertzke, *Echoes of Discontent: Jesse Jackson, Pat Robertson, and the Resurgence
of Populism* (Washington, D.C.: Congressional Quarterly Press, 1993), 129, 174.

13 See David Firestone, "Drive Under Way to Raise Turnout of Black Voters," *New York
Times,* 29 October 2000, www.nytimes.com; and Larry Elowitz, "An Analysis of the
1998 Midterm Elections" (paper on file with author).

14 See Chase Squires, "GOP Governors Put on a Brave Face," *St. Petersburg Times*
(18 November 2000), www.sptimes.com; and John M. R. Bull and James O'Toole,
"Success Surprised GOP in Philadelphia's Once Republican Suburbs," *Pittsburgh
Post-Gazette,* 9 November 2000, www.post-gazette.com.

15 Adolph Reed Jr., *The Jesse Jackson Phenomenon: The Crisis of Purpose in Afro-
American Politics* (New Haven: Yale University Press, 1986), 43.

16 Ibid., 67.

17 See James P. Young, *Reconsidering American Liberalism: The Troubled Odyssey of the
Liberal Idea* (Boulder: Westview Press, 1996), 6.

18 Stephen Carter, *The Culture of Disbelief: How American Law and Politics Trivialize
Religious Devotion* (New York: Anchor Books, 1993), 227–29.

19 Carter cites Gallup polling data in making the case about black religiosity. Ibid., 60.

20 These arguments gained a certain prominence with the 1965 publication of Daniel
Patrick Moynihan's *The Negro Family: The Case for National Action* (Washington,
D.C.: Department of Labor). Similar treatments of these themes have come from
Charles Murray in *Losing Ground: American Social Policy, 1950–1980* (New York:
Basic Books, 1984); and, within the African American community, from scholars
such as Shelby Steele in *The Content of Our Character: A New Vision of Race in
America* (New York: St. Martin's Press, 1990).

21 See, for example, Glenn C. Loury, "A Prescription for Black Progress," *Christian Century* (30 April 1986): 434–38; and Glenn C. Loury and Linda Datcher Loury, "Not by Bread Alone: The Role of the African-American Church in Inner-City Development," *Brookings Review* (winter 1997): 10–13.

22 See, e.g., John Leland, "Some Black Pastors See New Aid Under Bush," *New York Times,* 2 February 2001; and Elizabeth Becker, "Republicans Hold Forum With Blacks in Clergy," *New York Times,* 26 April 2001. Black clergy who have been at the center of these discussions have included Bishop Charles Blake, Reverend Eugene Rivers, Bishop Harold Ray, and Bishop Carlton Pearson.

PART I

Institutional Characteristics, Historical Contexts,

and Black Church Civic Involvements

1

REVISITING THE "ALL-COMPREHENDING INSTITUTION":

HISTORICAL REFLECTIONS ON THE PUBLIC

ROLES OF BLACK CHURCHES

Lewis Baldwin

Commentary concerning the involvement of the black church in public affairs and public policy issues reflects a range of tendencies. Some hold that
the black church has always majored in an otherworldly outlook and compensatory hope, thus relegating public service and social welfare to either
secondary status or no place at all.[1] Others downplay the otherworldly-
compensatory model, contending instead that the black church has always
embraced a reformist-activist ethic aimed at the transformation of society
and culture in the *here and now*.[2] Still others point to the dual function of the
black church, noting that that institution, throughout its history, has combined an emphasis on the rewards of heaven with an active participation in
temporal affairs.[3] This keen sense of the interrelationship between worldly
and other-otherworldly concerns provides the best avenue for understanding both the nature and the extent of black church involvement in American
public life.

This essay uses functional analysis to determine the various ways in which
the church and religion have traditionally served the individual and collective needs of African Americans. Drawing on Carter G. Woodson's image
of the black church as "all-comprehending institution," the general contention is that there has always been a tradition in the black church that encourages faith-based social action, social service, and involvement in public
policy issues. This tradition is rooted in a social gospel that upholds Christianity's historic concern for the poor and oppressed and that encourages the
involvement of the church in virtually every aspect of African American life.

A century before black churches originated and assumed various institutional forms, Africans in the American colonies approached their struggle for freedom and justice as a pressing moral and public policy issue. In 1661 an African petitioned the governmental authorities in the colony of New Netherlands (later New York) for freedom, suggesting that there was no necessary disjunction between being Christian and appealing to the political realm in the interest of the common good. Similar petitions were presented to the colonial governments of Virginia, North Carolina, and Massachusetts during the period from 1675 to the American Revolution, as enslaved Africans drew on the Christian ethic, Enlightenment principles, and democratic values in advancing their claims.[4] Apparently, such actions were designed to shape public opinion and policy regarding slavery at a time when many colonists refused, on religious grounds, to challenge the fundamental structures and ethos of their society.

In any case, the black church was born into a culture that did not separate private devotion from public duty. Invariably, this meant that the church had to move beyond the strictly *spiritual* and *ecclesiastical* to promote positive change in vital areas of life — social, political, economic, intellectual, and otherwise. This became all the more important for Africans in eighteenth- and nineteenth-century America, many of whom claimed the church as the only visible institution that they owned and controlled on a wide scale.[5] This is what Carter G. Woodson had in mind when referring to the black church as "an all-comprehending institution":

> The Negro church touches almost every ramification of the life of the Negro. As stated elsewhere, the Negro church, in the absence of other agencies to assume such responsibilities, has had to do more than its duty in taking care of the general interests of the race. A definitive history of the Negro church, therefore, would leave practically no phase of the history of the Negro in America untouched. All efforts of the Negro in things economic, educational and political have branched out of or connected in some way with the rise and development of the Negro church.[6]

This image of the "all-comprehending institution" helps explain how black churches, from their origins, found a special or unique expression. First established during the late eighteenth century, as Americans resisted British colonial domination, black churches of various denominations became meetinghouses of faith and social action. This was especially the case with black churches in the North, where Africans had more freedom than those in the South to create institutions for their own liberation and uplift. The politico-prophetic role that these churches would consistently assume in public affairs had become clear by the early 1800s, as they pointed to the paradox of a new nation born in freedom while more than 700,000 Africans languished in bondage. Richard Allen's African Methodist Episcopal Church (AME), James Varick's African Methodist Episcopal Zion Church (AMEZ), Peter Spencer's African Union Church, Thomas Paul's African Baptist Church, and other black churches were forced into the public arena by the very nature of the black condition, and their tendency to combine a strong African consciousness and spirituality with an emphasis on racial advancement proved that there were centrifugal forces at work inside them.[7]

The pioneers in the black church embodied a sense of mission and a depth of vision and leadership that were virtually nonexistent even at the highest levels of the nation's political life.[8] Knowing that society's institutional structures were racist and unjust, Allen, Varick, Spencer, Paul, the African Episcopal leader Absalom Jones, and countless others refused to reduce religion to matters of individual or personal ethics. They measured up to heroic standards of virtue while making the Christian faith relevant to the struggle for equal rights and social justice, and their voices remained uncompromising and undaunted in pursuit of the public good. Drawing on the Exodus, the crucifixion, and other stories, characters, and images from the Bible, they encouraged church-based activism while identifying their cause with the will of God. Moreover, their activities contributed to the rise of a host of benevolent societies and other ethnic associations to sustain their people's social, political, economic, educational, and cultural interests.[9] Consequently, black churches assumed a significance that was not duplicated by other ethnic churches. Winthrop S. Hudson says as much and more as he describes black churches as the repositories of black identity, the prime institutional embodiment of folk values, and the treasuries of religious folk life:

> Cut off from most areas of social and political life, the Negroes found in the church an opportunity for self-expression, recognition, and leadership. It was hardly a coincidence that until well into the twentieth century most of the outstanding Negro leaders had been ministers, for the ministry pro-

vided one of the few opportunities for leadership open to a Negro. Further-more, the church was the primary agency of self-help, and it played an im-portant role in maintaining group cohesion under difficult circumstances and in fostering the self-respect which is gained only through the exercise of independent responsibilities.[10]

While the earliest black churches differed to some degree in terms of their denominational identities, systems of polity, doctrinal standards, and modes of discipline, this did not obscure their fundamental agreement concerning the need to challenge the status quo. They had a common understanding of the Christian faith and its implications for addressing human need and in-equality. In other words, there was a consensus of beliefs, attitudes, values, and expectations that bound them together despite the incidentals that dis-tinguished them from one another. Thus, they were able to establish a broad, interdenominational tradition of shared involvement in the struggle for a just and inclusive society, one that contributed enormously to the vitality of black churches as social institutions.[11] This tradition was embodied to the fullest in the National Negro Convention Movement, which cultivated the spirit of self-reliance and uplift in black churches in the period between 1830 and 1860.[12]

Slavery was the one issue that drew black churches into the public arena in ways not yet captured in the scholarship on the subject. Indeed, the abolition of slavery figured quite prominently among the mission priorities of black churches. At a time when many white Christians viewed slavery as a civil mat-ter that justified the strict noninterference of the church, most black clergy and laypersons saw it as a great evil that had to be challenged and eliminated through the efforts of both ecclesiastical and governmental representatives.[13] This explains why slavery was consistently under attack in the sermons of the AME Zion leader Peter Williams Jr., the African Baptist pastor Nathaniel Paul, the AME spokesman Daniel A. Payne, and numerous others. In keeping with his quest for "the economic and political betterment of black people," Richard Allen went beyond preaching antislavery sermons to the boycotting of slave-made goods. Moreover, both the AME and AME Zion churches barred slaveholders from membership.[14] Such activities were geared in part toward shaping public opinion and policy in opposition to slavery. The efforts of churchmen such as Williams, Paul, Payne, and Allen were immensely important for African American churchpersons in the slave South, who were more limited in terms of movement, function, and opportunities of leadership, and who possessed fewer mechanisms to mold public opinion in favor of their cause.

There were more colorful figures in black churches that epitomized the African American component of abolitionist agitation. Inspired to some degree by the militant phase of abolitionism that followed the publication of David Walker's *Appeal to the Coloured Citizens of the World* (1829), James Forten of the African Episcopal Church, Henry H. Garnet of the African Presbyterian Church, and Frederick Douglass, Harriet Tubman, and Sojourner Truth of the AME Zion Church were among those who agitated against slavery with a determination and intensity rarely witnessed in antebellum times. Forten and Douglass contributed substantially to abolitionist societies and to antislavery newspapers such as *The Liberator,* and they consistently challenged the view, advanced in both religious and political circles, that the alleged inferiority of Africans made their enslavement necessary. Garnet pursued the notion that slavery could be abolished through political action or the legislative process, Truth constantly raised her eloquent voice in defense of abolition, and Tubman became widely known as an operator on the Underground Railroad.[15] Although black churches did little as a collectivity to influence legislation on the question of abolition, the antislavery efforts of these persons not only contributed in some measure to public discourse on the subject but also carried implications for social policy.

The Underground Railroad symbolized the lack of faith that many in the black church had in the efficacy of political action as a solution to the slavery problem. At a time when debates over slavery were occurring in the U.S. Congress, black churches from Virginia to parts of Pennsylvania and New York served as stations on the Underground Railroad, assisting untold numbers of escaped bondspersons to free territory. A towering symbol of the AME Zion Church's resistance to bondage, Harriet Tubman, as an Underground Railroad conductor, is said to have led more than two hundred to freedom.[16] The Bethel AME Church in Philadelphia and the parsonage of Bishop Richard Allen were important stations on the Underground Railroad. The same occurred with Peter Spencer's African Union Church in Wilmington, Delaware. Its Big August Quarterly Festival, which began in 1813, was known for its unique mixture of revivals, abolition rallies, and escaped slaves. Describing the African Union Church as "a gateway to freedom," one source recalled in 1889 that:

> As the years passed the church enlarged. The day grew in importance and the number of visitors increased from a few hundreds to many thousands. The desire for freedom grew stronger and stronger, and pilgrims did not always return to their masters, but found homes in the free states and in Canada. Thus, "Big Quarterly" came to be regarded with suspicion by slave owners. During the latter days of slavery, sheriffs, constables, and sometimes U.S. Marshals were busy watching for runaways. The old people now refer to these meetings as big excursions on the Underground Railroad, and smile at the remembrance of the tricks to which they resorted to hide and aid the fugitives.[17]

A particularly vexing problem for black churches was the colonization movement, which dominated the politics of "the anti-slavery cause from its founding in 1816 to the end of the 1820s." Widely supported by white politicians and abolitionist leaders, and "motivated by Christian missionary zeal," this movement "maintained that emancipation of the slaves could best be brought about if accompanied by expatriation to Africa."[18] Although this movement promoted the whole issue of black emigration to Africa, a political strategy extending back to the black church founder Paul Cuffee at the beginning of the 1800s, most black churchpersons rejected it because it "violated professed American principles" and encouraged "the perpetuation of human bondage" by "seeking to remove free blacks" from "their enslaved brethren." The very thought of renouncing American citizenship appeared absurd to free blacks like Richard Allen and Peter Spencer. Echoing the publicly expressed sentiments of Allen and James Forten, Spencer declared in 1831 that "we have our attachment to the soil, and we feel that we have rights in common with other Americans."[19] Although the African Methodist leader Martin Delany was among the few who considered African emigration essential to the political destiny of his people, such a strategy was never seriously entertained by the vast majority of black churches.[20] Indeed, it was never embraced by the National Negro Convention Movement, which considered a range of possible political options when confronting the slavery issue.[21]

The National Negro Convention mobilized black churchpersons in an effort to address matters that went beyond abolitionist agitation. While competition between groups like the AMES and AMEZS sometimes occurred within its ranks, it considered issues ranging from education to economic empowerment to political strategies and the physical health of African Americans. Its advocacy of temperance, grounded in the belief that alcoholic beverages merely exacerbated problems for the oppressed, was as significant as its affirmation of black autonomy and its debate concerning violence as a means to ending oppression.[22] The National Negro Convention Movement provided one avenue for black Christians to fulfill any political ambition or aspirations they may have had. In other words, the power they were denied in the secular politics of the larger culture was experienced to a great extent within the arena of church politics.

The pervasiveness of racism led black church leaders to conclude that economic power was perhaps the most significant ingredient in their people's efforts to establish themselves as a force in both their own communities and in the society as a whole. This is why economic values, along with the virtues of education, were highlighted even in the books of doctrine and discipline put forth by African Methodists.[23] In conformity with the Protestant work ethic, black churchpersons were taught to be industrious, to avoid dealing in lotteries, to be prompt in paying debts, to be saving in their means, to deal fairly with one another, and to support each other in business ventures. Such teachings could not have been more important since slavery not only forced scores of African Americans into situations of dependency but also robbed them of the capacity to establish a strong economic base for themselves and their descendants. This sense of being powerless compelled black churches, along with mutual aid societies and Masonic orders, to take the lead in establishing "an economic ethos for the uplift of the race."[24]

This stress on economic development and mobility supports the conclusion that the black church was "an early expression of Black Power or Nationalism."[25] This spirit of nationalism was engendered not only by Allen, Spencer, Paul, Jones, and other black church founders and organizers, who felt that their people's needs could not be met in white church settings, but also by Robert A. Young, David Walker, Henry H. Garnet, Martin Delany, Alexander Crummell, and others who contributed so profoundly to the radicalization of the antebellum black churches. Racism heightened their self-awareness and reinforced in them the centripetal tendency to view themselves as a people apart, as a different and separate people, even as they struggled in many ways to win acceptance in the United States. But even as the churches were infused with this nationalist consciousness, they refused to embrace the political dream of territorial separatism based on race. Furthermore — despite the actions of Henry H. Garnet, Denmark Vesey, Nat Turner, and others that served as invitations to violent revolution — they did not call for the overthrow of existing political and economic structures as a prerequisite for black liberation. To the contrary, the black churches testified to the need for all Americans to peacefully coexist on terms of equality, mutual acceptance, and shared power, and they made nonviolence and moral suasion their primary means of affecting public policy.[26]

Antebellum black churches were characterized by a pervasive and holistic evangelism, whose function was to produce religious conversions while reforming society at all levels. These churches appropriated the perfectionist ideas that attended an emerging holiness movement in American religious culture, and they were grounded in the conviction that the multitude of problems in the public arena could be solved only through the perfectibility of both the individual and the social order. This accounted in part for their importance to society as prophetic institutions. But the most pronounced prophetic dimension of the black churches was in their consistent critique of society's failures to deal justly and constructively with racial issues. They not only challenged white society with a more prophetic vision of liberty but also with a more inclusive understanding of the role that religion can play in public debate and political decisions regarding racism, the mistreatment of the poor and oppressed, and militarism.

The coming of the Civil War in 1861 confronted black churches with both old and new challenges. The war proved to be yet another issue of public policy that these institutions could not avoid, especially since the conflict grew largely out of sectional differences (North and South) over slavery. Unlike the white churches, black churches had always found common ground in their opposition to slavery, despite disagreements over how this evil could best be eliminated. In other words, their "millennial goal," or "Kingdom of God on earth," did "not include the continuation of slavery" under any circumstances.[27] This essentially united stance carried over into attitudes toward the Civil War. Because the position of black churches was shaped largely by racial considerations and commitments, there was virtually no public debate about the justice of the war itself. In the minds of those who comprised these institutions, the Civil War signaled the enactment of biblical principles that foretold the coming of the millennium. Indeed, it was God's vehicle of deliverance, or a sign that the God who delivered the ancient Israelites and led them toward a new and more liberating political destiny was still active in history. It was this assessment that led black churchmen such as Frederick Douglass, Martin Delany, and Henry M. Turner to support the enlistment of thousands of African Americans in the war effort on behalf of the Union cause.

President Abraham Lincoln's signing of the Emancipation Proclamation and the Union victory in the Civil War created a catastrophic social and political crisis that demanded special attention from black churches. Some four million slaves had been set free in the South by 1865, the vast majority of whom were virtually homeless, penniless, and illiterate. Having a desire to establish their own independence, these former slaves joined existing black churches or formed their own. The organization of the Colored Methodist Episcopal Church (CME) in Jackson, Tennessee, in 1870 was symbolic of their desire to be self-governing, and so were the many other black churches of different denominations that originated in various parts of the South. The very survival and expansion of these institutions virtually insured the preservation of a system of spiritual and cultural values that centered on freedom, self-help, and self-determination.[28]

This new freedom compelled African Americans to revisit the question "What is the relationship of the church and religion to society?" The answer to the question proved axiomatic for black churches, for once again they were forced to assume the nation's burdens around the question of race. Furthermore, these churches, as the crucial institutional centers of the folk, necessarily had to reclaim their image as "all-comprehending institutions." Only in this fashion could they become pivotal in reorganizing the culture, and in bringing structure, stability, and order to African American life.[29] Social welfare, economic structures, educational development, political enfranchisement, physical and psychological health, and racial justice remained the major public policy issues that black churches addressed. No less important was the cultural question of identity, which reinforced group solidarity, self-reliance, and a sense of social responsibility.

During the period of Reconstruction, the churches became what E. Franklin Frazier terms "the most important agency of social control among

Negroes." In this capacity, these institutions sought to reunite families and to restore kinship ties fragmented by slavery, to strengthen the roles of father and mother figures in the family structure, and to create a home environment in which cleanliness, intimacy, warmth, self-discipline, and Christian witness were allowed to mature. This could not have been more important, since the family was perceived as the fundamental unit of society — the center from which the church and other institutions evolved. Also in this connection, black churches encouraged respect for the marriage vow and monogamous family life, discouraged unregulated and unconventional sexual behavior, and expelled or excommunicated sex offenders and those guilty of adultery, fornication, and conceiving children out of wedlock. The goal was a more "organized social life among Negroes," an experience heightened in significance as African Americans were denied participation in a truly integrated society.[30]

There was an economic component to this vision as advanced by black churches. African Americans were urged to be industrious, to avoid dealing in lotteries, to practice frugality, to be prompt in paying debts, to deal fairly with each other, to pool their meager resources, and to support each other in business ventures. Moreover, the churches spawned the first black banks, insurance companies, funeral homes, business leagues, and a range of beneficial or mutual aid societies designed to assist the widowed and the orphaned and to respond to the crises arising out of poverty, malnutrition, sickness, and death.[31] Leaders as diverse in their philosophies as Booker T. Washington and W. E. B. Du Bois felt that such involvements on the part of the churches were indispensable, although they seriously doubted the capacity of those institutions to succeed in this area as long as they remained dominated by a largely uneducated leadership.[32]

The African Methodist leader Henry M. Turner extended his focus beyond economic empowerment and cooperation within the ranks of his people, to become the first "to raise seriously the issue of reparations for the years of slavery" endured by them. While the vast majority in black churches undoubtedly considered such a strategy unrealistic or impractical, especially given the nature of racism in the United States, Turner's forcefulness in raising it was indicative of his belief that economic power was perhaps more essential than anything else to the elevation of the race.[33] In any case, the effort to significantly improve the material resources of the folk had led Du Bois, by 1907, to conclude that "a study of economic cooperation among Negroes must begin with the Church group."[34]

Equally important were the contributions made by black churches to the educational development of African Americans. Denied education in many instances during slavery, the churches were given far more latitude after emancipation to provide education on all levels for blacks in the South. This was due in part to "the great educational crusade" implemented by both northern white and black missionaries among the freedpersons.[35] E. Franklin Frazier alluded to the great work of black preachers and churches in establishing schools during and after Reconstruction, noting that this was particularly important "since the southern States provided only a pittance of public funds for the education of Negro children."[36] By 1900, the AMEs were sustaining thirty-two secondary schools and colleges, the AMEZs were underwriting eight, and the CMEs five. Black Baptists proved equally successful in this venture. A number of seminaries and Bible schools were also organized, a development that significantly reinforced the "moral and religious outlook" that permeated church-related education. The impetus to build such institutions grew primarily out of the need for a more educated and progressive-minded ministry.[37]

This type of leadership was in greater demand than ever given the increased role of black churches in politics during Reconstruction. From their origins, the churches had had "a political meaning" for both preachers and the masses, for they provided opportunities that compensated for the virtual exclusion of all African Americans from full participation in political processes at the local, regional, and national levels. As E. Franklin Frazier noted, "The church was the arena in which the struggle for power and the thirst for power could be satisfied," and this held special significance for ambitious preachers, especially in the South, who were determined to achieve distinction and status. Also, the churches afforded the context in which African Americans "could vote and engage in electing" their bishops, pastors, convention delegates, and other church officers.[38] These political functions were significantly increased when the U.S. Congress enacted the Fourteenth and Fifteenth Amendments to the Constitution in 1868 and 1870, actions which, at least in principle, gave blacks full citizenship and the right to vote and hold public office.

With these developments, new questions emerged in black communities

about how the church should function in the public domain. While continuing as centers of ecclesiastical politics, the churches now entered the realm of
secular politics as they not only trained African Americans in the wise use of
the ballot but also became the training and proving ground for black political leadership. Black preachers, all of whom were Republicans who "shared
on the whole the conservative political philosophy of that party," joined hundreds of laypersons as political leaders of the race, and they all drew financial
and moral support from the churches. Black pulpits became the most important single force in national, regional, and local political campaigns, and
also for shaping and controlling opinion among African Americans on public policy issues. During Reconstruction, two of the twenty blacks elected
to the U.S. House of Representatives from the South were ministers, and
one of the two black U.S. Senators, Hiram R. Revels of Mississippi, was a
Methodist preacher. The AME preacher Henry M. Turner organized blacks
in the Republican Party in Georgia and later served the state in the legisla-
ture and as postmaster. Other black preachers served in state legislatures and
in local politics, and James W. Hood, a minister in the AME Zion Church in
North Carolina, was elected president of "perhaps the first political convention called by Negroes after they gained their freedom." Hood also served
as a local magistrate and Assistant Superintendent of Public Instruction in
North Carolina and was appointed Deputy Collector of Internal Revenue for
the United States.[39]

Black churchmen entered the realm of American politics with the conviction that they had to engage forthrightly the political processes in order to
effect much-needed change for all of the nation's citizens. Furthermore, they
went in with the belief that religion and morality should have some role in
democratic politics and law making, despite the constitutional boundaries
between church and state, a position they arrived at instinctively considering
their rootedness in a culture that did not draw a sharp dichotomy between the
sacred and the secular. Driven by this conviction, black legislators pioneered
in bringing public education to the South and in abolishing imprisonment
for debt, thus substantiating W. E. B. Du Bois's contention that democracy
pervaded the region for the first time in its history.[40]

While religion never became the basis of black political decision making,
it did have a role in the public debates among African Americans about

political choices. Moreover, the political choices of black politicians were always grounded in both moral and practical considerations, despite "the myth of black domination and debauchery" promoted by white southerners and painfully echoed in the motion picture *The Birth of a Nation* (1915). The burning of black churches by the Ku Klux Klan and other white terrorists, which emerged in the three decades after the Civil War, was reflective of how those institutions were perceived from the standpoint of their political significance.[41] Many white southerners saw black churches' heightened political role as a major contributor to the sharpening of antagonisms between them and African Americans. While it is true that black churches never achieved perfection in their political functions, they did not produce politicians bent on leading the South and the nation away from excellence or virtue in politics. In any case, once African Americans had been almost completely disenfranchised by white racists in 1898 and forced out of secular politics in the South, the churches again became the primary arena of black political activities.[42]

The Klan and the mob mentality among whites in the South injected a poison into the body politic that interfered with the black churches' capacity to fulfill their traditional role as "all-comprehending institutions." African American citizenship rights were eroded, and Jim Crow and racist social policies found expression in the Black Codes of the South and in the *Plessy v. Ferguson* decision of the Supreme Court, which upheld the doctrine of "separate but equal" in 1896. Black churches had to come to terms with what was essentially a heartbreaking and crushing defeat. The theology of hope that found expression in black songs and sermons after emancipation and the Civil War surrendered to feelings of despair and hopelessness in many circles. Some nationalists, such as the African Methodists Henry M. Turner and John E. Bruce, predicted that the rights of African Americans would never be respected in America, and they responded to the failure of Reconstruction politics by reasserting black identity, by encouraging "organized resistance" or the meeting of "force with force," and by calling for mass emigration to Africa.[43] In the midst of the anger, confusion, frustration, and despair, the churches became the most effective morale-building agencies for African Americans. In a real sense, they became both a religious and psychological refuge for the folk, and "religion offered a means of catharsis for their pent-up emotions and frustrations."[44] This essentially therapeutic function, which embraced a concern for both the physical and mental health of the folk, helps explain why mass insanity did not overwhelm blacks in the South.

Black churches never really abandoned the belief that the Christian faith should speak to and address public policy issues. However, their enduring role as "all-comprehending institutions" seemed endangered by the end of the nineteenth century, as African Americans, according to Gayraud S. Wilmore's interpretation, "retreated into a folk religiosity that lacked the social protest emphasis of the antebellum black denominations." This process of the "deradicalization of the black churches," as Wilmore calls it, continued into the early twentieth century and was completed by the end of World War II, as those institutions appeared more concerned about a puritanical moral code, salvation in the afterlife, proselytizing, church building, and creating an ecclesiastical framework to sustain themselves than they were about organizing and crusading against the personal and institutional racism of white America:

> During the 1920s and 1930s most black churches retained a basically rural orientation and retreated into enclaves of moralistic, revivalistic Christianity by which they tried to fend off the encroaching gloom and pathology of the ghetto. As far as challenging white society, or seeking to mobilize the community against poverty and oppression, most black churches were too other-worldly, apathetic, or caught up in institutional maintenance to deal with such issues, even in the good years following the Second World War.[45]

The "deradicalization of the black churches" was heightened by the abandonment of African Americans by the Republican Party after 1877, by the further deterioration of race relations at the turn of the century, and by the declining influence of radical voices like Henry M. Turner. Turner had tried desperately to radicalize the black churches, or to transform them into nationalist institutions with ecclesiastical connections in Africa, but his death in 1915 essentially deprived those institutions of this kind of strong and uncompromising leadership.[46] Also, the black churches were literally overwhelmed by the magnitude of the problems that confronted them, especially during the years of economic depression and the Great Migration. Devoid of the resources needed to address these problems adequately, most churches turned their sense of mission inward. Moreover, they subscribed to a curious blend of Christian fundamentalism and the conservative politics of Booker T. Washington, which called for racial self-uplift and education in the educational and mechanical arts, while rejecting agitation for civil rights, political power, and higher liberal arts education:

> Washington's gradualism, while opposed by a few who were not dependent upon his influence for personal advancement, was adopted by most black preachers not only because they lacked the courage to fight back, but because it was consonant with the ethics of white Christianity by which they were increasingly influenced. The picture of the nonviolent, self-effacing, patiently-suffering white Jesus held up by the conservative evangelicals and revivalists at the turn of the century became for many black preachers the authoritative image of what it is like to be a Christian. That image provided irrefutable confirmation, supported by Scripture, of the wisdom and expediency of Washington's position.[47]

The fundamentalism that captured the imagination and loyalty of most black churches in the early decades of the twentieth century attached great significance to biblical literalism, doctrinal conformity, evangelism, and soul-winning mission. Furthermore, it declared that revivalism and getting people saved, not social, political, and economic reform, was the best cure for society's ills. In other words, this kind of "grassroots revivalism" emphasized the metaphor of God as Savior in the afterlife to the essential neglect of God as Liberator in this life.[48] This apparent indifference toward religion's role in public affairs, however well-meaning, led to levels of pacifism and dysfunctionality on the part of many churches that helped trigger the rise of "alternative" and "unconventional" expressions of religion, among which were the Father Divine Peace Mission Movement, Daddy Grace's United House of Prayer for All People, and a number of Islamic and Jewish-Hebrew sects in African American communities. By challenging racism, affirming the identity and worth of African Americans, and addressing issues ranging from poverty and economic injustice to prison reform to matters of personal ethics and health care, these new religious movements compensated for the lack of a strong social and political witness by many of the churches.

But there were a few "prophetic radicals" who never advocated the strict noninterference of churches in public affairs and public policy matters. As racial conflict and urban problems worsened in the 1890s and during the three decades that followed, black Social Gospelers such as the AME preacher Reverdy C. Ransom, the AME Zion leader Alexander Walters, the Methodist laywoman Ida B. Wells, the Presbyterian clergyman Francis J. Grimke, and many others affirmed that the Christian has duties and a moral responsibility to redeem corporate life, and they applied the biblical principles of love and justice in their efforts to transform the church, the state, the economy, and other institutions.[49] For these leaders, the coexistence of Christianity and racist social, political, and economic structures could not be justified on the basis of scriptural interpretation and Judeo-Christian values. Reverdy Ransom said as much and more in his powerful essay "The Race Problem in a Christian State" (1906).[50] The Baptist preacher George W. Woodbey went even further in his claims, suggesting, in works such as *The Bible and Socialism* (1903) and *Why the Negro Should Vote the Socialist Ticket* (1908), that socialism and Christianity were not only compatible but that the combined values upheld by both afforded the best answer to America's racial dilemma.[51]

Social Gospelers in the black churches supported both local church-based activism and larger, more organized Christian movements designed to positively influence national public policy issues and much-needed institutional change. They encouraged local churches to interact with governmental structures in the interest of the public good and supported, at least in principle, the work of the Federal Council of the Churches of Christ in America (1908), the national centerpiece of the Social Gospel Movement, which aimed to secure a larger combined influence for churches in all matters pertinent to public affairs, human relations, and national policy. "Denominational lines, doctrinal lines, and color lines were all brushed aside by the greater thought of human salvation and the best way to bring it through the churches," asserted the AME Bishop Levi J. Coppin, who, along with the AME Zion Bishop Alexander Walters and others, held memberships in the FCCC.[52]

Black Social Gospelers pioneered in the founding of civil rights organizations. Reverdy Ransom, Francis Grimke, and the Baptist clergyman J. Miton Waldron represented the churches among that group of black intellectuals who, under the leadership of W. E. B. Du Bois and William M. Trotter, organized the Niagara Movement near Niagara Falls in 1905. This movement reflected the vision of reformed-minded black churches and their leaders when

it, during its meeting a year later at Harpers Ferry, issued its first address to
the nation:

> We will not be satisfied with less than our full manhood rights. . . . We
> claim for ourselves every right that belongs to a free-born American — po-
> litical, civil, and social — and until we get these rights, we will never cease to
> protest and assail the ears of America with the story of its shameful deeds
> toward us. We want full manhood suffrage, and we want it now, henceforth
> and forever.[53]

The Niagara Movement failed in part because it did not get strong support
from the masses of black churchpersons. Most black churches were not prepared to endorse such a radical challenge to the whole country. Nonetheless,
the Niagara Movement prepared the ground for the organization of the National Association for the Advancement of Colored People (NAACP) in New
York in 1909. Social Gospelers such as Reverdy Ransom, Francis Grimke, and
Bishop Alexander Walters joined with black militants like Ida B. Wells and
white liberals like Mary W. Ovington in establishing the NAACP, which re-
placed the Niagara Movement as "the guardian and advocate for black rights
in the political arena."[54] Black churches provided meeting space and financial
and moral support for the NAACP in its legal crusade to influence national
policy on the issue of race. Churches were also related to the founding of
the National Urban League in New York in 1910, an interracial organization
that employed the techniques of persuasion and conciliation in addressing
the social problems of urban blacks. The Urban League helped provide food,
clothing, shelter, and jobs for hundreds of blacks who left the rural South
and settled in the urban areas of the North during the periods around World
Wars I and II.[55]

Some of the large black churches became "social welfare agencies," serving
"a broad spectrum of the needs of the burgeoning urban populations."
Reverdy Ransom's Institutional AME Church in Chicago, H. H. Proctor's First
Congregational Church in Atlanta, L. K. Williams's Olivet Baptist Church
in Chicago, Adam C. Powell's Abyssinian Baptist Church in New York, and
Alfred D. Williams's Ebenezer Baptist Church in Atlanta became widely
known for their impact on issues ranging from labor relations and politics
to education, child care, housing, and recreation.[56] These churches provided

ministries of social service while seeking to influence local, regional, and national public policy on racial concerns.

Attempts to radicalize the black churches in the first three decades of the twentieth century were very rare. Marcus Garvey's Universal Negro Improvement Association (1916) intersected black ministers of different faiths and denominational affiliations in a movement that promoted African identity and repatriation. Randall K. Burkett has reported that "no black denomination as such ever formally opposed" Garvey's UNIA and that a "surprisingly large number of clergy, from virtually every black denomination," were "themselves active Garveyites." The AME Zion preachers James W. H. Eason and William H. Ferris, the Baptist pastors James R. L. Diggs and Junius C. Austin, and the CME minister William Y. Bell were among those churchpersons who gave strong physical, financial, and moral support to the activities of the UNIA.[57] But many black preachers rejected Garvey and the UNIA, and the organization failed to make inroads into black churches in the South. Even so, those black churchpersons who did join Garvey were trying to make a statement to the United States about its attitude, policies, and practices toward African Americans.

When Benjamin E. Mays and Joseph W. Nicholson wrote *The Negro's Church* in 1933, they detected a strong strain of conservatism in black churches that encouraged "withdrawal from social and political involvement in their communities."[58] This trend continued through the 1940s and early 1950s, reinforced, as it was on many levels, by a seemingly invincible racist system and fears ignited by the McCarthyite witch-hunt. Local and regional church-based activism was extremely rare, and one could only dream of gaining the vast spiritual, moral, and material resources of black churches in support of efforts to change institutions and to shape national public policy issues. However, black churches experienced a reawakening in the mid- and late-1950s, as clergy and laity came together in the struggle for basic civil or constitutional rights. Gayraud S. Wilmore offers the best description of the dimensions of this reawakening process, taking into account both its vastness and its limitations:

> If the period from the end of the First World War to the middle of the century saw growing disillusionment with the church because of a reactionary traditionalism, it must be said that it was the young Baptist minister Martin

Luther King, Jr., who reversed that trend and gave new vitality and relevance to Black Christianity in the United States. Black radicalism in the late 1960s found its most conspicuous expression in the highly secularized Black Panther Party which was justifiably suspicious of the churches and their leaders. But King's contributions to the civil rights movement gave the lie to the allegation that black preachers were nothing but Uncle Toms and that Christianity was hopelessly out of tune with the times. Despite the fact that he was never able to muster the full power of the churches behind the movement and received only token support from many of the most prestigious ministers, King nevertheless projected a new image of the church upon the nation and a new awareness of the possibilities inherent in black religion.[59]

With the coming of the freedom movement, the "deradicalized" black church faded into the background and the idea of church as "all-comprehending institution" was to a great extent revived. Under the leadership of King and others, the resources of the Christian tradition were applied to the structures of injustice, to the practical problems of daily life, and to national public policy issues. The church-centered civil rights movement addressed concerns ranging from voting rights to poverty and public health, and from full access to public facilities and accommodations to education to structural violence and world peace.[60]

Since King's death in April 1968, black churches have gradually shifted back toward what Wilmore calls "a reactionary traditionalism." Others call it "the disillusionment of a 'post-civil rights malaise.'" The pattern of young, vigorous, and activist black church leadership, represented by King, Ralph Abernathy, and other prophetic personalities in the 1950s and 1960s, had largely faded by 1980, and, since that time, churches have increasingly turned to revivals, massive crusades, a gospel of prosperity positivism, and matters of personal salvation as a substitute for active involvement in social, political, and economic change.[61] As quite a bit of recent scholarship on black churches has noted (including Michael Owens's chapter in this volume), black churches have too often been unresponsive to social urgencies in the period since the civil rights movement. Samuel Roberts points out in this volume that the black church's loss of prophetic edge has sometimes resulted from its overly close relationship with government in recent years.

While church involvement in public affairs still occurs in some measure on the local and regional levels, and with organizations like the Congress of National Black Churches on a broader scale, black churches generally can no longer claim the kind of prophetic posture that made them the object of suspicion and violent attack a half-century ago.

The power and relevance of black churches today and tomorrow hinges on their capacities to strongly impact public policy and public discourse around such issues as structural injustice, human oppression, public health and welfare, and the sacredness of all life forms. If black churches fail to translate religious fervor and moral passion into efforts to constructively address these issues, and if they do not develop stronger mission priorities aimed at youth, families, the elderly, the sick, and the imprisoned, then they will find it increasingly difficult to justify their existence.

The central questions, then, are: (1) Will the church remain relevant to virtually every aspect of African American life, or will it continue to surrender many of its traditional functions to other religious and so-called secular institutions? (2) Has the black church outlived its usefulness as the "all-comprehending institution"—as that institution devoted to the redemption of individual as well as corporate life? The answers to these and other questions will emerge as black churches continue to redefine and revitalize their ministries and missions to meet the challenges of a new century and a more insecure and uncertain world.

Notes

1   Hortense Powdermaker, "The Channeling of Negro Aggression by the Cultural Process," *American Journal of Sociology* 48 (1943): 755; E. Franklin Frazier, *The Negro Church in America* (New York: Schocken Books, 1963), 14; and John B. Childs, *The Political Black Minister: A Study in Afro-American Politics and Religion* (Boston: G. K. Hall, 1980), 1–2.

2   Gayraud S. Wilmore, *Black Religion and Black Radicalism: An Interpretation of the Religious History of African-Americans* (Maryknoll, N.Y.: Orbis Books, 1998), viii–x; and Lewis V. Baldwin, *"Invisible" Strands in African Methodism: A History of the African Union Methodist Protestant and Union American Methodist Episcopal Churches, 1805–1980* (Metuchen, N. J.: The Scarecrow Press, Inc., 1983), 37–239.

3   Vincent Harding, "Religion and Resistance among Antebellum Negroes," in August Meier and Elliott Rudwick, eds., *The Making of Black America: The Origins of Black*

Americans, 2 vols. (New York: Atheneum, 1974), 1: 177–97; James H. Cone, *The Spirituals and the Blues: An Interpretation* (Westport, Conn.: Greenwood Press, 1972), 86–107; and Childs, *The Political Black Minister,* 2–3.

4 Herbert Aptheker, ed., *A Documentary History of the Negro People in the United States* (Secaucus, N.J.: The Citadel Press, 1973), 1–16.

5 Winthrop S. Hudson, *Religion in America: An Historical Account of the Development of American Religious Life* (New York: Charles Scribner's Sons, 1965), 225.

6 Carter G. Woodson, "The Negro Church, an All-Comprehending Institution," *The Negro History Bulletin* 3, no. 1 (October 1939): 7.

7 Frederick A. Norwood, *The Story of American Methodism: A History of the United Methodists and Their Relations* (Nashville: Abingdon Press, 1974), 171; Woodson, "The Negro Church," 7; Baldwin, *"Invisible" Strands in African Methodism,* 37–70; Wilmore, *Black Religion and Black Radicalism,* 22–23; and Sterling Stuckey, ed., *The Ideological Origins of Black Nationalism* (Boston: Beacon Press, 1972), 6.

8 One source claims that the new American nation had "two versions" of its mission — one centering on its example as "a light to the nations," and the other on its role as "the liberator of the oppressed." It is no exaggeration to claim that black churches took this twofold mission much more seriously than whites in both the ecclesiastical and political realms. See Winthrop S. Hudson and John Corrigan, *Religion in America: An Historical Account of the Development of American Religious Life,* 5th ed. (New York: Macmillan, 1992), 113.

9 Robert L. Harris Jr., "Early Black Benevolent Societies, 1780–1830," *Massachusetts Review* 20 (autumn 1979): 603–25.

10 Hudson, *Religion in America,* 225 and 351.

11 Support for this claim is afforded in Wilmore, *Black Religion and Black Radicalism,* 99–124.

12 Ibid., 118.

13 Gardiner H. Shattuck Jr., *A Shield and Hiding Place: The Religious Life of the Civil War Armies* (Macon, Ga.: Mercer University Press, 1987), 1–5; Donald G. Mathews, *Religion in the Old South* (Chicago: University of Chicago Press, 1977), 156–57; Randall M. Miller and Jon L. Wakelyn, eds., *Catholics in the Old South: Essays on Church and Culture* (Macon: Mercer University Press, 1999), 14–17; and Wilmore, *Black Religion and Black Radicalism,* 103–24.

14 Philip S. Foner, ed., *The Voice of Black America: Major Speeches by Negroes in the United States, 1797–1973,* 2 vols. (New York: Capricorn Books, 1975), 1: 28–33, 45–50, 57–61, and 88–94; Norwood, *The Story of American Methodism,* 171; and Wilmore, *Black Religion and Black Radicalism,* 110–11.

15 John H. Bracey et al., eds., *Blacks in the Abolitionist Movement* (Belmont, Ca.: Wadsworth Publishing Company, 1971), 4–13 and 17–23; Benjamin Quarles, *Black Abolitionists* (New York: Oxford University Press, 1969), 121, 146, 157, 179, and 239;

Baldwin, *"Invisible" Strands in African Methodism,* 143–44; Wilmore, *Black Religion and Black Radicalism,* 57–59, 107–8, and 111–17; and Sterling Stuckey, *Slave Culture: Nationalist Theory and the Foundations of Black America* (New York: Oxford University Press, 1987), 153–54.

16   James B. Stewart, *Holy Warriors: The Abolitionists and American Slavery* (New York: Hill and Wang, 1976), 136; Quarles, *Black Abolitionists,* 146; and Wilmore, *Black Religion and Black Radicalism,* 113.

17   Wilmore, *Black Religion and Black Radicalism,* 111–13; *The Morning News,* Wilmington, Delaware (26 August 1889), 1 and 8; and Baldwin, *"Invisible" Strands in African Methodism,* 143–45.

18   Bracey et al., eds., *Blacks in the Abolitionist Movement,* 1; and Wilmore, *Black Religion and Black Radicalism,* 127.

19   Wilmore, *Black Religion and Black Radicalism,* 126–28; W. L. Garrison, *Thoughts on African Colonization* (Boston: Garrison and Knapp, 1832), 36–40; and Baldwin, *"Invisible" Strands in African Methodism,* 64.

20   M. R. Delany and Robert Campbell, *Search for a Place: Black Separatism and Africa, 1860* (Ann Arbor: University of Michigan Press, 1971); Stuckey, ed., *The Ideological Origins of Black Nationalism,* 21–27; and Wilmore, *Black Religion and Black Radicalism,* 136–39.

21   Wilmore, *Black Religion and Black Radicalism,* 118, 129, and 136.

22   Ibid., 118–21.

23   *The Discipline of the African Union Church in the United States of America and Elsewhere,* 3rd ed. enlarged (Wilmington: Porter and Eckel, 1852), 84–85 and 102–7; Jacob F. Ramsey, *Father Spencer, Our Founder: His Work for the Church and the Race* (Camden, N.J.: The General Conference of the Union American Methodist Episcopal Church, 1914), 11–13; Baldwin, *"Invisible" Strands in African Methodism,* 67–68; and Norwood, *The Story of American Methodism,* 171.

24   C. Eric Lincoln and Lawrence H. Mamiya, *The Church in the African-American Experience* (Durham: Duke University Press, 1990), 240–43.

25   Norwood, *The Story of American Methodism,* 171; Baldwin, *"Invisible" Strands in African Methodism,* 65–68; Alain Rogers, "The African Methodist Episcopal Church, a Study in Black Nationalism," *The Black Church* 1 (1972): 17–43; and Stuckey, ed., *The Ideological Origins of Black Nationalism,* 3–5.

26   Wilmore, *Black Religion and Black Radicalism,* 120–22; and Lawrence N. Jones, "Black Christians in Antebellum America: In Quest of the Beloved Community," *Journal of Religious Thought* 38, no. 1 (spring-summer 1981): 12–19.

27   William G. McLoughlin, *Revivals, Awakenings, and Reform: An Essay on Religion and Social Change in America, 1607–1977* (Chicago: University of Chicago Press, 1978), 138.

28   Hudson, *Religion in America,* 223–25; and Edward L. Wheeler, *Uplifting the Race:*

The Black Minister in the New South, 1865–1902 (Lanham, Md.: University Press of America, 1986).

29 Frazier, *The Negro Church in America*, 29–46; and Joseph E. Holloway, ed., *African-isms in American Culture* (Bloomington: Indiana University Press, 1990), x.

30 Frazier, *The Negro Church in America*, 31–34.

31 Ibid., 34–38.

32 Hart M. Nelsen et al., eds., *The Black Church in America* (New York: Basic Books, 1971), 40–43 and 77–81.

33 Wilmore, *Black Religion and Black Radicalism*, 150 and 165.

34 Frazier, *The Negro Church in America*, 34; and W. E. B. Du Bois, *Economic Cooperation Among Negroes* (Atlanta, 1907), 54.

35 Frazier, *The Negro Church in America*, 39–40.

36 Ibid., 38 and 40.

37 Ibid., 39–41; and Baldwin, *"Invisible" Strands in African Methodism*, 106.

38 Frazier, *The Negro Church in America*, 43–44.

39 Ibid., 42–43; Carter G. Woodson, *The History of the Negro Church* (Washington, D.C.: The Associated Publishers, 1985; originally published in 1921), 198–223; Henry M. Turner, *The Life of Henry M. Turner* (Atlanta, 1917), 23; and Samuel D. Smith, *The Negro in Congress, 1870–1901* (Chapel Hill: University of North Carolina Press, 1940), 8.

40 W. E. B. DuBois, *Black Reconstruction in America* (New York: Atheneum, 1975; originally published in 1935), 377–691.

41 John Hope Franklin and Alfred A. Moss Jr., *From Slavery to Freedom*, 6th ed. (New York: Knopf, 1988), 293; and Milton C. Sernett, ed., *African-American Religious History: A Documentary Witness* (Durham: Duke University Press, 1999), 247.

42 Frazier, *The Negro Church in America*, 42–43.

43 Foner, ed., *The Voice of Black America*, 489–91, 566–68, and 591–600.

44 Frazier, *The Negro Church in America*, 44–46.

45 Sernett, ed., *African-American Religious History*, 256; and Wilmore, *Black Religion and Black Radicalism*, 191. Wilmore's position is diametrically opposed to that of E. Franklin Frazier, who claimed that the antebellum black churches were other-worldly and compensatory in outlook, and that the black churches of the first half of the twentieth century were "secularized." "By secularization," wrote Frazier, "we mean that the Negro churches lost their predominantly otherworldly outlook and began to focus attention upon the Negro's condition in this world." See Frazier, *The History of the Negro Church*, 51.

46 Wilmore, *Black Religion and Black Radicalism*, 163–74.

47 Ibid., 164–66 and 168.

48 For important reflections on the impact of this "grassroots revivalist" tradition on black churches in the twentieth century, see Robert M. Franklin, "Religious Belief

and Political Activism in Black America: An Essay," *Journal of Religious Thought* 43, no. 2 (fall-winter 1986): 66.

49 The most important studies of these Social Gospelers are Calvin S. Morris, *Reverdy C. Ransom: Black Advocate of the Social Gospel* (Lanham, Md.: University Press of America, 1990); Anthony B. Pinn, ed., *Making the Gospel Plain: The Writings of Bishop Reverdy C. Ransom* (Harrisburg, Pa.: Trinity Press International, 1999); Ronald C. White Jr., *Liberty and Justice for All: Racial Reform and the Social Gospel* (New York: Harper and Row, 1990); and Ralph E. Luker, *The Social Gospel in Black and White: American Racial Reform, 1885–1912* (Chapel Hill: University of North Carolina Press, 1991).

50 Sernett, ed., *African-American Religious History,* 337–46.

51 Philip S. Foner, ed., *Black Socialist Preacher* (San Francisco: Synthesis Publications, 1983), and Larry G. Murphy et al., eds., *Encyclopedia of African-American Religions* (New York: Garland Publishing, Inc., 1993), 852–53.

52 Luker, *The Social Gospel in Black and White,* 314.

53 Lerone Bennett Jr., *Before the Mayflower: A History of the Negro in America, 1619–1964* (Baltimore: Penguin Books, 1969), 280–81 and 387; and Lincoln and Mamiya, *The Black Church in the African-American Experience,* 208.

54 Bennett, *Before the Mayflower,* 281; Lincoln and Mamiya, *The Black Church in the African-American Experience,* 208; and Wilmore, *Black Religion and Black Radicalism,* 166.

55 Wilmore, *Black Religion and Black Radicalism,* 170; and Franklin and Moss, *From Slavery to Freedom,* 289.

56 Wilmore, *Black Religion and Black Radicalism,* 190.

57 Randall K. Burkett, *Black Redemption: Churchmen Speak for the Garvey Movement* (Philadelphia: Temple University Press, 1978); and Randall K. Burkett, *Garveyism as a Religious Movement: The Institutionalization of a Black Civil Religion* (Metuchen, N.J.: The Scarecrow Press, Inc., 1978).

58 Lincoln and Mamiya, *The Black Church in the African-American Experience,* 209; and Benjamin E. Mays and Joseph W. Nicholson, *The Negro's Church* (New York: Russell and Russell, 1969; originally published in 1933), 70–71.

59 Wilmore, *Black Religion and Black Radicalism,* 204.

60 Ibid., Lewis V. Baldwin, *To Make the Wounded Whole: The Cultural Legacy of Martin Luther King, Jr.* (Minneapolis: The Fortress Press, 1992), 80–81; and Robert M. Franklin Jr., "Martin Luther King, Jr. as Pastor," *The Iliff Review* 42, no. 2 (spring 1985): 4–7.

61 Wilmore, *Black Religion and Black Radicalism,* 204; Carlyle F. Stewart III, *African-American Church Growth: 12 Principles for Prophetic Ministry* (Nashville: Abingdon Press, 1994), 15–160; and Clarence James, "Leadership Development Patterns in the African-American Community," unpublished essay (n.d.), 1–7.

2

WHAT A FELLOWSHIP:

CIVIL SOCIETY, AFRICAN AMERICAN

CHURCHES, AND PUBLIC LIFE

Allison Calhoun-Brown

The historic importance of black churches to the survival and liberation of individuals in an enslaved and segregated American society, and their importance to the interaction of individuals through the Great Migration, the civil rights movement, and electoral political efforts, should not be understated. As the primary institutions in civil society they helped perform the functions most often associated with institutions of civil society, including helping individuals to define community, understand norms, learn social trust, and develop civic skills and values. However, the ways churches have impacted and influenced individuals must be understood in relation to the uniqueness of the circumstances in which these institutions have emerged as well as the cultural and societal context in which they have had to operate. Moreover, the importance of black churches to civil society should not focus solely on how these institutions have helped individuals interact in community. Special attention must be given to black churches at the institutional level because the responses and resources of churches as voluntary organizations have been as important to empowering black people in the United States as actions taken by individuals.

Civil society has been defined as "those forms of communal associational life which are organized neither by the self interest of the market, nor by the coercive potential of the state."[1] For much of American history, racial segregation and exclusion extended to the market, state action, and communal associational life. These three spheres are usually conceptualized as independent of one another. However, the fact that blacks were neither free to organize according to the logic of the markets, nor free to organize politically to combat the coercive potential of the state, enhanced the role of this third component, communal associational life. In a racist context that did not allow blacks freedom to join mainstream voluntary organizations or the resources to establish many, even segregated civic institutions, the only widely accessible communal associations for black people were black churches.

This essay reviews the literature on civil society and the literature on black churches with the purpose of examining whether the ways in which the black church impacts public life adhere to or differ from the expectations suggested by the civil society literature. Broadly, that literature holds that participating in institutions is important to the development of civic skills and trust in individual citizens.[2] Civic skills and civic trust can then be translated into the type of social skills and trust that are necessary for democratic processes and democratic governance.[3] However, there are a number of challenges in applying the civil society literature to African American churches. Embedded in a large part of this literature is the assumption that participation in voluntary associations such as churches serves to reinforce the social order. Yet African American churches have been bases for challenging this order. They have historically been what Evans and Boyte referred to as "free spaces" — "environment[s] in which people are able to learn a new self-respect, a deeper and more assertive group identity, public skills and values of cooperation and civic virtue."[4] Harris refers to the ability of black churches to both reinforce civic loyalty and challenge racial inequality as "an oppositional civic culture."[5] He explains that black churches "serve as a source of civic culture by giving African-Americans the opportunity to develop positive orientations toward the civic order. The same institutions, however, also provide African-Americans with material resources and oppositional dispositions to challenge their marginality."[6] This duality affects each of the arenas in which the civil society literature suggests that voluntary activity matters — the development and utilization of individual capacities, the creation of community, and the protection and representation of interests in public life.[7]

The Impact of Voluntary Associations

DEVELOPING INDIVIDUAL CAPACITY

According to the civil society literature one of the primary benefits of participation in voluntary associations is the development of social capital. Putnam
defines social capital as the "features of social life — networks, norms, trust —
that enable participants to act together more effectively to pursue shared
objectives."[8] This perspective rests on a social-psychological understanding
about how good government and social institutions operate as the result of
the effective socialization of individuals into cooperative behavior patterns
through voluntary associations. Putnam describes how individuals who participate in such associations learn to work effectively with others in a group
context. They gain social trust, which spills over into trust in government.
The social trust that is developed through cooperative social interactions
serves to produce intelligent public policies that are beneficial to society as
a whole. Participation in voluntary associations helps to develop the social-
psychological resources that individuals need to participate in society and in
government.

Does participation in African American churches impact social capital?
There is little doubt that attending and being a part of churches is beneficial to the development of social skills. It has been said that the black church
"has no challenger as the cultural womb of the black community."[9] Historical
accounts have detailed the myriad of colleges, businesses, fraternities, sorori-
ties, secret societies and orders, musical groups, and civic and political organizations that have found their genesis in black churches. Frazier called the
church "a nation within a nation" in referring to the degree to which activities in and around these institutions structured the lives of African American
people as late as the 1960s.[10]

Other studies also support the observation that participating in church
can be beneficial to social-psychological well-being. Several studies have
found a relationship between church attendance and self-esteem, as well as
feelings of well-being and personal efficacy.[11] These observations are particularly significant because throughout much of American history, African
Americans were subject to the type of systematic racial oppression that was
purposely designed to dehumanize them.

Evidence also exists that participating in African American churches pro duces social trust. Harris found that during the civil rights movement church attendance and denominational affiliation encouraged inclusive, system-supporting political activities such as campaign activism and voter participation but discouraged exclusive, system-challenging forms of political participation such as political violence and black nationalism.[12] However, the social trust that is produced in black churches should not be interpreted as wholly system affirming. Reese and Brown report that messages presented in churches communicate civic awareness as well as feelings of racial identity and system blame.[13] Feelings of system blame and racial identification have been associated with racial consciousness and support for greater black autonomy.[14] Thus African American churches generate both trust and distrust in American society. This is not necessarily problematic. Theda Skocpol, for instance, asserts that "democracies [are] a product of organized conflict and distrust" more than the result of harmonious civil societies.[15] Still, though the oppositional civic consciousness that black churches communicate may not impact the actual development of social capital, this type of civic consciousness might be expected to impact the objectives for which that social capital is expended.

The civil society literature maintains that the development of social capital is not simply important because of the social-psychological benefits it offers to individuals but because these benefits motivate and support democratic participation and governance. Does participation in African American churches support political participation? Historically, this question is difficult to assess. While today we often presuppose available opportunities for political input in democratic societies, rigid systems of segregation, discrimination, and political disenfranchisement precluded these expressions by many African Americans until the latter part of the twentieth century. The level of racial exclusion by mainstream society left few outlets for available social capital. Thus, much of African American civil, political, and economic activity was redirected to the churches and to the other fledgling civic institutions that operated largely under their auspices.

Whether or not African American churches were supportive of the development of democratic processes is the subject of some controversy. Many point to the elections and politicking for leadership offices that went on in many churches as evidence of the presence of an understanding of electoral norms and processes.[16] Others caution that authoritarian patterns of control and organization nullified any education blacks might have received from black churches about democratic governance and practice.[17] While church leadership positions provided opportunities for acclaim to those who otherwise had no access to power in the wider society, Myrdal and other researchers concluded that the parallel nature of black church society was a "distorted development" and would ultimately serve to block access by blacks to the American mainstream.[18] Others suggested that the otherworldly nature of African American Christianity coupled with the apathy associated with lower socioeconomic groups rendered black churches "involuntarily isolated" and unable to engage their people politically.[19] Nonetheless, despite this history, more contemporary research reveals that individuals who attend African American churches can gain the social-psychological resources that are important to voting behavior[20] and that even otherworldly sentiments can be associated with racial empowerment.[21]

DEFINING COMMUNITY

The second reason voluntary associations are thought to be important to civil society is that they help to define community. The rationale is that in a "participant civic culture" like the United States conceptions of community are expanded through voluntary associations and that these types of expansions are beneficial to democracy.[22] Interactions in these associations facilitate the kind of cooperation and tolerance that are necessary for democratic governance. However, voluntary associations have certainly not always produced inclusive conceptions of community.[23] Indeed, the sorry, segregated history of the United States underscores this point.

Moreover, in looking at the relationship of African American churches to civil society and public life, it is important to realize that church communities were formed to a great extent in response to the fact that so many channels of activity outside the church were closed. As Mays and Nicholson commented, "it is not too much to say that if the Negro had experienced a wide range of freedom in the social and economic spheres, there would have been . . . fewer Negro churches."[24] To fail to account for the racially polarized context in which black churches had to operate is to misunderstand the history and nature of "voluntary communities" in American society.

The segregated churches and voluntary associations of many white Americans often served not to destroy but to reinforce the racial divide. Historically black churches have helped to constitute *black* community. This is not to say that black churches undermine a sense of American identity. To the contrary, Christian admonitions to love thy neighbor and to respect the equality of all people before God may instill a sense of broader community. There is little evidence to suggest that members of black churches are any less susceptible to the doctrines of American civil religion than others in American society. However, from their inception in slavery, churches represented more than just a place for religious expression. They provided a means of social cohesion to a people denied even the most rudimentary associations of language, home, and family.[25] Wilmore records that the relationship between churches and the black community also extended to free blacks. He writes that the black church independence movement "must be regarded . . . in every sense, [as] the first black freedom movement."[26] From the beginning, race and religion have ordered the lives of African American people, and there has always been a unique relationship between them. As Paris suggests, "black churches have always had a profound concern for the bitter and painful realities of black existence in America, as well as an abiding hope in a bright and radiant future (eschaton) free from any form of racial injustice." He continues, "the convergence of sacred principles with efforts for improved temporal conditions reveals the integral relationship of religion and politics in black churches."[27] It also reveals the minimal differentiation between the church and the African American community.

Given this history, how voluntary associations promote and define community in a context of racial polarization or stratification may be very different from how voluntary associations might define community in a more equal society. Notably, churches persist as the most segregated institutions in society. Contemporary empirical research indicates that participation in African American churches helps to define black group identification and black group consciousness.[28] This strengthening of minority identification may contribute to a more collective political orientation when individuals interact in other arenas of civil society and public life.

PROTECTION AND REPRESENTATION OF INTERESTS

A third area in which participation in voluntary associations is perceived to be important is in the protection and representation of interests. Scholzman, Verba, and Brady make some insightful observations about how civic engagement effects the protection of interests.[29] Rather than drawing on the conceptions of congruent community interests that inform much of the civil society literature, they focus on clashing individual and group interests that make issues of representation so important. For them what matters "is not only the amount of civic activity but also its distribution, not just how many people take part, but also who they are. In short, concern for democratic equality forces us not only to inquire how many people are bowling and whether they do so solo or in leagues, but also to ask who bowls."[30] While African American churches have been shown to encourage political and social activities through the church, Wuthnow's research indicates that church attendance among black evangelicals is not significantly associated with being a member of any other nonreligious civic group. Finding this true for both black and white evangelicals, Wuthnow explains that though evangelical churches generate social capital, the social capital that they generate is likely to be kept within their own organization.[31] Although studies have consistently shown that black churches can play a role in electoral mobilization dynamics,[32] the evidence that this context serves to influence political opinion formation within the congregation, or facilitate interest articulation outside of it, is virtually nonexistent.[33] The development of individual-level social capital in one voluntary association is no guarantee of interest representation by these individuals in broader societal contexts.

More importantly, the individual-level focus of much of the civil society literature obscures the fact that "voluntary associations matter as sources of popular leverage, not just as facilitators of individual participation and social trust."[34] It ignores how voluntary associations themselves can help to transform political institutions and relationships in society. Elisabeth Clemens discusses this point in examining the institutional effects of women's civic associations in American society.[35] "Beyond providing opportunities for individuals to develop political skills and to cultivate social networks or social capital, civic associations have often served as important sites for organizational experimentation." She continues, "To the extent that such associations are public but not fully integrated with formal political institutions, they may provide platforms for the invention of new forms of political mobilization."[36] The important organizational roles that black churches played during the civil rights movement are the clearest demonstration of this fact in regard to the black community.[37] Social movements, such as that for civil rights, demonstrate that the institutions of civil society are often the most effective means to protect and represent the interests of aggrieved groups.

The traditional way of studying the effects of black religion in the African American community has been to focus on the impact of African American churches as institutions.[38] However, Mukenge asserts that social scientists have neglected the structural dimension of the black church as the primary object of analysis since the mid-1960s.[39] He contends that the focus of more contemporary studies has been on ideology or ministerial style or various components of religiosity.[40] It is true that with an understanding of the multi-dimensionality of religion as well as survey research methodologies, the unit of analysis in studies of the black church has often become individuals and not the religious contexts in which these individuals operate. Moreover, as in much of the field of political behavior, an emphasis on survey research methodologies has shifted the favored measure of religiosity toward church attendance and the favored measure of political involvement toward voter participation. Although these aspects of both religiosity and political participation should be appreciated and assessed, this type of individual-level research has obfuscated the myriad of ways institutions such as churches can be involved in the political process beyond simply voting. Indeed, focusing on the individual level and voting behavior takes attention away from other important parts of the political process including agenda setting, interest articulation, policy formation, policy implementation, policy impact, and policy assessment — areas in which an institutional presence may be particularly significant. Certainly this was the experience of the African American community during the civil rights movement. The organizational presence of black churches and ministerial associations advocating for black people substantially impacted the favorable resolution of civil rights boycotts, protests, and demonstrations at the national level as well as in small and large cities all over America. This presence also led to significant policy changes. However, the effectiveness of black institutions in affecting policy today is a subject that too often goes unexamined.

Black Churches and Public Life

THE CHANGING SOCIETAL CONTEXT

However, if we are to examine the role of black churches today in representing interests (or developing social capital and defining community), it is important to appreciate not only the racial-historical context but the significant changes that have taken place in American civil society, the black community, and the nature and practice of black religion since the 1960s. Since the end of the civil rights movement there has been tremendous social change in America. In the last three and a half decades people's ideas and perceptions about community have been dramatically altered by developments like the end to codified racism and systematic segregation, a change in societal gender roles, and an information-communication technology explosion that has changed the nature of how we interact in the world. The past few decades have witnessed a rise in fundamentalist-oriented religion,[41] a rise in advocacy organizations, a decline in belief that the government has the ability to address social needs and concerns, and a decline in the hegemony of traditional Christianity in the American context.

These general societal trends have produced dramatic changes in the black community and in black churches as well. The end to legalized racism has allowed class differences among blacks to gain greater salience. The end to segregation has produced the suburbanization of the black middle class. This same trend has left the black underclass in decaying urban areas. Black churches often comprise members who do not live close to the institution. These churches are faced with the relatively new discussion about whether the community is the people who attend the church or the people who live in the neighborhood. Because the material interests of those two communities may not be synonymous, they have to prioritize the needs of their constituencies. Changes in racial, gender, and technology enhanced interpersonal relations have further affected how blacks define community. C. Eric Lincoln contends that though the black church has always been considered the "most formidable bastion of black identity, the 'Tiger Woods syndrome' which rejects the race of one parent as being defining to the exclusion of the other is awesome in its potential for the fragmentation of the church and the African-American community."[42] Black women are increasingly clear that racial identification cannot be constructed in a way that excludes gender. Many theorists contend that the political socialization that has occurred in African American churches tends to emphasize racial unity at the expense of gender concerns.[43] As in the rest of American society, the fastest-growing churches among blacks are the most theologically conservative. The rise in the numbers of parishioners attending denominations like the Church of God in Christ as well as independent churches that deemphasize racial issues in favor of a "prosperity gospel" has been dramatic.[44] The increase in the number of advocacy organizations has also impacted the black community. Debra Minkoff documents that the number of groups advocating for the interest of minorities increased sixfold between 1955 and 1985.[45] Thus, the centrality of black churches to the interests of the African American community may be undermined. The decline in the belief that the government can effectively address social problems might have served to enhance the public position of African American churches. However, because of the support of black churches for electoral representation as a means of addressing issues that have faced the black community, they too have become associated with the limited progress that electoral politics produces. This dissatisfaction has contributed to a loss of the traditional black churches' hegemony in social and political affairs. Increasing numbers of African Americans do not go church and do not look to the church for leadership. Whereas a generation ago as many as 80 percent of blacks went to church, today some contend that number is as low as 40 percent.[46] While this number is probably a little low, the feeling that black churches are in trouble persists. Much of the basis for this concern emerges from the fact that the unchurched come disproportionately from young, men, and the underclass. The irony of this is that these are precisely the communities that have traditionally been underrepresented and the communities toward which much contemporary sociopolitical action needs to be focused.

THE PERSPECTIVE OF BLACK LIBERATION THEOLOGY

Contemporary changes in society have left black churches at the proverbial crossroads with regard to their public role. Traditionally black churches have impacted civil society, albeit in somewhat different ways than the civil society literature suggests. However, their continued capacity, willingness, mandate, and effectiveness to carry out a public role may be altered in the light of societal changes. As James Cone explained, "If we want the black church to live beyond our brief histories and thus serve as the 'Old Ship of Zion' that will carry the people home to freedom, then we had better examine the direction in which the ship is going."[47] Lawrence Jones suggested more than twenty years ago that "religious institutions have not been sufficiently cognizant of the radical implications which the changing political, economic and social realities have for their life."[48] It is not that the existence of black churches is threatened. To the extent that poor blacks are marginalized in American society the role that black churches play in public life may be all the more significant. However, as Forrest Harris has observed:

> It has become increasingly obvious to the black community that access to nonsegregated public facilities and leadership in electoral politics has had a marginal impact on economic sources of black suffering as well as the need for organizing the community's resources for liberation. Black churches are discovering that some of the greatest needs are institutional, structural, systemic, and deeply rooted in the culture. These complex social crises require new ministry strategies and a refinement of the black church's theology and praxis.[49]

One such attempt to refine the theology and praxis of black churches has been through black liberation theology. James Cone was the first to formally explicate the tenets of black theology in the late 1960s and early 1970s. Black theology was the religious counterpart of the secular movement called black power:

> Black theology is a religious explication of black people's need to redefine the scope and meaning of black existence in white racist society. Black power focuses on the political, social and economic condition of black people, seeking to define concretely the meaning of black self determination in a society that has placed definite limits on black humanity. Black theology puts black identity in a theological context, showing that black power is not only consistent with the gospel of Jesus Christ: it is the gospel of Jesus Christ.[50]

However, some have questioned the extent of black liberation theology's integration and incorporation into everyday ministry. As Lincoln and Mamiya explain, "unless the movement of black liberation theology reaches beyond its present location in an intellectual elite and gives more attention to the development of hermeneutical traditions within the African-American community and to a mass education of clergy and laity in churches, the movement will continue to have minimal influence among its key constituencies."[51] Thus, although theologically linkages have been developed between spiritual functions and more public roles, the degree to which these linkages are practically applied and incorporated into ministry will determine whether black churches will continue to develop social capital, define community, and represent interests the way they have in the historic past.

The Black Church and the New Millennium

Given all of this, what can we expect the contemporary impact of black churches to be on public life? How can we anticipate that black churches as the primary voluntary associations in the black community will affect the development of social capital, the definitions of community, and the representation of interest?

First, the development of social capital through participation in churches is likely to continue. Though some have expressed concern that increasing professionalization and bureaucratization in African American churches undermines the opportunities for parishioners to develop civic skills,[52] current evidence suggests that simply attending many black churches increases social capital. However, to the extent that the environment in which the church operates is racially polarized, this social capital is likely to be expended primarily in support of the interest of the black community.

Second, churches will continue to struggle to define community in an increasingly complicated environment. Traditionally they have helped to develop racial identification and consciousness. Because churches are still the most segregated institutions in American society, the promotion of this identification is likely to continue. However, to the extent that the challenges of class, ethnicity, geography, and gender to unhyphenated racial identification frustrate the ability of black churches to define community in traditional ways, the institutions may have to seek alternative means of giving their people a sense of unity. In the era of fundamentalist religion this unity is often found in conservative religious and doctrinal beliefs. The effect of this on public life is that definitions of community begin to exclude those who may not subscribe to those opinions. Considering the dominant doctrines of the majority of black churches, groups like homosexuals, drug addicts, or people concerned with women's rights may increasingly be alienated from churchgoers in the black community.

Finally, one of the most exciting areas of research related to the function of social capital concerns how the church as an institution will represent or provide popular leverage for the interests of the black community. This subject is particularly intriguing in this time when the possibility exists for churches to have a significant policy impact as the government increasingly looks to partner with them to more effectively provide social services. Given its history as well as more contemporary developments we might expect the following:

The continued involvement of black churches in the area of civil rights. The black church has a rich history of advocating for these issues. As an institution it has most effectively developed and utilized its social capital in this area, and traditional civil rights issues involving race reinforce the more basic conceptions of community. However, it is increasingly difficult to define issues in a "rights" and not a "resources" framework. Pursuing rights has moral authority. Pursuing resources is subject to the hard realities of self-interested political pursuits. Resource politics is subject to the types of compromises that at the very least undermine moral authority and are often hard to reconcile with a "rights"-oriented framework. Thus, we might expect churches to be involved in traditional issues of civil rights and to continue to attempt to frame even resource-related discussions in rights-based terminology in an effort to maintain their moral authority. Church involvement will be most effective in cases where an issue is understood as a violation of a civil right. But rights-based arguments alone will not be adequate in resource politics — though the church as an institution may continue to make them because of the difficulties involved in their adopting more pragmatic positions.

Churches will oppose policies and programs that violate conservative doctrinal beliefs. Black churches will not powerfully advocate for issues having to do with matters such as women's rights, gay rights, or sexual-health issues. The conservative nature of the church's teaching on most of these subjects will prevent it from more substantive policy-oriented engagement around such topics. The church can most effectively advocate on issues that are tied clearly to the "right" side of a moral position. As long as other positions are by definition sinful there is little room to be accommodating to them. The ultimate answer of many conservative churches to social problems is deliverance not treatment. People need the Lord. Thus, it is difficult for churches to fully embrace or advocate for programs and policies that in the end offer but limited solutions. Moreover, the church has not dealt with issues of patriarchy and sexuality in the institution itself. Thus, it cannot be expected to be part of the vanguard around social problems related to these issues.

Churches will be interested in the issue areas of disprivileged segments of the community.[53] One of the most basic church missions is ministering to those in need. Most churches care deeply and many have programs to address the needs of people who are hungry, poor, elderly, sick, or hurting. However, in this area, church activity might be expected to be directed more toward enhancing its own ability to address the needs of its communities by outreaches in faith-factor-oriented programs than toward helping to develop or advocate for other government policies and programs that would address these needs.[54] Churches are better equipped to take on limited social services (like healthcare screening) than to enter the politics of substantive policy areas (like legislation to support greater access to health insurance). Social services are akin to the "ministries" in which churches have always engaged. Social service delivery, at least on the surface, does not represent a significant departure from that which churches have always done. However, there is a significant difference between delivering food baskets to needy families during the holidays and actually feeding the hungry. Rarely have churches offered ministries in the consistent, systematic, and sustained manner that would be required for them to actually be the primary deliverer of such services in the black community. Nonetheless, there may be willingness for some to explore an expanded role for their ministries in social services as well as a willingness to advocate for programs that facilitate such a role, because at the most rudimentary level social service activities look familiar to already functioning ministries of their churches.

Still, as Billingsley observed concerning black churches and social reform, "Many [churches] do not have the resources or the leadership to engage in such programs. And even if all churches did so, there would not be enough to meet the needs. The church, then, must serve as example and catalyst for the work which must be done by government and private agencies in collaboration with churches."[55] Whether or not churches will be this kind of catalyst remains to be seen. Many suggest that churches are better equipped to address issues of social service than the government. However, it is not a foregone conclusion that churches will be exemplary in this area. Potentially, there are considerable challenges. Do churches have the types of bureaucratic structures required to systematically deliver services? Do they have processes institutionalized in such a way that services will occur regardless of the personnel involved? How will the antidemocratic, highly personal nature of most church leadership interact with the routinized and bureaucratized standards of government work? Do churches have the administrative capacity and financial discipline to adequately deal with reporting issues? Moreover, being such a catalyst for effective government programs requires moving deeper into the policy-making process and developing skills and resources beyond the political mobilization so often associated with black churches.

Churches will be active in areas that enhance their own status, such as Community Development Corporation–related programs and publicly funded private schools. Such areas are appealing because in them churches can act largely on their own auspices and still engage in an expanded public role with public support. These areas provide them with good opportunities to have a substantial public impact but offer only broad guidelines on how they go about doing so. Therefore, they can act independently according to their own convictions and vision and still have significant policy effects free from many of the constraints of the public-policy-making process. In a time when churches are losing their hegemony, their authority may be strengthened if through such programs they can successfully demonstrate continued centrality and relevance.

African American churches are still the strongest institutions in the African American community and thus are well positioned to perform many of the functions of voluntary associations in civil society. However, the uniqueness of the African American experience in the United States, coupled with the tremendous changes that have taken place in American civil society and in the black community, structure the nature of the impact that churches have on the people who attend those institutions as well as the effectiveness and the willingness of the institution to represent the interest of the African American community in the broader American society.

Notes

1 Alan Wolfe, "Is Civil Society Obsolete?" in E. J. Dionne, ed., *Community Works* (Washington, D.C.: Brookings, 1998), 17.

2 James Coleman, *Foundations of Social Theory* (Cambridge: Harvard University Press, 1990).

3 Dietland Stolle and Thomas Rochon, "Are All Associations Alike?" *American Behavioral Scientist* 98, (1998): 47–66. See also Robert Putnam, "Robert Putnam Responds," *American Prospect* 25 (March 1996): 26–28.

4 Sara Evans and Harry Boyte, *Free Spaces: The Sources of Democratic Change in America* (New York: Harper and Row, 1986), 17.

5 Fredrick Harris, *Something Within: Religion in African-American Political Activism* (New York: Oxford University Press, 1999).

6 Ibid., 40.

7 Kay Scholzman, Sidney Verba, and Henry Brady, "Civic Participation and the Equality Problem," in *Civic Engagement and American Democracy* (Washington, D.C.: Brookings, 1999).

8 Robert Putnam, "Tuning In, Tuning Out: The Strange Disappearance of Social Capital in America," *PS: Political Science and Politics* (December 1995): 668.

9 C. Eric Lincoln and Lawrence Mamiya, *The Black Church in the African-American Experience* (Durham: Duke University Press, 1990), 8.

10 E. Franklin Frazier, *The Negro Church in America* (New York: Schocken Books, 1963).

11 Christoper Ellison, "Religious Involvement and Self Perception among Black Americans," *Social Forces* 71 (1993): 1027–55. See also Cheryl Townsend Gilkes, "The Black Church as a Therapeutic Community: Suggested Areas for Research in the Black Religious Experience," *Journal of the Interdenominational Theological Center* 8 (1980): 29–44; Benjamin E. Mays and Joseph Nicholson, *The Negro's Church* (New York: Russell and Russell (1969 reissue); Carter G. Woodson, *The History of the Negro Church,* 2d ed. (Washington, D.C.: Associated Publishers, 1945).

12 Harris, *Something Within.*

13 Laura Reese and Ronald Brown, "The Effects of Religious Messages on Racial Identity and System Blame among African-Americans," *Journal of Politics* 57 (1995): 24–43.

14 Richard Allen, Michael Dawson, and Ronald Brown, "A Schema-Based Approach to Modeling and African-American Racial Belief System," *American Political Science Review* 83 (1989): 421–41.

15 Theda Skocpol and Morris Fiorina, "Making Sense of the Civic Engagement Debate," in Theda Skocpol and Morris Fiorina, eds., *Civic Engagement and American Democracy* (Washington, D.C.: Brookings, 1999), 14.

16 Hart Nelsen and Anne Kusener Nelsen, *The Black Church in the Sixties* (Lexington: University of Kentucky Press, 1975).

17 Frazier, *The Negro Church in America.*

18 Gunnar Myrdal, *An American Dilemma: The Negro Problem and American Democracy,* vols. 1 and 2 (New York: Harper and Row, 1944).

19 Albert Cleague, "The Black Messiah and the Black Revolution," in J. Gardiner and J. D. Roberts, eds., *Quest for Black Theology* (Philadelphia: Pilgrim Press, 1971). See also Gary Marx, *Protest and Prejudice* (New York: Harper and Row, 1969); Anthony Orum, "A Reappraisal of the Social and Political Participation of Negroes," *American Journal of Sociology* 72 (1966): 33.

20 Allison Calhoun-Brown, "African-American Churches and Political Mobilization: The Psychological Impact of Organizational Resources," *Journal of Politics* 58 (1996): 935–53. See also Harris, *Something Within.* Other helpful works include Katherine Tate, *From Protest to Politics: The New Black Voters in American Elections* (New York: Russell Sage Foundation, 1993); Patricia Gurin, Shirley Hatchett, and James Jackson, *Hope and Independence: Black Responses to Electoral and Party Politics* (New York: Russell Sage Foundation, 1989).

21 Brian McKenzie, "Beyond Symbols: Examining the Political Impact of Black Liberation Theology." Paper prepared for the Southern Political Science Association meeting in Atlanta, 8–11 November 2000. See also Allison Calhoun-Brown, "While Marching to Zion: Otherworldiness and Racial Empowerment in the African-American Community," *Journal for the Scientific Study of Religion* 37 (1999): 427–40.

22 Gabriel Almond and Sidney Verba, *The Civic Culture: Political Attitudes and Democracy in Five Nations* (Princeton: Princeton University Press, 1963).

23 Michael Foley and Bob Edwards, "Escape from Politics? Social Theory and the Social Capital Debate," *American Behavioral Scientist* 40 (March/April 1997): 550–61.

24 Mays and Nicholson, *The Negro's Church,* 11.

25 Frazier, *The Negro Church in America.* See also Albert Raboteau, *Slave Religion: The Invisible Institution* (New York: Oxford Univeristy Press, 1978).

26 Gayraud Wilmore, *Black and Presbyterian: The Heritage of Hope* (Philadelphia: Geneva Press, 1983), 78.

27 Peter Paris, *The Social Teachings of Black Churches* (Philadelphia: Fortress Press, 1985), 2.

28 Clyde Wilcos, "Racial and Gender Consciousness among African-American Women: Sources and Consequences," *Women and Politics* 17 (1997): 73–94. See also Calhoun-Brown, "African-American Churches and Political Mobilization"; Christopher Ellison, "Identification and Separatism: Religious Involvement and Racial Orientations among Black Americans," *Sociological Quarterly* 32 (1991): 477–94; Michael Dawson, Ron Brown, and Robert Allen, "Racial Belief Systems, Religious

Guidance, and African-American Political Participation," *National Political Science Review* 2 (1990): 22–44.

29   Scholzman, Verba, and Brady, "Civic Participation."

30   Ibid., 429.

31   Robert Wuthnow, "Mobilizing Civic Engagement: The Changing Impact of Religious Involvement," in Theda Skocpol and Morris Fiorina, eds., *Civic Engagement and American Democracy* (Washington, D.C.: Brookings, 1999).

32   Harris, *Something Within.* See also Calhoun-Brown, "African-American Churches and Political Mobilization," and Tate, *From Protest to Politics.*

33   Maurice Mangum, "Otherworldly v. Thisworldly Concerns: Testing the Effects of Religion and Church on Black Political Attitudes." Paper presented at the Southern Political Science Association meeting in Atlanta, 8–11 November 2000.

34   Skocpol and Fiorina, "Making Sense of the Civic Engagement Debate," 15.

35   Elisabeth Clemens, "Organizational Repertoires and Institutional Change: Women's Groups and the Transformation of American Politics," in Theda Skocpol and Morris Fiorina, eds., *Civic Engagement and American Democracy* (Washington, D.C.: Brookings, 1999).

36   Ibid., 82.

37   Douglas McAdam, *Political Process and the Development of Black Insurgency: 1930–1970* (Chicago: University of Chicago Press, 1982). See also Aldon Morris, *The Origins of the Civil Rights Movement: Black Communities Organizing for Change* (New York: Free Press, 1984).

38   Lincoln and Mamiya, *The Black Church in the African-American Experience.* Other important works include W. E. B. DuBois, *The Souls of Black Folk* (New York: Avon Books, [1903] 1965); Woodson, *The History of the Negro Church;* St. Claire Drake and Horace Cayton, *Black Metropolis* (Chicago: University of Chicago Press, [1945] 1993); Mays and Nicholson, *The Negro's Church;* Myrdal, *The American Dilemma;* Wilmore, *Black and Presbyterian;* Albert Raboteau, *Slave Religion: The Invisible Institution* (New York: Oxford University Press, 1978).

39   Ida Rousseau Mukenge, *The Black Church in Urban America: A Case Study in Political Economy* (Lanham, Md: University Press of America, 1983), 4.

40   See, for example, John Brown Childs, *The Political Black Minister: A Study in Afro American Politics and Religion* (Boston: G. K. Hall, 1980). See also Charles Hamilton, *The Black Preacher in America* (New York: Schocken Books, 1972); Harris, *Something Within.*

41   Wade Clark Rook and William McKinney, *American Mainline Religion: Its Changing Shape and Future* (New Brunswick: Rutgers University Press, 1987).

42   C. Eric Lincoln, Introduction, in Andrew Billingsley, *Mighty Like a River: The Black Church and Social Reform* (New York: Oxford University Press, 1999), xxiv.

43   Bettye Collier-Thomas, *Daughters of Thunder: Black Women Preachers and Their*

Sermons, 1850–1979 (San Francisco: Jossey-Bass Publishers, 1998). See also James Cone, "Black Theology and the Black Church: Where Do We Go from Here?" in James Cone and Gayraud Wilmore, eds., *Black Theology and Black Liberation* (Maryknoll, N.Y.: Orbis Books, 1993); Paula Giddings, *When and Where I Enter: The Impact of Black Women on Race and Sex in America* (New York: William Morrow, 1984).

44 Harris, *Something Within;* Lincoln and Mamiya, *The Black Church in the African-American Experience.*

45 Debra Minkoff, *Organizing for Equality: The Evolution of Women's Racial and Ethnic Organizations in America, 1955–1985* (Philadelphia: Temple University Press, 1995).

46 Andres Tapia, "Soul Searching: How Is the Black Church Responding to the Urban Crisis?" *Christianity Today* (4 March 1996): 26–30.

47 James Cone, "Black Theology and the Black Church," in Milton Sernett, ed., *African-American Religious History: A Documentary Witness* (Durham: Duke University Press, [1977] 1999), 572.

48 Lawrence Jones, "Black Churches: A New Agenda," *The Christian Century* 96 (18 April 1979): 434.

49 Forrest Harris Sr., *Ministry for Social Crisis: Theology and Praxis in the Black Church Tradition* (Macon, Ga: Mercer University Press, 1993), 30–31.

50 Cone, "Black Theology and Black Liberation," 106.

51 Lincoln and Mamiya, *The Black Church in the African-American Experience,* 181.

52 Harris, *Something Within.*

53 Mark Chaves and Lynn Higgins, "Comparing the Community Involvement of Black and White Congregations," *Journal for the Scientific Study of Religion* 54 (1992): 147–69.

54 Ram Cnaan, *The Newer Deal: Social Work and Religion in Partnership* (New York: Columbia University Press, 1999). See also Mark Chaves, *Congregations' Social Service Activities. Policy Brief No. 6,* Center on Non Profits and Philanthropy (Washington, D.C.: Urban Institute, 1999).

55 Billingsley, *Mighty Like A River: The Black Church and Social Reform,* 188.

3

SYSTEM CONFIDENCE, CONGREGATIONAL

CHARACTERISTICS, AND BLACK CHURCH

CIVIC ENGAGEMENT

R. Drew Smith and Corwin Smidt

The concept of "dual citizenship" has been used to describe a feeling of political conflictedness — either by people whose discriminatory exclusion from citizenship rights has led them to pursue political alternatives to the formal politics within their national context, or by people wrestling within a modern national setting with enduring loyalties to "ancestral or primordial communities." The concept has been applied, in both instances, to contemporary social contexts in Africa,[1] but the dualities framed by the concept can be drawn on to talk about a type of tension felt within African American churches — churches pulled between political convention and political resistance, in one sense, and between temporal and spiritual imperatives, in another sense. Both dualities have guided choices by African American parishioners about whether, or how, to participate in American civic life. Fresh evidence of the persistence of these tensions within African American church life are presented and analyzed in this chapter.

This chapter also joins another kind of discussion about the interaction between African American religion and politics. Many African American churchpersons have chosen to participate in American political life — despite, or perhaps because of, the dualities they inhabit — and scholars have been increasingly interested in understanding some of the factors that have contributed to political participation in these instances. Attention has been given to factors such as the organizing skills of the congregation;[2] the congregation's institutional capacity, including the size of the membership;[3] religious inspiration;[4] and political inspiration.[5] A number of these factors will be explored here as well, primarily through analysis of data from the 1999–2000 Black Churches and Politics Survey (BCAP; see appendix for database characteristics). Specifically, the chapter examines contemporary trends in the civic involvements of black churches, noting the strong emphasis by black churches within the last few decades on electoral politics. In examining factors shaping the civic culture of black churches, we find that the likelihood of black church activism is influenced less by affinity or dissatisfaction with the American political system (system confidence) than by factors related to a congregation's resources.

Trends in the Civic Involvements of Black Churches

The heightened public activism and civic engagement by African American churches during the civil rights movement represented, for some, a political coming of age for black churches. With civil rights protest giving way to a renewed emphasis in African American communities on electoral politics, it was believed that a politically energized black church sector would be strategic to black electoral hopes.[6] The increase in the number of black elected officials—from approximately 100 in 1965 to over 8,000 in the year 2000—and the conspicuous involvement of black clergy in electoral affairs as political officeholders and as political brokers would seem to suggest that some of this black church political potential has been realized (see also introduction, pp. 4–6).

Data from the BCAP survey substantiate the strong election-oriented culture that exists among contemporary black churches. BCAP survey respondents were asked about their congregation's electoral involvements over the previous ten years, including participation in voter registration activities, transporting people to the polls on election day, passing out campaign materials, and advocacy related to ballot issues or referendums. Most pastors (84 percent) indicated that their congregations had been involved with voter registration initiatives, while nearly two-thirds (64 percent) reported congregational efforts to transport people to the polls, and approximately half that many said their congregations had been involved in passing out campaign materials (see table 1). These data related to voter registration and voter transport confirm impressions about the importance of black churches to black voter mobilization.[7]

TABLE 1 Select List of Congregational Activism

Q: During the last ten years has your congregation engaged in . . .

Voter registration	84%
Assisted with rides to the polls on election day	64%
Passed out campaign materials	31%
Advocated on behalf of a ballot issue or referendum	28%
Protest rallies or marches	17%

Source: 1999–2000 Black Churches and Politics Survey

A more conspicuous form of black church leadership in electoral affairs has been the holding of elective office by black clergy, and BCAP survey respondents were asked whether the congregation's pastor had ever held elective office. Nearly a tenth (9.2 percent) of the 1,956 BCAP survey respondents indicated that the pastor had served in such a capacity.[8] If the survey sample is truly representative of African American clergy in general, this suggests that hundreds of black clergy have served in elective office over the last thirty years. The most prominent of this group are the six black clergy elected to the U.S. Congress since 1971 (Walter Fauntroy, Andrew Young, William Gray III, Floyd Flake, John Lewis, and J. C. Watts). However, given that the majority of black officeholders have served as state and local legislators, county board members, and school board members,[9] it is likely that the vast majority of black clergy officeholders conform to this pattern as well.

Not only has there been a sizable percentage of black clergy who have served in elective office, the increase of such service during the 1990s was fairly dramatic. Of the pastors who indicated that they had served in elective office, 32 percent reported that they were serving at the time the 1999–2000 survey was conducted. However, 25 percent reported that they had served within five years prior to the survey, and 21 percent reported that they had served six to ten years prior to the survey. Another 16 percent said they had served during the 1980s, while only 4 percent had served prior to the 1980s. That means that among the pastors in the sample who have served in elective office, approximately 80 percent rendered that service no earlier than the 1990s (see table 2).

The BCAP survey asked respondents about participation by their congre-

TABLE 2 Period Elected Service by Pastors Took Place

Current	32%
Within last five years	25%
Six to ten years ago	21%
Eleven to twenty years ago	16%
More than twenty years ago	4%

Source: 1999–2000 Black Churches and Politics Survey

gation in a range of political activities that represent varying degrees of familiarity with and confidence in the formal political process. Voting-related activity and political protest are, undoubtedly, the political activities that are
most familiar to black churches. At the other end of the familiarity spectrum would be public policy formation. The public policy involvements of
black churches will not be covered extensively here,[10] although two measurements of public policy involvement will be included in the present discussion:
(1) whether the congregation has, over the past ten years, advocated on behalf of a specific ballot issue, proposition, or referendum; and (2) whether
the congregation is currently engaged in some civic or political organization.
The data in table 1 show that congregational involvement in advocacy related to ballot issues and in protest activities (despite its high degree of familiarity) significantly trails congregational involvement in voter-related activities (especially voter registration initiatives). Twenty-eight percent of the
congregations were involved in advocacy related to ballot issues, while only
17 percent of congregations reported involvement in protest activities. With
respect to current congregational involvement with civic or political organizations, 45 percent reported having such involvement (data not shown).

The extensive involvement by black churches in electoral affairs (as opposed to public policy formation or even protest) suggests fairly broad agreement among African American churchpersons about the necessity of a general involvement by their churches in political affairs. The emphasis here is
on the word "general," given that election-related activities — such as those
stressed by black church respondents — can be among the least demanding
forms of political engagement. After all, voting and organizing others to vote
occurs intermittently, and the voting process itself actually delegates some-

TABLE 3 Degree of Congregational Activism, Civil Rights Movement and Beyond

	CRM (%)	1980s (%)	1990s (%)
Very active	25	14	17
Somewhat active	64	75	72
Not very active	11	10	10
TOTAL	100	99	99
	N = 224	N = 321	N = 324

Source: 1999–2000 Black Churches and Politics Survey
Note: Column does not add up to 100% due to rounding.

one other than the voters to attend to day-to-day political matters. Therefore, one can actively participate in the voting process and still be relatively disengaged politically.

An indicator of this is that a subsample of BCAP respondents were asked how politically active the congregation was during the civil rights movement and, then, during the 1980s and 1990s. One-quarter of the respondents (25 percent) indicated that the congregation was "very active" during the civil rights movement, while only around 15 percent said the congregation was "very active" during the 1980s or during the 1990s. Roughly 10 percent admitted that the congregation was "not active at all" during those periods, while the overwhelming majority of the respondents indicated that the congregation was "somewhat active" during the three time periods (see table 3). What is especially revealing about these numbers is that only a small minority of congregations appears to have been decidedly active in political matters, despite the fact that much higher numbers of congregations reported involvement in some form of political activity.

Black Churches and Confidence in American Politics

In accounting for the scale and scope of black church activism within the context of American politics, there are attitudinal and procedural thresholds that are important to explore. For example, if black churches are not confident that specific forms of political participation have a reasonable likelihood of achieving the desired result — either because the procedural costs outweigh the benefits or because the system itself is deemed inherently unfair — this would have implications for whether or how black churches engage politically. Moreover, political engagement by black churches is affected by the way tensions between spiritual and temporal imperatives (that are common within many black churches) are negotiated. Factors such as these shape black church attitudes about the usefulness of participating in the American political process.

Black churches have differed widely in the extent to which they have communicated a sense of political utility. For many black churches, there are theological reasons for concluding that political matters are of limited importance and for directing their attention, instead, toward less temporal matters. But even where black churches have been politicized, there have been differing opinions among them about how likely African Americans are to gain from participation in the formal political process. Historically, there have been some African American Christians who have favored procedural approaches, while others have favored protest; there have been some who have advocated full integration into the American political system, and others who have advocated political separatism.

These contrasting views have drawn variously on two forms of "nationalism" — a "civil religious" form of American nationalism and a black racial nationalism.[11] The civil religious American nationalism, including its African American variants, expresses a belief in the potential religious significance of American politics and in the need to redeem the nation from its failures in order that it may achieve the moral purposes it is thought to possess. The U.S. Constitution is often invoked as a standard of the moral ideals that are part of the nation's charge, particularly its emphasis on the inalienable rights and freedoms of individuals.

Scholars have frequently pointed out how the political activism of black church leaders from the slavery era through the civil rights movement drew a sense of political confidence from these constitutional ideals. Peter Paris notes, for example, "it has been customary for the black churches to demonstrate unceasingly, in both thought and action, their strong patriotic spirit."[12] Evidence from the BCAP survey suggests that this confidence in American ideals remains constant among contemporary African American church

TABLE 4 Political Continuity Between African Americans and the U.S. Constitution

---

Q: African American social objectives are consistent with the social ideals expressed in the U.S. Constitution. What is your level of agreement with this statement?

Strongly agree	25%
Agree	36%
Uncertain	15%
Disagree	20%
Strongly disagree	4%
TOTAL	100%
	N = 863

Source: 1999–2000 Black Churches and Politics Survey

leaders. When asked if "African-American social objectives are consistent with social ideals expressed in the U.S. Constitution," slightly more that 60 percent of the respondents agreed, with 25 percent of that number agreeing strongly (see table 4).

A resonance with American political ideals, in combination with an increasing immersion in electoral affairs, has lessened some black church misgivings about exhibiting too close an association with the structures of American government. This is seen, in part, in the willingness of a number of black churches to enter into close programmatic collaborations with the government — something increasingly desired by governmental agencies as well, owing to a mounting emphasis on the "localization" of government services. This trend toward "localizing" government services has produced, among other things, a greater devolution of services from the federal to the state and local levels, and from government to private and community spheres. Churches have been heavily courted by government agencies as conduits for government program monies, particularly social services monies. The Charitable Choice provision of the Personal Responsibility and Work Opportunity Act of 1996 made it significantly easier for religious organizations to receive government monies, and numerous church-state collaborations around social service programs have developed as a result.

TABLE 5 Churches with Government-Funded Programs

Q: *Does your congregation have any programs for which it receives governmental funding?*

Yes	24%
No	76%
TOTAL	100%
	N = 1899

Source: 1999–2000 Black Churches and Politics Survey

BCAP survey respondents were asked, for example, if their congregations had programs for which they received governmental funding. Nearly a quarter (24 percent) of the respondents answered "yes" (see table 5). This percentage is three times the percentage reported by Lincoln and Mamiya in their 1990 study (8 percent).[13] A subsample of 324 BCAP respondents was asked, additionally, how they felt about churches receiving governmental funds for church-based programs. Of the subsample responding to the question, 9 percent strongly agreed with this practice and another 37 percent agreed. Nineteen percent of the respondents disagreed with this practice and 33 percent strongly disagreed (see table 6). Therefore, almost half of the sample favored programmatic collaborations between churches and government, which is a sizable level of support by black churches for such practices. The fact that more than half of the respondents were opposed to these partnerships, and that 33 percent were strongly opposed, is more in keeping with a historical wariness among black church leaders about too close an association with government.[14]

While these black church leaders generally profess a deep resonance with American ideals, and some even a willingness to collaborate closely with the governmental sector, these church leaders still reflect the currents of political discontent that exist within the black community at large. Aspects of black political discontent were captured in the 1993–1994 National Black Politics Study (NBPS), where a national sample of approximately 1,200 black respondents was asked questions pertaining to their political beliefs and attitudes. Seventy-seven percent of the sample felt, for instance, that "American society was unfair to black people," and two-thirds felt that "racial equality in

TABLE 6 Clergy Opinions on Churches Receiving Government Program Monies

---

Q: Please state your level of agreement with the following: It is helpful that the government is now encouraging churches to apply for and use government funds to provide social services.

Strongly agree	9%
Agree	37%
Uncertain	1%
Disagree	19%
Strongly disagree	33%
TOTAL	99%
	N = 323

Source: 1999–2000 Black Churches and Politics Survey
Note: Column does not add up to 100% due to rounding.

America" would either never be achieved or would not be achieved in their lifetime.[15] BCAP survey respondents were asked the same question about prospects for racial equality in America. The responses from the BCAP sample were similar to those in the NBPS sample, with 75 percent of BCAP respondents indicating either that racial equality would never be achieved or that it would not be achieved in their lifetime. Additional evidence of pessimism among the BCAP sample is evident in the fact that only 22 percent of the respondents expressed a belief that racial equality in America would soon be achieved, compared with 30 percent of the NBPS sample who expressed the same belief (see table 7). Thus, at least as it relates to the prospects for racial equality, black church leaders are somewhat more pessimistic about such prospects than the black population at large. Nevertheless, despite these indicators of political discontent among black church leaders, only a small percentage of clergy have been inclined to express their grievances through protest (17 percent, as mentioned above). Given the existence of the multiple procedural channels through which African Americans can now pursue their political interests and political grievances, these relatively low levels of protest activity may seem hardly surprising.

Sometimes political discontent among African Americans has been ex-

TABLE 7 Expectations of Racial Equality in the United States

Q: *Do you think blacks have achieved racial equality, will soon achieve racial equality, will not achieve racial equality in your lifetime, or will never achieve racial equality?*

	BCAP (%)	NBPS[a] (%)
Have achieved	3	5
Will soon achieve	22	30
Not in my lifetime	60	42
Never	15	23
	(N – 874)	(N = 1157)

[a]National Black Politics Study

pressed through forms of political separatism rooted in black nationalist philosophies. Black nationalism, which stresses the need for self-determined black cultural, institutional, and political terrain, has possessed a strong following among black parishioners since the formation of black denominations beginning in the late 1700s. That there is a continued emphasis by black churches on self-determined institutional and cultural space is supported by data from the BCAP survey. When asked if it is important that their congregation utilize black-owned businesses and banks, 95 percent of the respondents expressed agreement, with 66 percent strongly agreeing (see table 8). Moreover, the fact that 85 percent of African American Christians are estimated to belong to historically black denominations and conventions (as opposed to predominantly white churches) is further indication of the importance black churchpersons place on self-determined institutional and cultural space.[16] These are not necessarily indicators of a fully developed ideology of black nationalism—one that takes the form of political separatism, for instance—but the emphasis on institutional and cultural self-determination represents at least a foundational level of black nationalism nonetheless.

It is clear that the strong affinity black churches have expressed with core American constitutional ideals, despite prevailing currents of black political discontent, has helped to reinforce democratic and egalitarian instincts within both domains. In these respects, the intersection between black

TABLE 8 Patronage of Black-Owned Businesses

Q: It is important that our congregation utilizes the services of black-owned businesses and banks.

Strongly agree	66%
Agree	29%
Uncertain	2%
Disagree	2%
Strongly disagree	1%
TOTAL	100%
	N = 1917

Source: 1999–2000 Black Churches and Politics Survey

churches and American civic culture has been mutually enriching—though often not carried through to its fullest potential. For example, neither black churches nor American society more generally has been vigilant enough in applying their egalitarian convictions to longstanding problems of gender and economic-class inequality. Nor is it clear that black churches have engaged the broader American public sufficiently on contemporary manifestations of racial injustice, including racially biased policing and sentencing practices that have devastated black community life and eroded black civic confidence. Historically, grievances over racial matters in America have fueled black church activism. And while there is ongoing evidence of political discontent among black churchpersons about American racial practices and policies,[17] the urgency and insistence about addressing these matters is not nearly as evident as during the civil rights movement.

Congregational Characteristics and Civic Involvements

In assessing the involvement of black churches in political life, there are factors pertaining to a congregation's institutional resources and ecclesiastical context that need to be considered as well. That is to say, the nature and kind of resources at the congregation's disposal could well affect whether, and to what extent, a congregation is able to engage in particular activities. Likewise, the particular social theology associated with the denominational heritage of the congregation, or the kind of social theology expressed by the pastor, could serve to shape such congregational activity.[18] For example, the theological heritage of some denominations may emphasize and foster greater separation and withdrawal from the society than that of other denominations, while the theological heritage of other denominations may encourage greater engagement with society and efforts at cultural change. And, finally, the personal resources or characteristics of the clergy who pastor such congregations could also shape such activity. One might anticipate, for example, that the level of education attained by the pastor or the age of the pastor (in terms of generational experiences) might well affect whether the pastor encourages and enables the congregation to engage in particular activities.

Table 9 examines four types of congregational activism discussed above: (1) involvement in civic or political organizations; (2) voter registration; (3) advocacy related to ballot issues; and (4) political protest activities. As discussed previously, these four activities are suggestive of varying degrees of familiarity with and confidence in the formal political process — with congregational involvement in these activities having to do with, among other things, political assessments about the responsiveness of the political system. In order to examine the extent to which system confidence or, alternatively, church-institutional factors shape congregational participation in these various political activities, variables related to congregational resources, the pastor's social theology, the pastor's political perspectives, and the personal resources of the pastor are analyzed.

Congregational size and church income are clearly correlated with each of the four forms of congregational involvement examined in table 9. The larger the size of the congregation and the larger the level of church income, the greater the likelihood that the congregation is currently involved in the activities of a civic organization or has, in the past ten years, helped in a voter registration drive, advocated on behalf of some ballot measure, or participated in protest rallies or marches. For example, of those pastors who serve congregations of less than 100 parishioners, only 33 percent reported that their congregation is currently involved in the activities of some civic or political organization — as compared with 61 percent of pastors serving congregations of 500 or more that reported such involvement.

However, the extent to which congregational size and level of church income are correlated with these forms of activities varies in strength with the particular form of activity under examination. What the data reveal is that variation in congregational size is most strongly related to congregational voter registration initiatives (r=.27), and that congregational size is also somewhat strongly correlated with current involvement in organizational activity (r=.21). But, congregational size is less strongly related to either ballot or protest activity (r=.08), though these lower levels of correlation stem, in part, from the relatively low levels of involvement congregations reported having with ballot or protest activities.

Church income is related to the four forms of political engagement as well. For example, in congregations with an annual income below $50,000, only 27 percent of the clergy report that their congregation is currently involved in the activities of a civic or political organization. But when the congregation's annual income was $250,000 or more, 79 percent of the clergy report such involvement. Similarly, only 14 percent of congregations with incomes less than $50,000 report current advocacy related to ballot issues, while 50 percent of congregations with incomes of $250,000 or more report such advocacy. Also, 6 percent of congregations with incomes of $50,000 or less report current political protest involvements, while 35 percent of congregations with incomes of $250,000 or greater report recent protest involvements. Interestingly, 80 percent or more of congregations — whether in upper income, middle income, or lower income categories — report involvement in voter registration initiatives. Overall church income is more strongly correlated with the four forms of political engagement than is congregational size — as evidenced by the fact that the magnitude of the correlation coefficients is larger for church income than for congregational size in three out of the four cases examined.[19]

The two items bearing on social theology also tended to relate in important ways to the different forms of political engagement examined in table 9. The first measure of social theology has to do with the extent to which the responding minister agrees with the statement "Black churches should be involved in politics." Thirty-eight percent of the BCAP respondents "strongly agree" with this statement and 42 percent "agree." Not surprisingly, the greater the minister's agreement with this statement, the greater the likelihood that the congregation is currently involved in civic or political organizational activity. Only 12 percent of the ministers who disagree with the statement report current congregational involvement in civic or political organizations, compared with 56 percent of the ministers who agree with the

TABLE 9 Public Engagement and Forms of Political Activity by Selected Variables

	N	Involvement (%)	r	Voter Reg. (%)	r	Ballot (%)	r	Protest (%)	r
Congregation Size									
Less than 100	361	33		66		22		11	
100 to 499	733	44		84		27		17	
500+	500	61	.21	94	.27	33	.08	19	.08
Church Income									
Below $50,000	609	27		84		14		6	
$50,000 to $249,999	712	55		81		29		18	
$250,000 or more	273	79	.37	90	.04	50	.28	35	.27
Church Should Be Involved									
Disagree	246	12		83		9		4	
Uncertain	64	21		62		16		3	
Agree	1284	56	.33	85	.04	31	.17	19	.15
Denominational Family									
Historic Black Baptist	439	48		91		30		16	
Historic Black Methodist	236	63		91		36		24	
Historic Black Pentecostal	177	45		89		29		10	
Predominantly White	381	53		77		30		23	
Other	361	30	.22	76	.19	16	.14	8	.17
Racial Equality									
Never	27	64		65		43		23	
Not in my lifetime	169	70		72		42		30	
Will soon achieve	465	64		72		43		32	
Have achieved	112	67	−.01	56	.00	48	.01	32	.05
Objectives Consistent/Constitution									
Disagree	526	65		65		44		27	
Uncertain	133	51		60		18		17	
Agree	211	71	.08	72	.07	46	.06	33	.08

TABLE 9 *Continued*

	N	Involvement (%)	r	Voter Reg. (%)	r	Ballot (%)	r	Protest (%)	r
Education									
High school or less	343	19		92		8		4	
Some college/B.A.	586	47		85		23		12	
Postcollege	574	71	.41	76	−.17	45	.33	30	.29
Gender									
Female	215	43		73		23		9	
Male	1702	47	.03	85	.11	28	.03	18	.08
Age									
Young	463	55		77		33		23	
Middle	964	52		83		31		18	
Old	464	30	−.17	92	.15	14	−.15	7	−.15

Source: 1999–2000 Black Churches and Politics Survey

statement. The strength of this interrelationship is evident in the magnitude of the correlation coefficient between the two variables (r=.33). Variation in the level of the respondent's agreement with the statement about church engagement with politics is more moderately related to the congregation's involvement in ballot efforts (r=.17) and protest endeavors (r=.15). And, once again, the weakest correlation is evident with respect to voter registration drives (r=.04).

The particular denominational family of the congregation is also associated with the congregation's level and kind of public engagement. Differences in political engagement are evident, in fact, between congregations affiliated with historically black Baptist conventions, historically black Methodist denominations, historically black Pentecostal denominations, predominately white denominations, and smaller black communions or nondenominational churches.[20] Overall, congregations aligned with historically black Methodist denominations most frequently reported involvement in each of the four activities examined in table 9.[21] Black congregations aligned with predominantly white denominations were slightly less involved than the historically black Methodists in political organizational involvement, protest politics, and advocating ballot issues but were close to being the least involved of all the denominational families in voter registration initiatives. Congregations aligned with historically black Baptist conventions ranked third in three of the four categories of activity—although they were as frequently involved as historically black Methodists in voter registration initiatives. Congregations aligned with historically black Pentecostal denominations ranked fourth in three of the four activities, while congregations associated with smaller black communions or with no denomination at all were the least likely to report political involvement in the categories examined.

Two variables related to the system confidence of the clergy are also analyzed in table 9—perspectives on the attainment of racial equality and on the consistency of African American objectives with those of the U.S. Constitution. Generally speaking, responses to the item on racial equality revealed little relationship to any of the four forms of political activity—except perhaps to protest activity (r=.05) in which those who were more positive in their assessments were more likely to have reported engagement over the past ten years.

On the other hand, responses to whether African American objectives are consistent with the U.S. Constitution revealed a much more consistent pattern. Those clergy who expressed uncertainty with regard to the question were the least likely to report having engaged in any of the four forms of political activity, while those clergy expressing agreement that such objectives are consistent with the U.S. Constitution were the most likely to report having engaged in each of the four forms of political activity. Noteworthy, however, is the pattern of those disagreeing with the assertion. Somewhat surprisingly, they are also relatively engaged politically as they generally trail those who agree with the assertion by only a few percentage points. Given this curvilinear relationship between positions on the matter and levels of reported political activity (with those who disagree and those who agree being the most likely to engage in such activity), the magnitude of the correlation coefficients is, however, fairly modest in nature (ranging from .06 to .08).

Three variables related to the pastor's personal resources or characteristics are also examined in table 9—namely, level of educational attainment, gender, and age.[22] Given that many people find politics to be complex and political action to be daunting, greater educational attainment is likely to provide clergy with greater skills, knowledge, and perhaps even confidence that can be marshaled in political endeavors. Gender of the pastor is another characteristic that has been established by previous research as contributing to differences in political involvements. Feminist scholars, for example, have consistently pointed out gender-related differences in political styles and perspectives. In a more specific sense, sociological research undertaken recently has revealed that women clergy in mainline Protestant denominations have tended to possess different political agendas and different political goals than male clergy.[23] Finally, the age of the pastor may also shape the level and nature of political activity by congregations. For example, older clergy who experienced Jim Crow laws and/or the civil rights struggles of the 1950s and 1960s may well view the political world through different lenses than much younger clergy.

As might be expected, the level of education attained by the clergy is strongly related to congregational involvement in civic and political organizations (r=.41). Education is also strongly related to such political activities as ballot initiatives (r=.33) and protest efforts (r=.29). Surprisingly, educational attainment is negatively related to congregational voter registration drives (r=-.17), with pastors possessing the lowest levels of educational attainment being the most likely to report congregational efforts at voter registration.[24] Gender is only weakly related to the four forms of political engagement, with female clergy being less likely to report that their congregations have engaged in such activities. On the other hand, age is more strongly correlated with the four activities analyzed, though generally in a modest (the magnitude of the correlation coefficients ranging between .15 and .17) and negative direction.[25] Generally speaking, younger clergy are more likely than older clergy to report such endeavors. With regard to voter registration initiatives, however, the converse was true, with older pastors being more likely than younger clergy to report congregational efforts at voter registration.

Nonetheless, while such bivariate relationships are revealing and suggestive, they do not reveal the extent to which these variables remain related to political engagement once variation in the other variables is taken into account. Nor is it clear what specific factors emerge as primary in shaping the involvement of congregations in political and social life once these multiple factors are taken into account simultaneously. In order to address this issue, we employed a multiple classification analysis (MCA) — with each of the four forms of congregational political involvement serving as our dependent variables (tables 10–13, respectively). In each MCA, we employed two variables reflecting congregational resources (specifically, congregational size and church income), two variables reflecting social theology (specifically, responses to whether black churches should be involved in politics and to denominational family affiliation), and one variable reflecting personal resources (namely, the level of educational attainment reported by the pastor). Two additional variables were used as covariates, so as to control for their influence as well.[26]

Several conclusions can then be drawn from the multiple classification analysis of current congregational involvement in civic and political organizations as reported in table 10.[27] First, the overall set of variables does a fairly good job at explaining variation in the dependent variable, as the value of R squared is .28 — indicating that 28 percent of the variation in the dependent variable is explained by the five independent variables and the two covariates. Second, even when taking into account variation in the other independent variables, it is clear that variables related to congregational resources, social theology, and personal resources continue to shape the extent to which congregations are reported to be currently involved in the activities of civic or political organizations. Thirdly, once controls have been introduced, the pastor's educational attainment ranks as the most important variable influencing current congregational involvement in civic and political organizations (beta=.26). Social theology also continues to shape such involvement, but it is clear that the degree to which the pastor agrees that black churches should be involved in politics more fully shapes such congregational involvement (beta=.20) than does affiliation with a particular denominational family (beta=.09). Congregational resources also shape such involvement, with church income ranking third in importance in affecting such current activity (beta=.16) and congregational size serving as the least important factor affecting variation in the dependent variable once the impact of the other independent variables is taken into account (beta= .07).

These same independent variables and covariates are employed in a multiple classification analysis related to explaining congregational efforts at voter registration (table 11), congregational efforts at ballot advocacy

TABLE 10 Determinants of Congregational Civic Engagement:
A Multiple Classification Analysis

Independent Variables	N	Unadjusted mean scores		Adjusted for other independent variables and covariates	
		Mean	Eta	Mean	Beta
CONGREGATIONAL RESOURCES					
Congregational Size					
Less than 100	361	.33		.47	
100 to 499	733	.44		.45	
500+	500	.61		.53	
			.21		.07
Church Income					
$49,999 or less	609	.27		.39	
$50,000 to $249,999	712	.55		.50	
$250,000 or more	273	.79		.62	
			.37		.16
SOCIAL THEOLOGY					
Should Be Involved					
Strongly disagree	162	.06		.31	
Disagree	84	.23		.28	
Uncertain	64	.21		.37	
Agree	644	.47		.46	
Strongly agree	640	.65		.58	
			.37		.20
Denominational Family					
Historic Black Baptist	439	.48		.48	
Historic Black Methodist	236	.63		.55	
Historic Black Pentecostal	177	.45		.55	
Predominantly white	381	.53		.47	
Other	361	.30		.42	
			.22		.09
PERSONAL RESOURCES					
Education					
High school or less	343	.19		.30	
Some college/college grad.	586	.47		.47	
Postcollege	574	.71		.63	
			.41		.26

Covariates controlled: age and gender
R squared = .28

TABLE 11 Determinants of Congregational Efforts at Voter Registration:
A Multiple Classification Analysis

Independent Variables	N	Unadjusted mean scores		Adjusted for other independent variables and covariates	
		Mean	Eta	Mean	Beta
CONGREGATIONAL RESOURCES					
Congregational Size					
Less than 100	263	.66		.63	
100 to 499	629	.84		.84	
500+	466	.94		.95	
			.27		.30
Church Income					
$49,999 or less	487	.84		.89	
$50,000 to $249,999	617	.81		.80	
$250,000 or more	254	.90		.84	
			.04		.11
SOCIAL THEOLOGY					
Should Be Involved					
Strongly disagree	99	.95		.90	
Disagree	66	.67		.71	
Uncertain	51	.61		.65	
Agree	555	.82		.82	
Strongly agree	587	.87		.88	
			.19		.16
Denominational Family					
Historic Black Baptist	377	.91		.87	
Historic Black Methodist	229	.91		.91	
Historic Black Pentecostal	122	.89		.89	
Predominantly white	345	.77		.79	
Other	285	.76		.78	
			.19		.14
PERSONAL RESOURCES					
Education					
High school or less	339	.92		.92	
Some college/college grad.	503	.85		.85	
Postcollege	516	.76		.77	
			.17		.15

Covariates controlled: age and gender
R squared = .19

TABLE 12 Determinants of Congregational Efforts at Ballot Advocacy:
A Multiple Classification Analysis

Independent Variables	N	Unadjusted mean scores		Adjusted for other independent variables and covariates	
		Mean	Eta	Mean	Beta
CONGREGATIONAL RESOURCES					
Congregational Size					
Less than 100	264	.22		.32	
100 to 499	632	.27		.28	
500+	453	.33		.25	
			.08		.06
Church Income					
$49,999 or less	478	.14		.21	
$50,000 to $249,999	618	.29		.28	
$250,000 or more	253	.50		.42	
			.28		.16
SOCIAL THEOLOGY					
Should Be Involved					
Strongly disagree	94	.08		.26	
Disagree	65	.13		.15	
Uncertain	50	.14		.22	
Agree	557	.24		.24	
Strongly agree	583	.38		.34	
			.21		.13
Denominational Family					
Historic Black Baptist	370	.30		.31	
Historic Black Methodist	229	.36		.32	
Historic Black Pentecostal	133	.29		.36	
Predominantly white	342	.30		.25	
Other	275	.16		.22	
			.14		.10
PERSONAL RESOURCES					
Education					
High school or less	331	.08		.13	
Some college/college grad.	502	.23		.23	
Postcollege	516	.45		.42	
			.33		.26

Covariates controlled: age and gender
R squared = .17

TABLE 13 Determinants of Congregational Engagement in Protest Activities: A Multiple Classification Analysis

Independent Variables	N	Unadjusted mean scores		Adjusted for other independent variables and covariates	
		Mean	Eta	Mean	Beta
CONGREGATIONAL RESOURCES					
Congregational Size					
Less than 100	264	.11		.21	
100 to 499	632	.17		.18	
500+	443	.19		.13	
			.08		.08
Church Income					
$49,999 or less	475	.06		.09	
$50,000 to $249,999	615	.18		.17	
$250,000 or more	249	.35		.31	
			.27		.20
SOCIAL THEOLOGY					
Should Be Involved					
Strongly disagree	94	.02		.14	
Disagree	65	.06		.07	
Uncertain	49	.04		.10	
Agree	552	.13		.13	
Strongly agree	579	.25		.23	
			.21		.14
Denominational Family					
Historic Black Baptist	368	.16		.16	
Historic Black Methodist	227	.24		.21	
Historic Black Pentecostal	132	.10		.13	
Predominantly white	338	.23		.20	
Other	274	.08		.12	
			.17		.09
PERSONAL RESOURCES					
Education					
High school or less	331	.04		.11	
Some college/college grad.	494	.12		.13	
Postcollege	514	.30		.24	
			.29		.16

Covariates controlled: age and gender
R squared = .16

(table 12), and congregational engagement in protest activity (table 13).[28] What emerges from these three tables is that the particular variables that best account for variation in the dependent variable vary depending on the particular form of political activity analyzed. For each of the four forms of political activity analyzed in tables 10–13, the three strongest betas in each analysis involve a particular congregational resource, the pastor's social theology, and the pastor's personal resources. However, the relative importance of these three factors varies from table to table, with the particular congregational resource most shaping such political activity varying according to the specific activity analyzed. For example, whereas the pastor's level of education (a personal resource) exhibited the highest beta value related to a congregation's current engagement in civic organizational activities and to congregational efforts at ballot advocacy, congregational size (a congregational resource) exhibited the highest beta value for congregational efforts at voter registration. But when one examines congregational involvement in protest activity, church income (a congregational resource) revealed the highest beta value. Social theology consistently played a role in shaping such activities, as variation in clergy agreement or not on whether "black churches should be involved in politics" ranked either second or third in terms of the magnitude of its beta value for each of the four activities analyzed. And while the denominational family variable played a more modest role in explaining variation in such forms of political activity, the magnitude of its beta value never ranked last in any of the four activities analyzed. Thus, variation in congregational engagement in political activities appears to be a function of variation in congregational resources, the personal resources at the pastor's disposal, and the social theology expressed by the pastor. Which of these factors plays the strongest role in shaping congregational political activity depends on the particular form of political activity undertaken.

Conclusion

The BCAP data shed light on a number of important matters pertaining to black church civic and political involvement. First, black churches today report being far more involved in electoral affairs than any other form of civic or political activity. The data also show, however, that only about 15 percent of the churches surveyed considered their congregations to have been especially active in political matters of any sort during the 1980s and 1990s—as compared with 25 percent of the respondents who indicated high levels of political involvement by their congregation during the civil rights movement. Therefore, the activist core of black churches appears to be smaller than during the civil rights movement, and the political emphasis of that activism is far more on electoral matters than on the protest politics characteristic of black church activism during the 1950s and 1960s.

Nevertheless, black clergy remain somewhat ambivalent about the American political system. Most believe that the social objectives of African Americans are consistent with the social ideals of the U.S. Constitution, yet few black clergy believe that African Americans will achieve equality anytime soon. But in assessing the correlation between system confidence in such instances and a congregation's political involvements, few discernible patterns emerge, except that both affinity and dissatisfaction with the American political process motivate black church political participation, and that this political participation tends to take more conventional than insurgent forms.

The factors that account more strongly for variation in congregational involvement in civic and political affairs are related, instead, to congregational characteristics. The data analysis shows that variation in the political involvement of black churches is shaped by variation in: (1) the size and income of the congregation; (2) the theological heritage of the congregation; and (3) the social theology and educational attainment of the congregation's pastor. The fact that congregational resources more than affinity with the political system shape political involvements in these instances suggests that there are social resource requirements for participation in the formal political process that are difficult to overcome—especially within social contexts where pressures on limited resources call for constant calculations about costs and benefits and opportunities and obstacles inherent within a range of possible institutional actions and involvements.

Notes

1   See, for example, C. R. D. Halisi's application of "dual citizenship" to the South African context, and his discussion of uses of the concept with reference to other African contexts. C. R. D. Halisi, *Black Political Thought in the Making of South Africa* (Bloomington: Indiana University Press, 1999), 3.

2 Aldon Morris, *The Origins of the Civil Rights Movement: Black Communities Organizing for Change* (New York: Free Press, 1984); Doug McAdam, *Political Process and the Development of Black Insurgency: 1930–1970* (Chicago: University of Chicago Press, 1982).

3 C. Eric Lincoln and Lawrence Mamiya, *The Black Church in the African-American Experience* (Durham: Duke University Press, 1990); Andrew Billingsley, *Mighty Like a River: The Black Church and Social Reform* (Oxford: Oxford University Press, 1999).

4 Fredrick C. Harris, "Something Within: Religion as a Mobilizer of African-American Political Activism," *Journal of Politics* 56, no. 1 (February 1994): 42–68; Allison Calhoun-Brown, "African-American Churches and Political Mobilization: The Psychological Impact of Organizational Resources," *Journal of Politics* 58, no. 4 (November 1996): 935–53.

5 Allen D. Hertzke, *Echoes of Discontent: Jesse Jackson, Pat Robertson, and the Resurgence of Populism* (Washington, D.C.: Congressional Quarterly Press, 1993); R. Drew Smith, "African-American Protestants, Political Activism, and 'Liberal' Redemptive Hopes," *Theology Today* 53, no. 2 (July 1996): 191–200.

6 James M. Washington, "Jesse Jackson and the Symbolic Politics of Black Christendom," *Annals of the American Academy of Political and Social Science* 480 (1985): 89–105.

7 In fact, Deborah Kalb notes that during the 1996 elections black churches were involved in mobilizing black voters to the point of participating in sessions on voter mobilization sponsored by the Democratic National Committee (1996: 1067). See Deborah Kalb, "Effort to Register Blacks Could Sway Election," *Congressional Quarterly* (April 20, 1996), 1065–67.

8 The question was specific to the pastor, regardless of whether the respondent may have been an associate minister or, in a few cases, a layperson.

9 See Theodore Cross, *The Black Power Imperative: Racial Inequality and the Politics of Nonviolence* (New York: Faulkner Books, 1987), 332–39; and Manning Marable, Foreword, in Rod Bush, ed., *The New Black Vote* (San Francisco: Synthesis Press, 1984), 3.

10 A subsequent volume in this series on black churches and public life will focus exclusively on public policy involvements by African American churches.

11 R. Drew Smith, "African-American Protestants, Political Activism, and 'Liberal' Redemptive Hopes"; R. Drew Smith, "Black Religious Nationalism and the Politics of Transcendence," *Journal of the American Academy of Religion* 66, no. 3 (fall 1998): 533–48; and David Howard-Pitney, *The Afro-American Jeremiad: Appeals for Justice in America* (Philadelphia: Temple University Press, 1990).

12 Peter Paris, *The Social Teaching of the Black Churches* (Philadelphia: Fortress Press, 1985), 31.

13 Lincoln and Mamiya, *The Black Church in the African-American Experience*, 189.

14 It is important to note that the support for government partnerships among BCAP respondents is almost 20 percent less than levels of support indicated in a study by Ram Cnaan of 401 Philadelphia congregations. See Ram Cnaan, *Keeping Faith in the City: How 401 Urban Religious Congregations Serve Their Neediest Neighbors* (Philadelphia: CRRUCS, 2000), 20. Cnaan's respondents, like BCAP's respondents, were predominantly clergy, but, unlike the BCAP sample, only 59 percent of the churches surveyed by Cnaan were African American (14). The BCAP survey results on this matter also differ significantly from survey results reported by Mark Chaves, "Religious Congregations and Welfare Reform: Who Will Take Advantage of 'Charitable Choice'?" *American Sociological Review* 64 (December 1999): 841; and by the Pew Forum and the Pew Research Center (PF/PRC), "Faith-Based Funding Backed, But Church-State Doubts Abound" (Washington, D.C.: PF/PRC, 2001), 8. The survey data reported by Chaves show that 64 percent of the respondents affiliated with African American churches expressed an interest in government funding of church-based programs, while the survey data reported by PF/PRC show that 81 percent of the African American respondents support such funding. However, both the Chaves survey respondents and the PF/PRC survey respondents were from the general population and were not primarily clergy as was the case with the BCAP sample. This suggests, at the very least, that black clergy are much less receptive to government funding for church-based programs than is the general African American population.

15 Michael Dawson, "Black Discontent: The Preliminary Report on the 1993–1994 National Black Politics Study" (on file with author).

16 Lincoln and Mamiya, *The Black Church in the African-American Experience,* 407.

17 For example, 41 percent of BCAP respondents reported that their congregations have engaged in advocacy during the last ten years on affirmative action policies, and 52 percent reported engaging in advocacy during the last ten years on civil rights.

18 The term "social theology" refers to the social and political perspectives expressed by the individual that are (likely) derived from one's more general theological understanding. More specifically, it refers to one's theology related to the role of the church in the world. See James Guth, John Green, Corwin Smidt, Lyman Kellstedt, and Margaret Poloma, *The Bully Pulpit: The Politics of Protestant Clergy* (Lawrence: University Press of Kansas, 1997), chapter 4.

19 Variation in church income is most strongly correlated with whether the congregation is currently involved in civic or political organizational activity ($r=.37$), while variation in church income is more moderately correlated with advocacy on behalf of a ballot issue ($r=.28$) and participation in a protest rally or march ($r=.27$). However, while there was a strong correlation between variation in congregational "size" and voter registration initiatives ($r=.27$), there is barely any correlation at all between congregational income and voter registration initiatives ($r=.04$).

20 Historically black Baptist conventions include the National Baptist Convention, USA, Inc.; the National Baptist Convention of America; the Progressive National Baptist Convention; and the National Missionary Baptist Convention. The historically black Methodist denominations include the African Methodist Episcopal Church; the African Methodist Episcopal Zion Church; and the Christian Methodist Episcopal Church. The historically black Pentecostal denominations include the Church of God in Christ; the Pentecostal Assemblies of the World; and the Full Gospel Baptist Fellowship. Predominantly white denominations refer to the Roman Catholic Church, Episcopal Church, Presbyterian Church, United Methodist Church, and other "mainline" Protestant denominations. The category "other" includes congregations that identified themselves as nondenominational or that were aligned with relatively small black communions.

21 Because the denominational family variable is a nominal-level variable, the correlation coefficient reported for this variable in table 9 differs from that used for the other variables examined in the table. The correlation coefficient reported for the denominational family variable is Cramer's V. As a result, the magnitude of the correlation coefficients for this variable cannot be directly compared to the other variables examined in the table — the value of a particular reported Cramer's V can only be compared in relationship to the other three Cramer's V values reported for the denominational family variable.

22 Survey questions on these matters were specific to the pastor, regardless of whether the respondent was an associate minister or (as in a few cases) a layperson.

23 James Guth, John Green, Corwin Smidt, and Lyman Kellstedt, "Women Clergy and the Political Transformation of Mainline Protestantism." Paper presented at the annual meeting of the Social Science History Association, Atlanta, 1995. See also Laura Olson, Sue Crawford, and James Guth, "Changing Issue Agendas of Women Clergy," *Journal for the Scientific Study of Religion* 39 (June 2000): 140–53.

24 These data cannot answer why this may be the case. However, it may be related to the fact that pastors with lower levels of education may tend to serve congregants who are, themselves, less educated and in need of intervention and assistance with voter registration.

25 Age was recoded in such a manner to secure approximately one-quarter of the respondents in the youngest and oldest age categories, and approximately one-half of the respondents falling into the middle category. Given this objective, those pastors who were 45 years of age or younger were coded as "young," and those 66 years of age and older were coded as "old." Those clergy whose ages ranged from 46 through 65 were coded as "middle-aged."

26 We chose to drop the two items related to attainment of equality and consistency of African American objectives with the U.S. Constitution because analysis revealed that their contribution to explaining variation in the dependent variable was weaker

in nature than that of the variables included in the analysis. Moreover, when these two variables were included in the analysis, the model explained far less variance than the model presented. Overall, however, the variable related to consistency of black objectives with the U.S. Constitution was more strongly related to variation in each of the forms of political activity than was the variable measuring attainment of equality.

27 Several things about the analysis should be noted. First, since the dependent variable is dichotomous in nature (either the congregation is currently involved in the activities of such civic or political organizations or it is not), the unadjusted mean scores reported in the second column of table 10 are identical to the percentages for the same variables reported in table 9. Likewise, the value of eta (the correlation coefficient) for these same variables is identical to the correlation coefficients reported in table 9. The fourth column then reports the expected mean value for the category of the particular independent variable, once the effects of all the other independent variables and covariates have been taken into account. This expected mean value can be interpreted as the expected percentage of pastors per category reporting current congregational involvement in civic or political organizations—once the effects of the other independent variables and covariates have been taken into account. Thus, while 34 percent of those clergy serving congregations of less than 100 parishioners reported current congregational involvement in civic or political organizations, 47 percent of such clergy would be expected to do so once differences in the other variables (e.g., educational attainment, differences in social theology, and differences in church income) had been taken into account.

28 As was true with regard to the analysis in table 10, the dependent variable in each of these three tables is dichotomous in nature. As a result, the unadjusted mean scores reported in the second column of tables 11, 12, and 13 are identical to the percentages for the same variables reported in table 9. Likewise, the value of eta (the correlation coefficient) for these same variables is identical to the correlation coefficients reported in table 9. The fourth column once again reports the expected mean value for the category of the particular independent variable, once the effects of all the other independent variables and covariates have been taken into account. Once again, this expected mean value can be interpreted as the expected percentage of pastors per category reporting current congregational involvement in civic or political organizations—once the effects of the other independent variables and covariates have been taken into account.

PART II

Black Churches and Normative Assessments of the

American Political Context

4

"TO FORM A MORE PERFECT UNION":

AFRICAN AMERICANS AND

AMERICAN CIVIL RELIGION

David Howard-Pitney

Religion and politics in the United States have always significantly interacted. For no group is this more true than African Americans, particularly given the black church's traditional central place in African American social-political life. The connections between black religion and politics range from the disproportionately high numbers of black clergy and churches involved in electoral politics to a general extension of Christian-derived habits of mind, language, and sentiment into political affairs. These latter habits form an important feature of many African Americans' political culture. Political culture involves such matters as people's beliefs, attitudes, and general disposition toward their political system. This chapter focuses on one important strand of the cultural ideals supporting African American political action, the American civil religion. African Americans have long participated in and shaped this cultural tradition that endows the nation with transcendent meaning and millennial destiny. This civic faith joins religion and nationalism, mixing American religious themes such as messianism, deliverance, and redemption with U.S. political ideals such as democracy, freedom, and equality. The national faith, with its web of symbols, myths, and rituals, seeks to bind the highly diverse, heterogeneous U.S. polity into a single national moral-spiritual community.[1]

This chapter examines some of the ways that many African Americans, including those associated with the church, most characteristically practice American civil religion. No one generalization adequately characterizes African Americans' relation to the civil religion, as the black community is no more monolithic in this area than in most others. Religious scholar Martin Marty observes that American civil religion "has subspecies, much as the Christian faith has denominations," for "a construct as loose as civil religion" can be used by different people to "fill different needs at different times." Thus, while most forms of U.S. civil religion share many broad normative ideals (e.g., freedom and democracy) and symbols (e.g., Statue of Liberty or Constitution), their precise content and application vary enormously. Significant variations occur by cultural groups, by political ideology, by geographical region—even from individual to individual; indeed, Marty suggests there "may be as many civil religions as there are citizens."[2]

The chapter acknowledges the complexity of African Americans' relation to the civil religion and describes some of that diversity. Nevertheless, it makes three key generalizations. Disproportionately more than other groups, African Americans practice civil religion of the following sorts: (1) *"Nation Under God,"* or theistic (mainly Christian) forms of civil religion; (2) *Prophetic,* or socially critical, forms that call for reform and posit the nation's future, not current perfection; and (3) *Progressive* forms, or ones located in the U.S. center-left. These three main traits typically, though not invariably, cluster together.[3] Moreover, the chapter shows how these traits are quintessentially expressed in the African-American Jeremiad—both historically and currently the most pronounced rhetorical form of African American public protest and civil religion. This chapter also examines the purposes to which African Americans put civil religion as well as its primary ideological effects. I conclude that the civil religion's ultimate social-political function for African Americans is to inculcate hope for America's future and outcome of their public efforts, thereby encouraging black civic engagement.

African American Civil Religion's Three Main Traits

UNDER GOD

The single most salient trait of the African American civil-religious style is that it usually envisions the national mission and destiny as existing literally "under God." Martin Marty presents the dyad of "Nation under God" versus "Nation as Self-Transcendent" as one of the most fundamental divisions within American civil religion. The "Under God" form posits the Judeo-Christian God as the source of America's mission, which remains, therefore, always subject to divine authority and judgment. The "Nation as Self-Transcendent" form, on the other hand, regards America's social-political system and attributes such as democracy and free enterprise as having intrinsic transcendent meaning, with or without God. African Americans overwhelmingly embrace "Nation Under God" versions of the American faith.

Many African American leaders, both religious and political, stress the moral-spiritual dimensions of public issues, often alluding directly to God and the Bible. Reverend Jesse L. Jackson, whose public pronouncements are suffused with biblical references and imagery, for example, brings God and morality talk to public policy discussion often and unabashedly. "At the core of every political, economic, or social issue are religious, moral, and spiritual dimensions," Reverend Jackson has proclaimed. "The spiritual and the temporal, the sacred and the secular," he teaches, "are intertwined." America is strong because "God has blessed us mightily," and, to stay great, Americans must "trust God and lean not to our own understanding." Jackson ends many speeches with the scriptural paraphrase that "if my people, who are called by my name, will humble themselves and pray and seek my face, and turn from their wicked ways, then God will forgive their sins . . . and . . . heal their land."[4]

Public moralizing, typically within a theistic framework, moreover, transcends most black political and ideological divisions. Alan Keyes, who represents the opposite conventional political pole from Jackson's, also delivers the God-based moralisms so characteristic of black public figures. Holding a Harvard Ph. D. in government, Mr. Keyes has been a U.S. foreign policy official in the Reagan and first Bush administrations, two-time Republican nominee to the U.S. Senate for Maryland, and a Republican presidential candidate in 1996 and 2000. He is a successful media commentator and TV and radio talk show host as well as one of the most in-demand speakers in the American conservative movement.

Comparing Reverend Jackson and Mr. Keyes is instructive for this chapter's concerns, given their wide disagreement on almost every major public issue. First, Jackson and Keyes occupy analogous, though inverse, national political terrain. Jackson is on the left edge of the Democratic coalition and is supported mainly by liberal groups such as labor, environmentalists, and civil rights activists, while Keyes is on the far Republican right with his most fervent supporters being religious and so-called movement conservatives.

Each is outside the center of power and gravity in his respective party, though touching the center and always seeking to influence it. Their evangelical-like ideological fervor, and that of their followers, makes them important base constituencies in their respective parties. Party regulars value their potential for electoral energy and mobilization, courting them during primaries and using them during general elections. Keyes's powerful moral rhetoric during the 2000 Republican presidential primaries stirred many in the Christian right more deeply than had any candidate since Pat Robertson in 1988. Likewise the voter registration and turnout drives led by Jackson and other black Democrats in the closing weeks of the 2000 presidential campaign are widely credited as underlying Democrat Al Gore's late surge to carry narrowly the popular presidential vote. Both leaders are also fundamentally social-political activists who seek to shape public opinion and policy through diverse means. Both Jackson and Keyes are successful media commentators and talk show hosts, for example, and operate within various public organizations and bases. They are public moralists and gadflies in the business of shaping social opinion in the directions they favor. Electoral activity, including sometimes running for office, is one means of pursuing their larger public mission.[5]

While Keyes is a generic conservative, deeply hostile toward what he sees as activist centralized government, excessive taxation and regulation, and wasteful and harmful government social programs, his most singular emphasis is ever on values and morality. These are times, Keyes claims, when "America's social and economic ills" stem from "the sad disrepair of our moral infrastructure" and "when just about every domestic problem we face is, at root, a problem of moral character." In discussing the economy, he says, therefore, "we don't have [mainly] money problems. We have moral problems," for, though economics is important, "in the long life of a nation, it is ultimately subordinate to the moral facts." "Crime and violence," likewise, "aren't just social facts" but deep "moral realities," since "external violence" is but "the symptom and consequence of internal lawlessness and self-indulgence." To rid itself of violent crime America doesn't need gun control, he contends, it needs more moral control.[6]

Even as Keyes asserts that public matters cannot be addressed without reference to morality, so he contends values cannot be addressed without reliance on God. Failing to recognize that political freedom and self-government depend on citizens' moral virtue and self-control—and that such virtue comes only from knowing and obeying God's laws—is, for Keyes, the crux of society's crisis. Although "most Americans once believed that . . . the only secure foundation for freedom was God—the Source of unalienable rights and the Policeman stationed in every human heart," America's political leaders "don't want to talk about it anymore because they claim that it involves bringing religion into politics." Americans have strayed in this regard, Keyes holds, from the wisdom and example of America's founders. Keyes's signature thesis is that the Declaration of Independence "explicitly embodies an argument that relies upon religious belief" and the Founding Fathers held that a nation "based on the idea of human equality in freedom could not survive without an appeal to God."[7]

PROPHETIC

African American civil religion's second most salient feature is that it usually takes prophetic form—prophetic in the sense both of predicting the future *and* of vigorously protesting social injustice. It critically judges contemporary society in light of the sacred ideal, finds society wanting, and urges reform. Prophetic civil religion's "divine discontent" serves the purposes of social protest and reform movements by providing them ideological tenets and rhetorical weapons.

Former Supreme Court Justice Thurgood Marshall typified this attitude during the 1988 Constitutional Bicentennial when he voiced discomfort with a constitutional scholar's glowing assessment of the original Constitution as the product of a "Golden Age, the likes we shall not see again." Marshall expressed concern, lest such unqualified celebration invite "complacent belief" in the perfection of the original Constitution. This seemed particularly inappropriate given the Constitution's initial recognition of slavery and much later acceptance of racial segregation and disenfranchisement—to cite just two conceivable reservations about that original document's perfection. For most African Americans, what should be celebrated and is "sacred" about the Constitution is not what the Constitution once was, but what it eventually became—and, even more, may yet become. Many blacks' critical, prophetic stance toward present society and calls for corrective change are well expressed in the political rallying cry "to build a more perfect Union" (uttered alone or with the tag "leaving no Americans behind").[8]

PROGRESSIVE

Another distinguishing feature of African American civil religion is its tendency to take progressive reformist form. This political progressivism is basically the most liberal-to-socialist agenda possible within the existing political mainstream and supports government actions to serve both blacks' interests and the general welfare. This prophetic progressive tradition typically embraces liberal reformist policies seeking ameliorative change within middle-class American ideals and constitutional procedures. At its best, this tradition effectively utilizes current existing norms and procedural forms while also striving to expand and transform the prevailing ideological-political order.

This trio of predominant traits in black civil religion relates historically to what religious historian Vincent Harding calls "The Great Tradition of Black Protest." Most antebellum-era black protest, he notes, generally employed "white American political and religious assumptions," including "the Revolution's rhetoric and ideology" and Founding Fathers mythology. Although never the sole source of African American resistance rhetoric, "this sort of protest," he holds, "based on American democratic principles and too often on naïve faith, became the broadest single element — the mainstream — in the river of black struggle in America."[9] What Harding has dubbed the Great Tradition, the present essay characterizes as the chief black civil religious persuasion that — for good or bad and with inherent strengths and limitations — continues to inform African American national public discourse.

The African American Jeremiad

One of the chief ways blacks have contributed to the national civil-religious dialogue has been with the rhetorical tradition of the black jeremiad. From abolitionist times to the present, national leaders such as Frederick Douglass and Martin Luther King Jr. have employed a distinctly African American variant of a widespread American rhetoric of social criticism and prophecy known as the American jeremiad. Creatively adapting it to their ends, blacks have shaped and enriched greatly both American jeremiadic and general civil religious traditions.

Historians identify the jeremiad, or political sermon, of the seventeenth-century New England Puritans as the first unique American literary form. Since these early Anglo-Americans defined themselves as the chosen agents of God's providential design for humanity, they viewed their social failures as threatening that mission and, consequently, the world's salvation. Jeremiad sermons denounced the chosen people's misconduct and threatened coming punishment for it. Yet the "essence" of the jeremiad, writes historian Sacvan Bercovitch, was "its unshakable optimism," for the Puritan jeremiad invariably closed by affirming society's special promise and prophesying its coming perfection. This American jeremiad survived its Puritan origins and became attached to the Republic and U.S. society generally, as it evolved into a central feature of American national culture and civil religion.[10]

Offering a powerful cultural idiom for expressing strong social criticism within normative cultural bounds, the American jeremiad was frequently used and adapted by African Americans for protest purposes. Historian Wilson J. Moses defines the "black jeremiad" as "the constant warnings issued by blacks to whites concerning the judgment that was to come from the sin of slavery."[11] It was, he contends, the rhetorical mainstay of black Northern abolitionists. Forged in the heat of blacks' rhetorical assault on American slavery, the African American jeremiad outlived abolitionism and became an enduring staple of black protest rhetoric in subsequent struggles for justice in America.[12] At the start of the twenty-first century, African Americans still actively use it.

Jeremiahs, Left and Right: Jesse L. Jackson and Alan Keyes

Perhaps no better known practitioner of the black Jeremiad exists today than longtime civil rights activist, social-political leader, and two-time Democratic Party presidential candidate, Reverend Jesse L. Jackson. Jackson has voiced jeremiads consistently in his efforts to attract popular support for social and political reform. "Today," he proclaims, "we have a crisis in America" and "are a nation adrift . . . on a collision course" with disaster, making a national change of direction "imperative."[13] Ever a reformer-Jeremiah, Jackson denounces America's current immoral deeds, urges Americans to repent, and promises salvation contingent on the nation's return to right action.

Since the 1960s, Jackson has frequently stated disapproval of America's "state of spiritual decadence and despair." Jackson holds that during the 1970s, "a decade of moral decadence," the nation started drifting backward from the social progress and gains achieved by the civil rights movement. For him, this regression reached its nadir under Ronald Reagan. During Jackson's bid for the Democratic Party's 1984 presidential nomination, he crisscrossed the country proclaiming an "agony" and "darkness across the land" brought by Reaganomics. What was clear from Jackson's criticisms was that among the worst sins of the United States in the 1980s was its waning commitment to civil rights and racial justice. The "Reagan Revolution," Jackson declared, tried to roll back every major advance of disadvantaged groups in the last two decades and "must be seen as a reversal of all past White House and congressional actions" in these areas.[14]

"As a nation, we must change direction," he warned in the 1980s, as "our very lives are at stake." He exhorted Americans to reexamine "every aspect of foreign and domestic policy that has favored . . . the few over the many." Professing grave concern over the Union's state, Jackson ever stressed that Americans were at "a crossroad" between paths of "danger and opportunity." Choosing wrongly would lead to "greater danger," while taking the right path would lead to "greater opportunities." "I still believe the country can be saved" and progress to new, unprecedented heights, he exclaimed, *if* it would seek "new values and new vision."[15]

Jackson's grand political goal has been to build and mobilize a "Rainbow Coalition" of the poor, people of color, women, gays, workers, and farmers seeking progressive change. For Jackson, this national progressive alliance is destined to redeem the promise of a new and better America. His movement, he believes, heeds "the call of this nation's highest and noblest principles that we might fulfill our mission . . . and be the source of hope for people yearning to be free everywhere." Jackson has been unflagging in lifting up the best features of America's mission and seeking to stir people to its achievement. Addressing the 1984 Democratic National Convention, he stated that Americans, though imperfect, are "called to a perfect mission: to feed the hungry, to clothe the naked, to house the homeless, to teach the illiterate, to provide jobs for the jobless, and to choose the human race over the nuclear race." And it was the Rainbow Coalition's task, he declared, "to inspire our party and the nation to fulfill the mission" and make real "the promise of democracy."[16]

The jeremiad that Reverend Jackson delivers has changed little over the decades and mirrors, in both rhetorical form and in substance, Martin Luther King's jeremiad, especially during his later years, circa 1966–68. Jackson resolutely ties black imperatives, as did King, to interracial political reform focused on shared economic interests. This is expressed in Jackson's exhortations for Americans to seek "higher, common ground" and shift from "civil" to "silver" rights, paralleling King's final calls for a national "Poor People's Campaign" and a (mainly economic) "Revolution of Values." Jackson sees his movement as having been founded by the prophet King, who, he says, left America with a "charge" and a "promise." King charged Americans to defend the weak, fight discrimination and deprivation, and "reshape the priorities" of their nation; his "promise" was that "you'll get there one day," "that if you hold on and hold out, joy is coming," because "there is a new city whose builder . . . is God."[17] The basic reform message and prescriptions of Jackson's progressive jeremiad, however updated in slogan and context, still follow King's final vision.

In his 1999 address to the NAACP's annual convention, "Rebuilding the House: The Fourth Movement of the Freedom Symphony," Jackson laid out his "Covenant for the Next Century" to "transform our nation" and redeem its promise. "Today, as this century ends and the Millennium begins, we embark on the fourth stage of our struggle to make this a more complete union" with "shared economic security . . . for all." This coming rebuilding of the national house, he stressed, connected directly with America's past sacred achievements. "We can look back on the past hundred years with a sense of hope and . . . accomplishment," for "we . . . have changed the course of the nation together." "America entered this century in a condition of shame," locked in apartheid with voting restricted to white males, but "100 years later, much has changed." Despite setbacks, through courageous struggle progressives had won, he declared, for "today our dreams are the dreams of all America. We have changed the way that a majority of Americans think about race. And not just race. Civil Rights, women's rights, environmental protection—these are mainstream values now."

Now Americans stood poised to write a new movement in America's historic "Freedom Symphony," Jackson prophesied. The symphony's first three

movements — the "struggle to end slavery," "the struggle to end legal segregation," and "the struggle to give all Americans the right to vote" — were already
written. Now the fourth movement, which was "the climax . . . for which the
others were the prelude," awaited realization. It would, he admitted, be "the
hardest to compose"; it was "the movement begun by Dr. King just before
his death."

This generation's task was to complete America's business, "the unfinished
movement of Dr. King, the struggle to provide shared economic security and
justice." Though Jackson's agenda had many parts, including vigorous en-
forcement of civil rights, at its core was *economics*. King, he said, "knew that
a multi-ethnic, multi-cultural campaign for economic justice had to be the
final movement of the civil rights struggle." Therefore the pressing question
was "how do we build and lead a multiracial coalition for change?" Not by
focusing "on that which divides us," he answered, "but on that which unites
us," such as universal needs for quality jobs, health care, and public education
and for clean air and water, safe streets, and strong families and communities.
"We can move forward on this common ground."

Jackson closed by invoking America's better future and challenging people
to act to realize this dream. Reaching back to the last century's democratic
progress for encouragement, he stressed the moment's vast possibilities. With
the cold war and Reagan-era deficits gone, "we have an amazing opportunity
to make America better," he proclaimed, "to change the house to redress the
growing divide between the upstairs and downstairs." So, it was "time to lift
our sights . . . revive our spirits" and "begin to compose the fourth movement
in the Freedom Symphony, to finish Dr. King's unfinished work."[18]

Although Alan Keyes's public analyses and positions could scarcely be further from Reverend Jackson's, his rhetoric also parallels the American jeremiad. He always posits America's special promise and mission. According
to him, America's prime mission has always been to know and obey God,
from which knowledge will flow all God's blessings, first to Americans and
through them to the whole world. But he thinks contemporary Americans
are backsliding from achieving this mission and from the heroic model of its
founders. In jeremiadic tones, Keyes denounces the shameful conduct and
misdeeds of the current generation. Americans are in crisis and at a crucial
crossroads: one direction (the way Americans are now heading) leads toward

doomsday, the other (the righteous one) toward the millennium. The deplorable present foretells national grief and divine chastisement. Yet despite such gloom and doom, Keyes typically concludes by optimistically prophesying the chosen people's imminent reformation and resulting fulfillment of the promise. For example, he spent most of one scorching speech lamenting the "dismal state of our culture" but then noted that in the past when faced with such an ultimate moral decision "we have chosen what is right." "I believe we shall do so again," he closed, "then we shall hold up a beacon of light and hope for all of humanity to understand the true destiny of mankind."[19]

Throughout his collected volume of columns and speeches, *Our Character, Our Future: Reclaiming America's Moral Destiny,* Keyes expresses great moral-spiritual concern (though even while wearing his Christian commitment on his sleeve, Keyes cites the Declaration of Independence more than the Bible for moral authority). Commenting on a host of cultural issues, Keyes decries what he considers America's many grave social sins such as abortion, drugs, and sexual promiscuity. Elements of the jeremiad surface throughout this book but especially in its final chapter, a transcript of a speech titled "Spiritual Healing," which is among the purest expressions of a jeremiad found in the contemporary American context.

America's state of moral-spiritual decline, Keyes contends in "Spiritual Healing," is so severe that it threatens America's mission and invites God's punishing wrath. Assessing the "grave condition of our land" and state of the "Soul of America" makes him wonder: "Will America survive?" It is "sorely threatened. We are faced . . . today with a threat to our integrity and . . . future of this nation." Recalling that America's mission comes from the "God of judgment," Keyes pictures Abraham asking God about America, as he asked Him about Sodom, "Will you spare them?" Keyes similarly is haunted by a poet's image of "God rocking the cradle of aborted babies, as he commands his angels to dance on the grave of America."

Fortunately, there is a way to avoid such calamity, Keyes claims. But "to go forward, we must first reach back" and return to the truths of the Founding Fathers and Declaration of Independence—namely, that America depends on divine providence. It follows, therefore, that to reform, Americans must first acknowledge that the root of their woes is having strayed from God and God's laws. So, "we the people of the *Declaration,* and people of faith,"

Keyes declares, "have a special calling to call people back to the principles of the *Declaration* and . . . in doing so . . . back to God." Throughout the book, Keyes claims that America's essential nature is not material but spiritual: "The American dream . . . is not [mainly] a dream of materialism" but "a mission to seek the face of God and to rely upon his will": "The republic was not a dream. It was a prayer."

Notwithstanding its plaintive and ominous tones, Keyes's jeremiad ends hopefully, holding out the prospect of America repenting and fulfilling its promise. The situation is dire, he warns ("The hour is late" but "not *too* late"), and the choices stark ("if we continue down [our current] road" divine chastisement awaits). Yet "if we are faithful," he promises, "there is yet time to stave off such a fate." Averting destruction and finding salvation are "not impossible," though it *was* conditional: *If* the people will do *this, if* they do *that,* he concludes in a long list of repentant *if*s, then "we may yet still attain our great destiny."[20]

The jeremiad's salience in both the archliberal Jackson's and ultraconservative Keyes's oratory underscores its centrality to African American public discourse. Nevertheless, their sharp political-ideological differences are reflected in important differences in how each approaches and utilizes this black civil-religious tradition. The key difference in their use of jeremiadic rhetoric is the *kind* of issues they raise and positions they support with it. Although Jackson does regularly chastise Americans for acts of social-cultural immorality such as drug use, promiscuity, and media violence, his jeremiad *chiefly* targets inequities of political economy for which he urges structural reforms. Keyes, on the other hand, while saying relatively little about issues of economic and social justice, is truly prophetic, decrying social immorality (as he and the Christian right define it).[21] While Jackson's major focus on systemic ills and needed structural reforms versus Keyes's primary stress on personal piety and inner moral transformation is clearly the most basic divide in their prophetic modes, even that difference, while substantial, is not absolute. Interestingly, in his long catalogue of social iniquities, Keyes often excoriates hedonistic materialism and consumer culture, also favorite targets of moralizing liberals. Yet the left's co-optation of some of the right's "values" issues seems more pronounced than social conservatives' following more typically liberal practices such as criticizing unjust aspects of American economic and political institutions. Jackson and similarly inclined black progressives' fairly unique niche seems to be in combining economics-oriented political progressivism with morally traditional stands on many social-cultural issues.

Strategic and Ideological Uses of U.S. Civil Religion

Widespread as black civil religious expression is, whether, how, and to what end it is used varies greatly among African Americans. Black nationalists and Marxists, for example, usually reject America's civil religion outright, especially its hope for eventual freedom and justice for blacks in American society.[22] Black progressives and conservatives within the so-called mainstream naturally differ markedly in their versions and uses of the civic faith. More surprising, perhaps, is the considerable variability among progressives themselves relating to and using civil religion. Practically all black progressives use civil religion strategically to help achieve their ends, with some seeming to attach genuine inspirational and spiritual importance to civil religious formulations.[23]

Scholar and activist Vincent Harding typifies the most overtly spiritual approach to American civil religion among black progressives. In a volume of stirring essays about the civil rights movement's meaning and legacy, *Hope and History: Why We Must Share the History of the Movement,* Dr. Harding places the freedom struggle of the 1950s and 1960s squarely into civil-religious context. The "Black-led, multi-racial quest for democracy," he writes, was another "powerful outcropping of the continuing struggle for the expansion of democracy in the United States . . . in which African-Americans have always been integrally engaged."[24] Its flame of memory must remain lit and its transforming power kept alive today, he eloquently pleads. Telling young Americans the story of the movement, Harding asserts, is to call "them into communion with their Black and white ancestors in the struggle for a more humane American nation."[25]

The civil rights movement's ultimate gift to the nation, Harding asserts, was the new democratic realities and possibilities it created for realizing America's best and truest self. Most profoundly, the movement raised what it means "to redeem a land" and "remake a nation." Harding declares: "Our vocation of keeping hope and . . . memories (and therefore life) alive" will ascertain whether there are "still men and women whose hearts burn with great annealing flames on behalf of a new and just America." The answer to that fateful query, he predicts, will determine America's final result.[26]

The sharply differing tone of Congressman William Clay's book *Just Permanent Interests: Black Americans in Congress, 1870–1992* seems light-years from the lyricism of *Hope and History*. Whereas Harding voices an essentially ideal-spiritual vision, long-term Congressman and Congressional Black Caucus (CBC) founder Clay dispenses blunt, no-nonsense advice from the school of political hard knocks. Clay's history of African Americans in Congress to the present day invariably offers *real politique* lessons for African Americans engaging in American politics. Clay's "intense realism" considers politics "a deadly serious exercise" in which "only the strong survive" and "each group tends to devour its opponents." Thus, he stresses, African Americans must press in a practical, self-interested way for their fair share of government largess. "The CBC Fight for a Pro-active government," Clay asserts, aims to make government "a partner with our people to rectify three centuries of unfair, immoral treatment." To obtain this, he stresses, what blacks needed was the "exercise of raw power" — not the "idealistic, ideological pipedreams" of "wide-eyed optimists, hoping for the millennium when white politicians will share the spoils of victory" simply because it is fair to do so.[27]

Congressman Clay strongly advises blacks against attempts at moral appeal such as in the jeremiad. Ever insistent on advancing blacks' self-interest through determined practical pursuit of power, Clay thinks it foolishly naive to appeal to or believe in whites' conscience and goodwill. Intelligent people, he claims, "have come to realize that the so-called 'collective conscience' of this nation is a fantasy" and have awakened "to the fact that white Americans will only accede to black Americans those rights which we can negotiate through pressure or take by force." The Congressional Black Caucus has been effective, he claims, because it has relied solely on "tough talk and action" that has made the establishment "sit up and . . . notice."[28]

Clay also speaks harshly at times of key civil religious icons such as the Declaration and Constitution. For example, when "that glorious document the United States Constitution was the subject of so much fanfare and brouhaha" during the Bicentennial celebrations, he contends, only African American leaders "were addressing the sad truth of America's pitiful beginnings — a country conceived in sin, born in corruption, and continuing to live out the lies, contradictions, and hypocrisies embodied in the Declaration of Independence and Bill of Rights."[29]

Yet elsewhere Clay tempers such caustic descriptions of the nation's sacred texts and even depicts them as a source of blacks' political determination. At his book's end, he stresses how "despite the imperfections in the legacy of our founding fathers, the Congressional Black Caucus . . . has directed its efforts to perfecting the union." And he says of the heroic "sixty-seven black men and women who have served in the United States Congress" that these

> pioneers for justice and equality . . . [though] all victims of discrimination [and] . . . schooled in the hard knocks of reality . . . believed more deeply in the promises of democracy than did the framers of the Constitution. . . . They embraced the essence of the Constitution as did no other group in America, perhaps *because they had no other choice,* as their very survival depended on adherence by the majority to the tenets embodied in that document [emphasis added].[30]

Clay's statement implies that black congressional leaders (including himself, presumably) have invoked the Constitution "because they had no other choice." The civil religion is so publicly ubiquitous and strategically necessary, it seems, that even a relatively nonidealistic black politico such as Clay will sometimes play that card.

Civil Religion's Ideological Function and Effects

It is clear that blacks' own distinctive versions of the national faith have supplied a major portion of the ideals that have supported African American political activism. Conceivably, though, employing civil religious rhetoric might simply reflect pragmatic determination to employ every possible lever of influence. On the other hand, rituals such as the jeremiad work subtly, partly unconsciously, to alter people's moods and beliefs and dispose them toward prescribed acts and behavior. The civil religion's chief ideological function seems to be to inculcate hope and optimism about American possibilities.

Civil religion's optimism-producing effect regularly surfaces in Jesse Jackson's rhetoric. Addressing new graduates at Mitchell College commencement ceremonies, Jackson declared that "our nation must rely on the young" and their optimism and idealism to meet America's challenges. Today's youth would inescapably "make choices" of great "consequence" for themselves and a better society, Jackson declared, as every American "generation faces special challenges." Past democratic achievements such as establishing public education, ending legal segregation, and extending democratic rights happened "because past generations, at their moment of truth, were willing to stand" and do the right thing. So Reverend Jackson recited his version of the nation's sacred history to inspire the youthful graduates likewise to rise heroically to meet their day's urgent issues for advancing the common good.

However, acts by which people improve society, he contended, presuppose belief in the very possibility of social progress. "The sworn enemy of those who would do justice," he preached, is "cynicism" and "the collapse of faith." So he implored youth not to yield to despair. As it is "difficult to maintain optimism" and "act in faith," he declared, "to combat cynicism we must rely on the . . . characteristics of youth—idealism, optimism, enthusiasm, and courage," because "great things are not achieved by cynics; they are achieved by believers" such as Martin Luther King, Cesar Chavez, Robert Kennedy, and other heroes of the American past. So, "let us call one other to act in faith. Remain faithful. Remain optimistic . . . fight the good fight," he closed, exhorting, "Keep hope alive!"[31]

Jackson's Mitchell College address gives an indication of how American civil religion is used to induce hope for America's brighter tomorrow. The civil religion's impossible-to-disprove faith in a prophesied but never-quite-here perfect America provides some with a needed antidote to the faith-corroding effects of past and present discouragement. Such invincible faith in America's mythic future is expressed in poet Langston Hughes's lines: "O, let America be America again—The land that never has been yet—And yet must be." It parallels, too, Vincent Harding's sense of being a citizen of a nation not yet realized, of having as home "a land that does not yet exist." It is in this mythic American realm that Harding locates the "power to transcend history and create a better future for ourselves with others" and not "perish in hopelessness, mutual terror, and despair."[32]

Whether such faith is either warranted or desirable as a means of spurring action or, rather, a delusion that diverts attention and energy from the tasks necessary for racial liberation is essentially a matter of faith and worldview. At the same time, one can note how African Americans' use of the civil religion — particularly as voiced in the black jeremiad, or "Great Tradition of Black Protest" — contains characteristic strengths *and* weaknesses. At times, the civil religion has been imagined and articulated magnificently — and leveraged effectively — by such key figures as Martin Luther King. Harding, while often admiring the "Great Tradition," also criticizes some of its features, especially its proclivity toward naive, unrealistic optimism about blacks' struggle for freedom in America. At "its most dangerous levels," he warns, "such an approach encouraged black identification with the goals and interests of an oppressive white society," thereby inhibiting black self-determination and consideration of more radical alternatives than those offered by the oppressor culture.[33]

Sacvan Bercovitch argues that the American jeremiad's primary ideological function is to maintain social order and control. According to him, this hegemonic jeremiad offers a symbolic formulaic analysis of social ills that cuts off consideration of more objective, potentially radical analyses.[34] Indeed, to the extent that many African American leaders have employed a culture-affirming rhetoric grounded in consensus, they have had to fit their goals within its nonrevolutionary bounds. Yet the jeremiads most often voiced by national black leaders have more boldly condemned America's social failings and demanded more sweeping corrections than have most similar white spokespersons. Whether fighting against slavery, for civil rights, or for adding economic substance to the legal forms of democracy, historical black jeremiahs such as Frederick Douglass, W. E. B. Du Bois, and Martin Luther King struggled — sometimes successfully, sometimes not — to transform what were once considered radical, suspect causes into what most Americans eventually regarded as eminently respectable, moderate goals. Moreover, when the parameters of tolerable reform shifted in their direction, such leading black jeremiahs have typically repositioned themselves leftward to champion new, more "radical" social goals.[35]

Paradoxically, the African American jeremiad tradition has been both conservative and radical in social-political effect. On the one hand, it adopts the terms of the existing social-political consensus and affirms society's underlying cultural norms. On the other hand, the black jeremiad operates dynamically within an evolving consensus and is most typically found on the forward outer edge of that consensus, prodding it toward ever more thorough and inclusive social change. For even while mainstream progressives such as

Jackson opt to work within the ideological and procedural norms of the current system, their larger aim remains to transcend and transform that system.

The Future of the African American Jeremiad

Although this chapter documents past and ongoing participation of African Americans in American civil religion, the future of blacks' engagement with this civic-cultural tradition remains to be seen. Its future seems particularly questionable in view of the shifting social-political contexts in which African American public involvement and activism operate. Blacks' much-heralded shift from "protest to politics" or "unconventional to conventional" politics since the 1960s is particularly relevant.[36] The great political changes since passage of civil rights–era reforms such as the 1965 Voting Rights Act have steadily expanded black access to formal political institutions and influence. Blacks' transition from practicing outsider- to insider-politics, furthermore, could conceivably lessen blacks' traditional political appeal to conscience.

African Americans' tendency to link their political struggles to national ideals may stem historically from the race's relative powerlessness. Forms of moral suasion such as the American jeremiad seem most needed by groups with fewer alternative means of influence. It is possible, therefore, that as black political representatives become more fully integrated and empowered within the conventional political system, black leaders may appeal less often to the nation's highest civic-religious values. If so, then a nonidealist, "realistic" approach such as that advocated by Congressman Clay may be the future direction in which black politics moves.

There are other reasons, however, to anticipate continuing African American appeal to American civil religion. First is the evidence of civil religion's ongoing brilliant articulation and artful manipulation by such national figures as Jesse Jackson and Alan Keyes. Also crucial is that, despite African Americans' many post-1960s legal gains and electoral "firsts," black success in substantially affecting U.S. public policy since the 1960s is unclear and open to question.[37] Further, if significant disparity between black and white Americans in political resources and power persists, African Americans may continue to find it strategic to appeal to the dominant culture's professed values.

Finally, little reason exists to assume that the black public tradition of moral civil-religious appeal will cease to have value and utility in an era of blacks' increasing absorption into U.S. procedural politics. Moral conviction and appeal, while not the only or necessarily the main part of effective politics, will likely remain a necessary component of successful political discourse. Even more to the point, it is a false dilemma to present African Americans' only choice as being either pragmatic self-interest pursued exclusively through conventional politics or idealistic protests against injustice without related attempts to utilize institutional mechanisms of power. Rather, these two approaches have always tended to be mutually supportive and work best together. Indeed, during the civil rights movement's heyday, pressure generated by street protests worked in tandem with traditional political activities such as lobbying Congress. Moreover, when the stirring civil-religious language of leaders such as King enhanced both sets of activities was precisely when blacks achieved greatest national political success. It seems that African Americans have always most effectively combined idealistic protest with pragmatic politics—being, so to speak, simultaneously *as wise as serpents and guileless as doves.*

Strategic considerations alone suggest that most politically engaged African Americans will wish to have every usable arrow in their quiver, including American civil religion. Furthermore, one must acknowledge many individuals' evidently sincere belief in national civic ideals. It seems altogether likely, then, that most African Americans engaged in mainstream politics will keep invoking American civil religion in the ongoing struggle to shape U.S. society's present and future.

Notes

1 The term "civil religion" entered common scholarly language with Robert Bellah's seminal article "Civil Religion in America," *Daedalus* 96 (winter 1967): 1–21. Civil religion remains the most common, though not sole, term that scholars use to describe such civic religious phenomena.

2 Martin E. Marty, "Two Kinds of Two Kinds of Civil Religion," in *American Civil Religion,* ed. Russell E. Richey and Donald G. Jones (New York: Harper and Row, 1974), 141–42. It is important to note that black nationalist civil religions, other than variants of the American national faith, also exist. See, e.g., Randall K. Bur-

kett, *Garveyism as a Religious Movement: The Institutionalization of a Black Civil Religion* (Metuchen, N.J.: Scarecrow Press and American Theological Library Association, 1978). Charles Reagan Wilson skillfully describes a distinctive Southern regional variant of the civil religion; see, e.g., *Judgment and Grace in Dixie: Southern Faiths from Faulkner to Elvis* (Athens: University of Georgia Press, 1995) and *Baptized in Blood: The Religion of the Lost Cause, 1865–1920* (Athens, GA: University of Georgia Press, 1980). Despite his many valuable insights about shared regional culture among white and black Southerners, Wilson overreaches to claim that Southern blacks' civil religion is simply or purely a subset of the surrounding larger white Southern civil religion, especially since the latter, he says, revolves around veneration of the Confederate "Lost Cause." In my opinion, it is wrong to suggest that revering the Confederacy is *any* part of most African Americans' civil religion, North or South.

For investigation of *diverging* race-specific American civil religions in the South during the 1950s, see Andrew Michael Manis, *Southern Civil Religions in Conflict: Black and White Baptists and Civil Rights, 1947–1957* (Athens: University of Georgia Press, 1987). There is as much basic disagreement in the majority of white and black Southerners' civil religions over the Civil War, I hold, as Manis's study shows there was disagreement over civil rights during the civil rights era.

3   The "Nation Under God" versus "Nation As Self-Transcendent" civil religious dyad as well as the "Priestly" versus "Prophetic" dyad are described in Marty, "Two Kinds of Civil Religion," 139–57.

Of the three chief traits of black civil religion I identify here, "Nation Under God" seems the *most* pronounced, as most African Americans' public symbolic language, whether from a liberal, conservative, nationalist, or other perspective, posits a deity; blacks' prophetic and progressive tendencies, though still predominant among blacks overall, appear somewhat less hegemonic. For example, political progressives overwhelmingly employ prophetic rhetoric toward major national economic and political issues and often on social-cultural issues as well, while conservatives generally decline taking a prophetic stance on issues of political economy (though significantly, many of them *are* prophetic on social-cultural issues such as abortion and school prayer). Similarly, more African Americans operate social-politically within a theistic context than are either liberal or conservative. Nevertheless, if any cluster of tendencies may be considered modal or mainstream for African Americans, it is the theistic-prophetic-progressive triumvirate.

4   Rev. Jesse Jackson, *Legal Lynching: Racism, Injustice and the Death Penalty* (New York: Marlowe and Co., 1996), 166–67; for an example of his stock "If my people . . ." reference, see "Rebuilding the House: The Fourth Movement of the Freedom Symphony," Remarks of the Rev. Jesse L. Jackson, NAACP 90th Annual Convention, 14 July 1999, online: Rainbow/Push Coalition, http://www.rainbowpush.org/

speech/index.html, 23 September 1999. Jackson is, of course, besides a political leader, an ordained Baptist minister. But nonclergy African American leaders of overtly secular organizations seem equally comfortable bringing the divine into their discussions. NAACP President Kweisi Mfume, for example, opened the civil rights organization's 1998 Annual Convention by invoking "as the first order of our business, the blessing of Almighty God . . . on these delegates at this hour in our nation's history . . . [and asking] God . . . to bless America as we work to bring about real and meaningful change." Kweisi Mfume, speech given by NAACP President Kweisi Mfume (rough transcript), First Plenary Session, 13 July 1998, NAACP online, http://www.naacp.org/president/speeches/archived, 19 March 1999.

5   On Keyes's rhetoric's resonance with conservative evangelical activists in the 2000 Iowa Republican caucuses, see Ellen Gamerman of the Baltimore *Sun,* "Keyes Scores Iowa Coup: No. 3 Place," printed in San Jose *Mercury News,* 25 January 2000, 14A. On the national Democratic leadership's view of the effectiveness of Jackson's energetic voter registration drives and campaigning in the 2000 election, see pages 57–58 in Peter J. Boyer, "Man of Faith: Can Jesse Jackson Save Himself?" *The New Yorker,* 22 October 2001, 50–65. Jackson utilizes, for example (besides the Democratic Party), such organizations as PUSH (People United to Serve Humanity)/Rainbow Coalition and a nationally syndicated TV talk show, while Keyes hosts a TV public affairs show, "Alan Keyes Makes Sense," established the Declaration Foundation, and works with many other conservative organizations. Most critical for this chapter's purposes are the important similarities between the two African American leaders' civil religious styles and rhetoric. Both Keyes and Jackson typify, for example, African Americans' strong preference for "Nation Under God" civil religion and for infusing public debate with strong moral-spiritual content. Jeremiadic elements likewise are salient in both men's public rhetoric. Thus, Keyes like Jackson also typifies black civil religion's tendency for prophetic rhetoric—although of the two, it is Jackson who completes the triad of most common African American civil religious tendencies, including political progressivism.

6   Alan Keyes, *Our Character, Our Future: Reclaiming America's Moral Destiny,* ed. George Grant (Grand Rapids: Zondervan Publishing House, 1996), 24, 29, 11, 34–35.

7   Ibid., 20, 37.

8   Marshall quote in Stuart Taylor Jr., "Marshall Sounds Critical Note on Bicentennial," *New York Times,* 7 May 1987, 1 ff; see examples of the "More Perfect Union" phrase used by sources later in this chapter.

9   Vincent Harding, *There Is a River: The Black Struggle for Freedom in America* (New York: Harcourt Brace, 1981), 83–84, 60, 42.

10 Sacvan Bercovitch, *The American Jeremiad* (Madison: University of Wisconsin Press, 1978), 6–7. For Bercovitch, the complete rhetoric has three defining elements: affirmation of America's *promise;* criticism of current *declension,* or retrogression

from that promise; and a concluding *prophecy* that society will soon reform to complete its mission and redeem the promise. Bercovitch's description of the Puritan jeremiad's transformation into a more secular national version is detailed in chapter 4, "The Typology of America's Mission."

11   Wilson Jeremiah Moses, *Black Messiahs and Uncle Toms: Social and Literary Manipulations of a Religious Myth* (University Park: Penn State University Press, 1982), 29–31. Moses was the first to use in print the term "black Jeremiad."

12   The fullest treatment of the African American jeremiad tradition is the writer's *The Afro-American Jeremiad: Appeals for Justice in America* (Philadelphia: Temple University Press, 1990).

13   Rev. Jesse L. Jackson, "Save the Family Farm and the Farm Family," Chicago, 26 January 1985, in *Straight from the Heart* [SFH hereafter], ed. Roger D. Hatch and Frank E. Watson (Philadelphia: Fortress Press, 1987), 287; "Equity in a New World Order," New Orleans, 16 July 1980, *SFH*, 290; "Equity in a New World Order," *SFH*, 291.

14   "Religious Liberty: Civil Disobedience, Conscience, and Survival," Philadelphia, 27 April 1976, in *SFH, 147;* "Equity in a New World Order," *SFH*, 290; "In Search of a New Vision and a New Focus," Washington, D.C., 17 May 1980, *SFH*, 97; "Jackson Criticizes Anti-Affirmative Action Actions," press release, 3 December 1983, Jesse Jackson for President Committee.

15   Jackson, "Equity in a New World Order," *SFH*, 290; "Political Votes, Economic Oats," Washington, D.C., 20 January 1978, quoted in *SFH*, 35.

16   "The Quest for a Just Society and a Peaceful World," Washington, D.C., 3 November 1983, quoted in *SFH*, xiv; "The Candidate's Challenge: The Call of Conscience, the Courage of Conviction," Democratic National Convention, San Francisco, 17 July 1984, in *SFH*, 3.

17   "Brown: Twenty-five Years Later," *New York Daily News,* 17 May 1979, in *SFH*, 89; "Protecting the Legacy of Dr. Martin Luther King, Jr.," Atlanta, 15 January 1986, *SFH*, 130–31. King also, said Jackson in the latter speech, reminded Americans of God's promise (as Jackson regularly does) that "if my people, who are called by my name, will . . . pray and seek my face," God will redeem them.

18   "Rebuilding the House: The Fourth Movement of the Freedom Symphony," Remarks of the Rev. Jesse L. Jackson, NAACP 90th Annual Convention, 14 July 1999, online: Rainbow/PUSH Coalition, http://www.rainbowpush.org/speech/index.html, 23 September 1999.

19   Keyes, *Our Character, Our Future,* 14.

20   Ibid., 27–28, 132–35.

21   Jackson and Keyes's rhetorical similarities as well as content differences parallel those found between the evangelical 1988 presidential candidates Pat Robertson and Jesse Jackson examined so incisively in Allen D. Hertzke, *Echoes of Discontent: Jesse*

Jackson, Pat Robertson, and the Resurgence of Populism (Washington, D.C.: Congressional Quarterly Press, 1993). Most fundamentally, in Hertzke's analysis, Jackson and Robertson each articulated a brand of populistic-prophetic protest against the standing liberal order. The key difference was that Robertson's prophetic populism mainly scored the cultural evils of liberal American society (leaving the standing order's economic immorality untouched), while Jackson's prophetic message targeted mainly social and economic injustice and (secondarily but also) society's attendant moral-cultural decadence.

22 See R. Drew Smith, "Black Religious Nationalism and the Politics of Transcendence," *Journal of the American Academy of Religion* (fall 1998): 533–48.

23 Admittedly, it is problematic confidently to impute from someone's public words alone their true intent or sincerity; no one, after all, can read hearts. Nevertheless, the nature of one's language usually does suggest underlying attitude, which is what I have tried, no doubt imperfectly, to discern from the texts.

24 Vincent Harding, *Hope and History: Why We Must Share the Story of the Movement* (Maryknoll, N.Y.: Orbis Books, 1990), 6–7. Harding also stresses the civil rights movement's global impact, noting that wherever popular democratic movements arose in the 1980s, there were usually voices or banners proclaiming the African American freedom movement's inspirational anthem, "We Shall Overcome" (see 27–29).

25 Ibid., 9, 17, 198.

26 Ibid., 158.

27 William L. Clay, *Just Permanent Interests: Black Americans in Congress, 1870–1992* (New York: Amistad, 1992; updated edition, 1993), xx–xxi, 345–47, 7, xix.

28 Ibid., 7, 340.

29 Ibid., 349

30 Ibid., 352.

31 Rev. Jesse L. Jackson Sr., "Choices/Consequences: A Call to Courage with Conviction," Address at Mitchell College Commencement Ceremonies, New London, Conn., 15 May 1999, online: Rainbow/PUSH Coalition, http://www.rainbowpush. org/speech/index.html, 22 May 1999.

32 Langston Hughes, *The Dream Keeper* (New York: Alfred A. Knopf, 1946), 7, as quoted in Harding, *Hope and History*, 182; Harding, *There Is a River*, xii–xiii.

33 Harding, *There Is a River*, 42, 132–33.

34 See especially Bercovitch, *American Jeremiad*, 160, in chapter 4, "Ritual of Consensus" on the jeremiad's basically conservative social function.

35 For treatment of these major historical figures' evolving jeremiads through the course of their public careers, see the writer's *The Afro-American Jeremiad*.

36 E.g., Katherine Tate, *From Politics to Protest: The New Black Voter in America* (Cambridge: Harvard University Press, 1993); Robert C. Smith, "Black Power and the

Transformation from Protest to Politics," *Political Science Quarterly* (fall 1981): 431–43; and Fredrick Harris, *Something Within: Religion in African-American Activism* (New York: Oxford University Press, 1999).

37   For a strong expression of the thesis that blacks in recent decades have been marginalized, co-opted, and generally rendered politically ineffective and irrelevant in American politics, see Robert C. Smith, *We Have No Leaders: African-Americans in the Post-Civil Rights Era* (New York: State University of New York Press, 1996).

5

RECOGNITION, RESPECTABILITY,
AND LOYALTY: BLACK CHURCHES
AND THE QUEST FOR CIVILITY

Walter Earl Fluker

Historically, the overwhelming majority of African Americans have been ensconced in the morals and manners of American civil society without the benefits of its social and political merits. The most loyal (and at times the most reverent) allegiance to constitutional faith[1] and the most vigorous defense of American civil life have come from its benighted sons and daughters who have been denied access to participation and benefits of these practices. This contradiction is a statement about the hypocrisy and disloyalty of a nation that has continually uplifted the ideals of democratic society as attainable to those who play by its moral rules and customs. It is also a damning commentary on the anguished dilemma of African Americans who have had to deal with the psychosocial dynamics of civility in respect to public life and political participation.

The black church is at the center of this portraiture of misplaced loyalties and reverence. More than any other institution in American society, the black church has demonstrated what political scientist Fredrick C. Harris calls *the dualistic orientation of oppositional civic culture.* Despite the ways in which black church life and practices mirror and reinforce the conflicting loyalties of faith and nation, these faithful civil practitioners have been able to bridge the relationship between their internal religiosity and unrewarded civility into political organizing and participation.[2] The roots of these practices, as they relate to civility, can be best understood by examining the historical entrapments of race and ideology within the American civil context and identifying the discursive formations that represent the broad and often conflicting practices of civility in black life. These discursive formations, it will be argued, provide heuristic instruments that allow us to look at the sources of conflicting social practices and to identify ways in which acts of civility may serve as *social capital* and transforming praxis within social and political spheres of influence.

Civility, as understood within the black church tradition, is both problematic and redemptive.[3] It is problematic because of its historical roots in what has been variously described as *the American dilemma,* that is, the problem of *doubleness* in African American history and culture. It is redemptive because black churches have dealt with the problematic in ways that have also produced three underlying social practices informing a transformative praxis that has sought the best in American democratic idealism. These three practices, *recognition, respectability,* and *loyalty,* have been the cornerstones of African American strivings within a society that has misnamed, disrespected, and disenfranchised African Americans in civic life. Nonetheless, because of the ironic, even paradoxical manner in which black churches have continued to maintain their loyalty to a system that has historically abused their commitment, I am suggesting a theological reevaluation of our public commitments in light of these three underlying practices.

The operative assumption throughout this essay is that black churches, by virtue of their allegiance to democratic idealism and long-standing practice of civility as a means of accessing the social rewards and benefits of civil society, have invested largely in *social capital.* But their investments have often been disallowed or manipulated in ways that have rendered them ineffectual and nonnegotiable in political life. Nonetheless, the practice of civility is a *good* in and of itself; and its benefits extend beyond the political sphere. Civility, in black churches, and in African American life generally, provides the moral and spiritual infrastructure that makes its *own* community life possible. Furthermore, civility as subversive speech and action provides the moral and spiritual material that sustains its place within political life and public discourse. Because of black churches' long-standing commitment to American democratic society and their commitment to civility as normative for participation in public life and polity, it is necessary to inquire regarding its theological rationale for participation in civil life. The church, unlike other social institutions, claims loyalty to a sphere of influence and being beyond the political. Its inner life and practices point to a higher value than the political. Black churches, variously constructed and sanctioned, claim loyalty to God as the highest value and source for their participation in public life. How, then, might civility in black church life and practices be explored as a historical, political, and theological phenomenon without violating its raison d'être?

The approach in this analysis is first to inquire concerning black churches' sociohistorical entrapment in race and ideology expressed most profoundly in the language of *the American dilemma* and to explore the genesis of civility in black churches as a postbellum phenomenon. Secondly, I will examine the role of education in inculcating certain habits and practices that conspired with the ideology of race that promoted patriarchal formulations and race-management as primary moral grammatical expressions of civility among black elites, including black clerical leadership. The historical implications of this white-sponsored and politically manipulated moral training found creative resonance with the psychosocial need among freedmen and freedwomen for recognition, respectability, and loyalty. Finally, I offer a brief proposal for a theological rationale for civility among black churches that is subversive and transformative as a prolegomenon to a larger effort in process.

The Quest for Civility

The quest for civility is a popular subject in various media and discussions about the decline and renewal of community in American society. Civility as intellectual discourse has received increased attention since the publication of Stephen Carter's popular book by the same name.[4] The publication of Carter's work coincided with the publication of *A Call to Civil Society: Why Democracy Needs Moral Truths*[5] by the Council on Civil Society chaired by Jean Bethke Elshtain of the University of Chicago, which was also home to yet another distinguished scholar concerned with civility as an intellectual and practical discipline, the late Edward Shils.[6] The subject of civility, however, has been a matter of serious intellectual debate preceding the rise of the nation-state.[7]

In American civic life, our earliest progenitors found social and political merit in practicing civility. Fourteen-year-old George Washington is reported to have copied from a seventeenth-century English translation of a sixteenth-century French book of manners for what later became his *Rules of Civility and Decent Behavior in Company and in Conversation*.[8] Civility, as a quest for social dignity and political reward, promised its most loyal practitioners a place within democratic polity, but for those who failed to abide by the rules or who by virtue of race, ethnicity, gender, class, or sexual lifestyles were deemed unfit for civil society, the etiquette, manners, and ways of civility were punitive and damning.

CIVILITY, CIVIL SOCIETY, CIVIC LIFE, AND CIVIC CAPACITY

Civility is used in a variety of contexts often masking complex historical, sociological, and methodological issues. Civility in common usage refers to a set of manners, certain etiquettes, and social graces that are rooted in specific class orientations and moral sensibilities.[9] Civility, however, does not refer simply to etiquette, manners, and social graces but is inclusive of *social capital* and the inherent benefits accrued by these *networks of reciprocity*. Civility also has to do with the individual's social dignity within that system. In the following discussion, the term "civility" is used as a framework for discussing the role of social capital within the context of black church life and practices.[10] I do not limit civility, however, to social capital but refer more broadly to the concept as the social-historical script or contract that the individual citizen negotiates within the context of the larger society. Civility is the psychosocial ecology of the individual, a certain understanding or self-referential index of the individual's place within a social system as it relates to individual character.

Civic life, in this discussion, covers broad territory—including questions of what constitutes *civility, civic capacity,* and *civil society.* For instance, Robert Wuthnow suggests that civil society is "the arena in which individual freedoms, even those that are self-interested, are kept in tension with collective values and community participation."[11] Michael Walzer defines civil society as "that 'space of uncoerced human association' and 'the set of relational networks' and institutions that fill it, all trying to harmonize the conflicting demands of individual interests and the social good. Families, schools, churches, synagogues, mosques, voluntary societies, nongovernmental organizations, and communications media all belong to civil society."[12] The critical point of leverage in both definitions is the role of *values* (freedom, self-interest, collective good, community). Included in the idea of civic life is this larger understanding of the role of values that make civil society possible. Undergirding these values, or, better, the practice that infuses and sustains values within a democratic social and political culture, is civility. Civility, in this context, treats social capital and civic capacity as synonymous in that they both refer to "connections among individuals — social networks and the norms of reciprocity and trustworthiness that arise from them." Moreover, social capital is related to civic virtue in that the latter is "most powerful when it is embedded in a dense network of reciprocal social relations." Putnam opines, "A society of many virtuous, but isolated individuals is not necessarily rich in social capital."[13] This description of *social capital* and its role in creating and sustaining community is important for the following discussion in two ways. One is that *social capital* provides networks for community engagement that can be inclusive and socially beneficial even for those who are not civically engaged; and secondly, social capital derives its life and power from the norms of reciprocity that it engenders and sustains.

Black Civility and the American Dilemma

THE NEGRO PROBLEM

Any serious accounting of the genesis of civility within black church life must investigate the underlying discursive practices wrought by *dilemma* and its civilizing effects on black freedmen and freedwomen. Since Gunnar Myrdal's classic study, *An American Dilemma*,[14] the term *dilemma* has come to represent broad and conflicting ideologies in respect to African American life and culture.[15] The subtitle of Myrdal's work, however, underscored the fundamental character of the issues at stake: he characterized the dilemma as "The Negro Problem and Democracy." The Negro Problem (sometimes The Negro Question) has been the staple ideological statement defining and representing the life and place of the African in American society since slavery. The Negro Problem, formulated by all sides of the male-dominated white power elite, was "What shall we do with the Negro?"[16] The Problem, however, reached its most significant historical impasse during the last two decades of the nineteenth century and the first two decades of the twentieth. With increased African American political participation, economic development, and the large population of blacks in the South during Reconstruction, these years witnessed a rise in racially motivated violence, lynchings,

and legislative and judicial practices aimed at stripping agency from freedmen and freedwomen and returning the country to a place that was safe
for "white women."[17] At the same time former abolitionists, emigrationists,
mostly Northern white religious leaders, politicians, industrialists, and philanthropists worked diligently to solve the Negro Problem through education as a means of civilizing the child/savage generally depicted in bestial
and minstrel images.[18] Such was the social and political context that greeted
the African American entrance into the twentieth century and informed the
moral and civic practices of black intellectual elites and religious leaders.
Myrdal's formulation of the American dilemma, however, betrayed a deeper
and more fundamental problem seldom echoed in quiet, genteel places where
the *problem of whiteness* was suppressed and ignored.

THE PROBLEM OF WHITENESS

The problem of whiteness had its roots in bourgeois acquisitiveness and was
deeply related to religion, culture, and morality. Since the "founding" of this
nation, the culture-shapers and policy-makers have struggled with "the republican dilemma." The dilemma was how to salvage "freedom" to pursue
wealth from the inbred contamination that accompanied it. The resolution,
of course, was to promote republican ideology and Protestant asceticism,
the toxic mixture of which had striking implications for the development
of possessive individualism in American society and the problem of race.[19]
More precisely, the question that plagued white evangels and the founders
of the republic was "How does one justify the nefarious trade in human
cargo and bondage through religious and moral means without a scapegoat?"[20] All acts of public piety that erase shame and guilt demand a ritual-
istic sacrifice to insure the *order* of civilization. The child/savage imagery of
Africans was used by white elites to first justify the barbarous treatment of
freedmen and freedwomen, but underneath this imagery was a more subtle
and sinister need—the perpetuation of class and gender ideology. The strife
between lower classes of indigent whites fighting to protect the "virtue of
white women" and the demonic depiction of African Americans as beasts
and minstrels provided for white elites both the justification and the means
for capital accumulation and dominance through race and gender construc-
tions. But the resolution of the problem of whiteness had mixed results. According to Toni Morrison, it made the white perpetrators of this madness

sicker and sillier; and it made African Americans worse — it planted jungles within them.[21]

Moreover, the failed resolution of the problem of whiteness produced "iron cages" that held both enslavers and the enslaved in bondage.[22] The duality of the image of child/savage created even greater anxiety for white ruling classes — it also created a dilemma. White elites had to decide whether to continue dominance through psychological, cultural, economic, political, and physical coercion or to adopt elaborate emigration schemes. White philanthropic and religious leadership was split on this issue and, not surprisingly, so was African American leadership at the turn of the century.[23]

Recognition, Respectability, and Loyalty

Before Myrdal's highly acclaimed study of the Negro Problem, W. E. B. Du Bois's, in artful prose, forthrightly captured the nature of the problematic in black life:

> After the Egyptian and Indian, the Greek and Roman, the Tueton and Mongolian, the Negro is a sort of seventh son, born with a veil, and gifted with second-sight in this American world, — a world which yields him no true self-consciousness, but only lets him see himself through the revelation of the other world. It is a peculiar sensation, this double-consciousness, this sense of always looking at one's self through the eyes of others, of measuring one's soul by the tape of the world that looks on in amused contempt and pity. One ever feels his twoness, — an American, a Negro; two souls, two thoughts, two unreconciled strivings; two warring ideals in one dark body, whose dogged strength alone keeps it from being torn asunder.
>
> The history of the American Negro is the history of this strife, — this longing to attain self-conscious manhood, to merge his double self into a better and truer self. . . . He simply wishes to make it possible for a man to be both a Negro and an American, without being cursed and spit upon by his fellows, without having the doors of Opportunity closed roughly in his face.[24]

Du Bois's depiction of doubleness is a meditation on the psychosocial condition of the African American at the turn of the century, but it is even more. At the core of the problematic is the plea for recognition, respectability, and loyalty. Recognition, respectability, and loyalty were also cornerstones of racial uplift ideology that dominated the landscape of post-Reconstruction activities among black leadership. These civic goods were sought through education, suffrage, political leadership, and jury service based on natural rights arguments.[25] Most prominent among these strategies, however, was education.

EDUCATION AS THE BATTLEGROUND
FOR SOCIAL CONTROL FOR FREED PEOPLE

In his now-classic study *The Education of Blacks in the South, 1860–1935,* James D. Anderson contends that beyond the specific arguments regarding the utility and efficacy of industrial versus classic education among freedmen and freedwomen was a larger, more significant ideological design promoted by race and capital. Anderson demonstrates the ways in which white patriarchy conspired with Negro leadership, most notably with Booker T. Washington, to maintain the subordinate status of black and white laborers through industrial education expressed most dramatically in the Hampton-Tuskegee Model. Critical to Anderson's analysis is the formation of an alliance of Northern white philanthropists, politicians, religious leaders, and industrialists who met in secret with the landed gentry of the South from 1899 to 1901 and later forged a campaign for Southern education from 1901 to 1914 in order to insure the perpetuation of hegemonic practices of the planter class. At stake in this alliance was the resolution of two contending ideologies on the Negro Problem. One was the proposal offered by Northern and Southern religious and social leaders for universal education as a substitute for older and cruder methods of socialization and control.[26] The resolution of this dilemma for those on all sides was universal education, but with an important caveat: freedpeople would benefit best from industrial education based on the Hampton Model.[27]

Key to the success of this campaign was collaboration with Negro leadership. Before Booker T. Washington and W. E. B. Du Bois became the popular representatives of industrial versus classical education for freedpeople, the ideological die was cast by the growing white resistance to a literate black leadership through the work of General Samuel Chapman Armstrong, the founder and principal of the Hampton Normal and Agricultural Institute.

Armstrong believed that political participation by literate black leadership spelled the death of the South as an economic force, and that with the failure of the South, the economic stability of the nation would founder. His solution was to ensure that freedmen and freedwomen would maintain a labor force for the agricultural wealth of the South. His strategy was to train a generation of laborers who would teach the values of hard work, thrift, and subservience to other blacks. His pedagogy reinforced belief in black subordination to the planter-class ideology of minstrelsy and infantilism, that is, an educated black leadership was detrimental to the political economy of the South. He found his perfect pupil in one Booker T. Washington.

The dilemma is hardly resolved; it still exists at the heart of African American life and practices and has far-reaching implications for the ways in which African American leaders understand and participate in civic life. In recent years a number of scholars working in critical race theory and in historical, literary, cultural, multicultural, and philosophical studies have addressed the problematic in other terms.[28] Most relevant to the purposes of the present discussion is the treatment afforded by cultural critics who ask the question of *dilemma* or *doubleness* as it pertains to binary oppositions in black life that grow out of adaptation to a North Atlantic aesthetic. These studies seek to understand the ways in which attachment to the heroic ideal of the European aesthete prevents and further complicates progressive critiques and strategies for agency and peoplehood. Preoccupation with dilemma as a one-dimensional causal phenomenon is unproductive and akin to riding two horses galloping in different directions, which is a strain on the anatomy. More progressive critiques look at the question of dilemma in respect to macroeconomic and political variables and their relationship to cultural meanings.

EDUCATION, UPLIFT IDEOLOGY, AND THEIR CIVILIZING EFFECTS

Broadly speaking, education among freedpersons was utilized as a means of racial uplift, but it had the paradoxical advantage of inculcating certain habits and practices that encouraged bourgeois manners and morals.[29] The civilizing influences of education, despite great ideological divides as to which type was most effective for uplift, had much the same impact on recognition, respect, and loyalty to democratic values. Black intellectuals and race leaders such as Ida B. Wells, Anna Julia Cooper, W. E. B. Du Bois, Booker T. Washington, Thomas T. Fortune, and Mary Church Terrell all embraced the polite and gentle pursuits of bourgeois morals embodied in thrift, industry, self-control, piety, temperance, and the work ethic — all necessary, they believed, for successful citizenship and economic independence. Kevin Gaines adds, "Education of the freedpeople was often tied to moral evolution and industrial training rather than citizenship and political independence."[30] Gaines's observation is important in that it demonstrates the ways in which discursive formations provide the means for the articulation of moral languages that over time become distinct from habits and practices originally related to, or assumed to be related to, the historical project of their discursive features — in this case to the ideology of racial uplift.

Black elite ideology of racial uplift was accompanied by a specific moral vocabulary, born of the rigors of slavery and Jim Crow, but in its most basic formulation it was a language that sought recognition, respectability, and loyalty to an ideal embodied in democratic life and practices. Furthermore, the moral vocabulary of black elites evolved over time to embrace a bourgeois worldview that promoted self-reliance and social egalitarianism. This worldview proved to have complex and aggravating features that impacted ways in which black people, especially black churches, understand civility.

The ideological divide in the education of freedpeople, industrial versus classical, was symptomatic of a deeper fissure between self-reliance and social egalitarianism, reflected most radically in the accommodationist stance of Booker T. Washington and the protest discourse of W. E. B. Du Bois. Even more was at stake in this division — self-reliance and social egalitarianism also had specific gender and politicoeconomic alliances. Gaines suggests, "Racial uplift, in order to function ultimately depended on the recognition of the other, namely those often contemptuous whites and insubordinate blacks. And racial uplift ideology seemed to function best for those of its adherents who had internalized the language of patriarchal power."[31]

NONSPECIFICITY AND ERASURE OF FEMALE AGENCY

Joy James's critique of patriarchal power among black elites provides insight into the moral discourse that perpetuated itself beyond its distinct discursive formation and mission. According to James, two poles of intellectuals represent black leadership: *instrumental* and *consensus building.* The instrumental leader, according to James, is primarily functional and administrative,

whereas consensus-building leaders are concerned with speech and agreement. The two types mark two distinct yet related modalities of leadership
and moral perspectives. Both modalities are necessary for effective leadership
in African American life and practice, yet the most popular form is consensus
building because at the heart of its discourse are democratic values. On the
other hand instrumental leaders are concerned with institutions and more
formally with public life. The two forms have produced two main types of
black leaders — public intellectuals and leaders guided by a sense of vocation
and public responsibility.[32]

   Classic examples of this divide are representations of gender and class
associations in respective ideological clans. Paul Robeson and W. E. B. Du
Bois versus Ella Baker and Claudia Jones are examples cited by James. James
further suggests these respective divisions also tend to promote fictive and
nonfictive characterizations of black women intellectuals. Nonspecificity and
erasure of black women leaders are the means by which the charismatic public intellectual perpetuates the divide and fosters a certain kind of moral
vocabulary not unlike the accommodationist rhetoric of their predecessors.
"*Nonspecificity* promotes the disappearance of the detailed historical or empirical record. In some respects, it erases subject, deeds and events, while
simultaneously discussing them. *Nonspecificity* promotes *erasure*."[33] Nonspecificity and erasure, as we will see, significantly impact conversations regarding the role and place of women in black church leadership.

RACE MANAGEMENT AS ELITE CATEGORY OF MORAL PRACTICES

Hierarchical dominance is a key element that emerges in the moral discourse and practices of black elites, male and female (not to be confused with
patriarchal practices and self-reliance ideology). Black elites also functioned
as "race managers," according to James. Perhaps there is no example more
powerful than the figure of Booker T. Washington at the turn of the century. But Washington is not alone. The hierarchical/functional model that
accompanies leadership practices among black elites has a direct correlation
with ways in which race and capital have functioned within patriarchal systems.[34] The moral vocabulary, however, that undergirds the practices is even
more invasive and disrespectful of the masses. Gaines suggests that black cultural elites saw self-help and Negro improvement as a statement about "the
moral and cultural deficiency of impoverished Blacks rather than economic

exploitation and coercion."[35] Moreover, the language of leadership sought to dislodge itself from those whom it sought to manage.

The Black Church and Civic Life

The black church is not immune from the doubleness of black life and its role in civic life and practices, specifically black church leadership. Historically, black church leadership has and still maintains the primary function of race management for political and social elites. Gayraud S. Wilmore notes that since Reconstruction there has been a deradicalization of the black church in respect to political engagement and prophetic practices. Although Wilmore's thesis has been criticized as providing a convenient narrative of decline in black church activism in order to promote the project of black theology, with few notable exceptions the political posture of black churches has been essentially defensive and accommodationist. This was witnessed most recently in the Gore-Bush campaign of 2000 and subsequent meetings with church leaders.[36] In addition, the patriarchal formulations of black church leadership and the accompanying race-management discourse have functioned in deleterious ways to subvert black political participation and organization. At the same time, these leaders still function as the hope and possibility of transformative practices in black civic life. The ideological and cultural precedents for black church leadership have their genesis in the doubleness already described.

Edward L. Wheeler, in a neglected study of black ministerial leadership from 1865 to 1902, underscores the problematic in respect to dilemma. He suggests that for black ministerial leadership during Reconstruction and at the turn of the century, doubleness was portrayed in respect to *accommodation* and *possibility.* Given the horrific circumstances of black life during white political reentrenchment, the censure of black economic and cultural agency through lynching and racial strife, freedpeople had limited options. Temperance and education provided the fundamental options of possibility for black ministerial leadership. Education, of course, became the dominant cultural mechanism for uplift and provided the cultural lens through which civic life was engaged.[37]

Wheeler's analysis points to the ideological sequences in the later work of contemporary black theologians, sociologists, and church historians who

tend to overlook the role of accommodation and possibility as twin constructs in a larger historical narrative that either romanticizes the protest
traditions of black churches or condemns them for their embrace of normative cultural values that promote accommodation and acquiescence.[38] In
the following pages I will argue that ideological and cultural precedents of
black civic life represented in racial uplift remain as essential moral guides for
black church leadership. Also, the modalities of recognition, respectability,
and reverence will be revisited as central, heuristic loci for the reformulation
of civic life in black church practices, especially as they pertain to leadership
and agency.

CIVIC LIFE AND PRACTICES IN BLACK CHURCH LEADERSHIP

Stephen Carter compares civic life to a train ride with many passengers with
competing needs and interests. He argues therefore that

> Civility . . . is the sum of the many sacrifices we are called to make for the
> sake of living together. When we pretend that we travel alone, we can also
> pretend that these sacrifices are unnecessary. Yielding to this very human
> instinct for self-seeking . . . is often immoral, and certainly should not be
> done without forethought. We should make sacrifices for others not simply
> because doing so makes social life easier (although it does), but as a signal
> of respect for our fellow citizens, marking them as full equals, both before
> the law and before God.[39]

While I am in agreement with Carter's suggestion that civility requires a
certain kind of sacrifice for the common good, far more is at stake in the
question of civility in black church life and practices. Carter's understanding of civility tends to be sympathetic to the ways in which black church
leadership has often succumbed to the suffering-servant ideology that leads
to quietism and accommodationism.[40] The metaphor of a train ride, as it relates to the historical experience of African-Americans, is even more problematic. In black life generally, civility as a social and political option is
severely limited. In fact, some scholars even question its utility as a political
good.[41] Nonetheless, in black churches, because of the ideological and cultural precedents mentioned earlier, civility has come to represent precisely
that—a social and political good elevated to the level of *civic virtue*. In this
respect, it has to do with "the rules of association of free members (of society)

and so the basis of social dignity."[42] Evelyn Brooks-Higginbotham's examination of the "politics of respectability" signals part of what is at stake in the
usages of civility as a social and political strategy for citizenship rights among
women of the Negro Club Movement. Higginbotham writes, "The politics
of respectability assumed a fluid and shifting position along a continuum
of African-American resistance. Through the discourse of respectability, the
Baptist women emphasized manners and morals while simultaneously as-
serting traditional forms of protest, such as petitions, boycotts, and verbal
appeals to justice."[43]

Similarly, early architects of the modern civil rights movement utilized
civility as a means of cultivating habits and practices that conspired toward
engagement in democratic society. Most notable among these leaders in the
mid-twentieth century were black religious elites and pastors such Reverdy
Ransom, Mordecai Wyatt Johnson, Howard Thurman, Benjamin Mays, and
William Stuart Nelson.[44] Mordecai Wyatt Johnson, in a memorable speech
titled "The Faith of the American Negro," declared,

> Since their Emancipation from slavery the masses of American Negroes
> have lived by the strength of simple but deeply moving faith. They have
> believed in the love of and providence of a just and holy God; they have
> believed in the principles of democracy and in the righteous purpose of
> the Federal Government, and they have believed in the disposition of the
> American people as a whole and in the long run to be fair in all their
> dealings.[45]

It is not surprising the most outstanding exemplar of this legacy of civility
is represented in the person of the Reverend Martin Luther King Jr. and his
leadership in the modern civil rights movement. Perhaps better than any
other church leader of the twentieth century, King was able to forge civility
into a subversive weapon in the struggle for equal rights.[46] Stephen Carter indicates that the modern civil rights movement is a case in point of the efficacy
of civility in public life.[47]

The value of education among these ministerial elites was, without question, of the highest importance. At stake in the education of black religious
elites was the quest for recognition and respectability. The pioneer black sociologist E. Franklin Frazier wrote in his classic study of the black bourgeoisie
that among the Negro middle class there was a quest for social status and

prestige that developed from an "inferiority complex." The fixation with so-cial recognition was manifested in the aspirations of the middle-class Negro in puritanical family and sexual mores, which set them apart from the black masses. "But the chief compensation for their inferior status in American society," writes Franklin, "was found in education."

> While their racial heritage and conventional standards of morality only gave them a privileged position in the Negro community, education gave them access to a world of ideas that provided an intellectual escape from their physical and social segregation in American life. Therefore, they placed an exaggerated importance upon academic degrees, especially if they were secured from white colleges in the North. If one secured the degree of doctor of philosophy in a northern university, he was regarded as a sort of genius. Consequently, for the relatively small group of edu-cated Negroes, education was an indication of their "superior culture" and a mark of "refinement."[48]

Tied to the drive for educational accomplishments were also certain morals and manners not unlike those of their ideological predecessors. Among these morals and manners were the deeper and more problematic issues of patriarchal power, race management, and honor and shame. One cannot read the histories, biographies, and proceedings of black church leaders and denominational meetings without acknowledging the fierce strife, political maneuvers, and, to use James M. Washington's language in describing black Baptists, "frustrated fellowship."[49]

CIVILITY AND CIVIC CAPACITY IN BLACK CHURCHES

R. Drew Smith has suggested that the issue of *civic capacity* among African American churches merits critical analysis and review because of churches' long and well-documented history of "engagement of the public space in the pursuit of a public good that extends beyond the religious and social con-cerns of [their] immediate ecclesiastical constituencies."[50] Smith's concern is with the intersection between church and society and the ways in which African American churches have impacted specific public policy — or, in the larger orb, the public good. An important yet grossly neglected dimension of this phenomenon is the interstices of civic associations within black com-munities and the ways in which they have impacted public policy. Implicit in this suggestion is the argument that civic associations provide the social capital and the moral and spiritual infrastructure for political and social movements that conspire toward political participation and public activism. This has been especially true in black civil society. Cornel West claims that

> The two most effective forms of organizing and mobilizing among black people were the black women's club movement led by Ida B. Wells and the migration movement led by Benjamin "Pap" Singleton, A. A. Bradley, and Richard H. Cain. Both movements were based in black civil society — that is, black civic associations like churches, lodges, fraternal orders, and sororities. Their fundamental goals were neither civil rights nor social equality, but rather *respect and dignity*, land and self-determination.[51]

Without strong and active civic associations like the black church, the moral fiber and industry essential for political engagement among African Americans are scarce if not absent altogether. Fredrick C. Harris has demonstrated the ways in which the civic capacity of African Americans in voting behavior has been influenced by church membership and attendance. Harris also suggests that internal religiosity is causally linked to self-esteem and personal efficacy. Personal efficacy, he believes, is causally related to political efficacy and consequently to political activism among black churches.[52] Harris favors a focus on religious institutions rather than clerical leadership as a way of conducting a valid scientific investigation of these claims. I would suggest that the issues at stake warrant a closer look at black church leadership as well, especially in respect to the ways in which leadership in these religious institutions impacts internal religiosity, self-esteem, and personal efficacy. The task of leadership in respect to these dimensions is both ethical and theological.

CIVILITY AND ETHICAL LEADERSHIP IN BLACK CHURCHES

The cultivation and practice of civility in black churches cannot be understood outside the larger narratives of moral traditions and the ways in which leaders are formed in these communities. The suggestion here is that leaders are formed in specific communities of discourse and practice and that *character* as "the unity of a narrative quest" is a fundamental ingredient of the civic infrastructure that Smith and Harris address.[53] One of the critical yet unexamined dimensions of African American churches' civic engagement in matters that impact the public good is the role of ethical leadership.[54] Ethical leadership includes the complex and often conflicting notions of the role of religion, ethics, and leadership in influencing public life, as well as how these notions impact the ways in which civic engagement is understood and practiced. At stake for African American churches in the examination of civility is the dynamic tension created by the need for adequate political, economic, and social structures and the increasing void in the value infrastructures that make civic life and political engagement possible. Consequently, we must inquire regarding the critical resources and methods available to enhance the civic capacity of African American churches through religious experience and give particular emphasis to the place of religion, ethics, and leadership. It is in this context that the troublesome and controversial notion of doubleness must be revisited both as a problem for civility and black life and as a critical theological resource for creative engagement and possibility for black church civic practices.

A REEVALUATION OF RECOGNITION, RESPECTABILITY, AND REVERENCE AS THEOLOGICAL CONSTRUCTS

I would like to propose a closer look at civility in black church life from a theological perspective that takes seriously recognition, respectability, and loyalty as inherited discursive features in the quest for participation in American democratic life and practice. Loyalty, however, with respect to this quest for civility in black church life, has been more closely related to reverence or to a sense of ultimacy and hope. It should be kept in mind that the quest for civility for African Americans has been a quest for community, a sense of belonging and acceptance. Ideally, civility as a goal has promised access to this community through recognition, respectability, and loyalty. Theoretically, each focus represents a dimension of human experience: self/personal (recognition); society/public (respectability); and spirit/piety (reverence).

Recognition. *Recognition* in black life has a long and painful history and does not require extensive commentary here. For Orlando Patterson, the drive for recognition from the master was the basis for the social dignity and honor sought by enslaved Africans—and consequently was the means by which their masters manipulated them. Civility, as a response to the insatiable need for social dignity and respectability, became the chief aim of black church leadership as it did for their secular counterparts.[55] I simply refer the reader to chronicles of black literature that attest to the inordinate need in black life for recognition from the Other—the Other being the normative gaze that judges, condemns, and sentences black agency to despair, destruction, and death. Whether Du Bois' eloquent meditation cited earlier or Ralph Ellison's *Invisible Man* or Louis Armstrong's theodicial lament, "Lord, what did I do to make me so black and blue?" the quest for civility is in its first moment a quest for social recognition and agency. Concerning civility as a religious question, Howard Thurman captures best what is at stake in black church life and practices. In a meditation he writes, "It is a strange freedom to be adrift in the world of men without sense of anchor anywhere. . . . It is a strange freedom to go nameless up and down the streets of other minds where no salutation greets and no sign is given to mark the place one calls one's own."[56] Martin Luther King's famous sermon on recognition, titled "The Drum Major Instinct," is another example of the central place that recognition plays in the life of black people, especially in African American churches.[57]

The quest for recognition, in black religious life and practices, finds its apotheosis in the search to be understood and to be named by God. Many of the spirituals attest to this search. "I've got a new name o'er in Zion," "I told Jesus it would be alright if he changed my name," or "I once was lost, but now am found" speak to the namelessness, lostness, and invisibility in American civic and political life. To be seen, heard, and intimately understood as an individual in a community with others is one of the marvelous ministries performed by black churches. At the same time, the black church has participated in the often vicious and violent practices of nonspecificity and erasure of female agency and voice. A theological perspective that takes seriously the place of recognition would inquire about the specific roles of female leadership and agency within its own ranks and the ways in which churches must not sanction in their own inner lives the related practices they decry in public life.

Respectability. Closely related to recognition is *respectability*. In the construal of civility I am proposing, respectability has more to do with the rules of association of free people (citizens) and with social dignity. In this view, respectability includes (1) a certain self-referential index that recognizes oneself as inhering and therefore deserving certain acknowledgments of one's human dignity in public space; and (2) an obligation or duty to the Other to demonstrate in public space one's obligation to the Other as inhering and therefore deserving certain acknowledgments of human dignity. Undergirding this twofold definition of respectability is the need for empathy and balance in relation. In this view, Sarah Lawrence-Lightfoot's excellent and creative exploration of respect as a nonhierarchal expression of human relationship is invaluable for the theological task of the black church.[58]

The Negro Women's Club Movement's politics of respectability should be viewed in this perspective as a civic virtue raised to political engagement. Similarly, along with recognition, respectability was a key goal sought by the modern civil rights movement. Fredrick C. Harris refers to this distinctive phenomenon as the *dualistic orientation of black oppositional civic culture.* Harris captures in this statement the paradoxical strivings of black church life and practices that combine the quest for social dignity with political activism. Throughout the modern civil rights movement this dualistic orientation of black oppositional civic culture provided black church leadership with the critical skills and competencies to wage an unorthodox campaign against social inferiority and segregated statutes. James H. Evans has argued that this quest for respectability is part and parcel of black church life and practices and serves as the theological rationale for the larger question of honor and grace.[59]

In addition, a theological treatment of respectability would also inquire concerning the ways in which race management of the masses violates the fundamental theological norm of respectability within black life and culture. Leadership would stress nonhierarchal associations that breed and nurture equal dignity and freedom of individuals in covenant relationships that perceive power as opportunity for empathy and balance.

Loyalty (and Reverence). One of the supreme tests of civility among black churches has been, and continues to be, the question of *loyalty.* In his book *The Social Teachings of the Black Churches,* in a chapter titled "Autonomy in Dilemma," Peter Paris discusses the long-standing struggle within African American communities between loyalty to faith and loyalty to the nation.[60] The dilemma, Paris informs us, is how do we reconcile these contending demands for loyalty: the inclusive moral demand of faith versus the more particularized, and often self-annihilative, demand of the nation. These loyalties, he suggests, "represent, respectively, theories of politics and ecclesiology that imply moral conflicts in theory and practice."[61] Historically, African American church leaders have tended not to reconcile these conflicting demands but rather acquiesce to the demands of the national loyalty.[62] Our whole-hearted participation in all American wars is an illustration of this position. Such a posture has not only stymied our "power" within the political scenario of the United States but has prevented black churches from authentically participating in the world community. Politically, this conflict of loyalties has played out in an inept embrace of public policy that adversely impacts black life and culture and renders church leadership vulnerable to charges of accommodationism and invisibility.

Theologically, the quest of loyalty to faith versus loyalty to nation is highly problematic. The dearth of prophetic proclamation within the ranks of black church leadership rests on conflicting ideologies that are at once political, cultural, theological, and existential. The elucidation of the web of inter-action among these complex interrelated variables is not the task of this discussion. Suffice it to say that the prevalent theological presuppositions sur-rounding dilemma, exodus, and the problem of suffering in black life are not unrelated but are essential nodal points for further investigation into the resolution of the problem of loyalty addressed above. Such an investigation would aim toward a resolution of the problematic by stressing a new para-digm for black church leadership that moves beyond fixation with dilemma as an authentic and redemptive category for thought and praxis. Similarly, the exodus motif, which has played such a central role in theologizing about black political and cultural existence within the United States, would need to be reexamined in light of a broader theological category that incorporates the exilic state of black life both nationally and globally. Finally, the existen-tial state of black people, nationally and globally, would need to be raised as the catastrophic and disproportional black suffering is juxtaposed to the image of a God of mercy and justice. Theologically, the question might be raised as John the Revelator's depiction of the "second death," the theological equivalent of Orlando Patterson's concept of "natal alienation."[63] The critical theological issue in this instance as it relates to loyalty and the larger question of civility is "How can black life be saved from eternal namelessness, invisi-bility, and profanation of civic inclusion and participation?" The theological response must be formulated beyond *repair* (as in reparations, justice) but must seek a profoundly spiritual and social remedy not unlike the answer given in the utopian vision of the Revelator, "a new heaven and a new earth" of which Pentecost is a divine foretaste. In this respect, loyalty to nation versus loyalty to faith gives way to reverence for the creation. Here, the ideal of a beloved community serves as normative vision for civil life and practice.

In many respects, Martin Luther King's last prophetic vision of the World House mirrors what he had in mind with the idea of the beloved community. At once, in a singular vision of possibility, King articulated the dream of the beloved community in which civility was inspired and undergirded within the context of global communion — a vision in which it was possible to see the movement of black life from dilemma to diaspora; exodus to exile; and the "frying pan" (second death) to the fire (Pentecost). Many believe he was speaking in many languages as the Spirit gave utterance — languages that speak in loving and just ways to the agonizing yet redemptive possibilities inherent in recognition, respectability, and reverence for an ideal of community more grand that even the nation can ever hope for — *a new heaven and a new earth.*

Notes

1 Sanford Levinson, *Constitutional Faith* (Princeton: Princeton University Press, 1988).

2 Fredrick C. Harris, *Something Within: Religion in African-American Activism* (New York: Oxford University Press, 1999), 40.

3 The definition of "the Black Christian tradition" offered by Peter Paris best captures the distilled formulation of the syncretistic perspective that informs this view. In *The Social Teachings of the Black Churches* (Philadelphia: Fortress, 1985), Paris claims that "the tradition that has always been normative for the black churches and the black community is not the so-called Western tradition per se, although this tradition is an important source for blacks. More accurately, the normative tradition for blacks is the tradition governed by the principle of nonracism which we call the black Christian tradition. The fundamental principle of the black Christian tradition is depicted most adequately in the biblical doctrine of the parenthood of God and the kinship of all peoples" (10). This critical principle of nonracism, according to Paris, is fundamental for "justifying and motivating all endeavors by blacks for survival and social transformation." Moreover, the black Christian tradition has functioned both in priestly and prophetic functions: "the former aiding and abetting the race in its capacity to endure racism, the latter utilizing all available means

to effect religious and moral reform in the society at large." A biblical anthropology, which affirms the equality of all persons under God, is the locus of authority and basis for the moral and political significance of black churches (10–12). This tradition boasts of a distinguished company of African American theological visionaries who sought to carve out of American democratic liberalism, as represented by the "founders" of this nation, a basis for a just society that is inclusive and responsible to the high moral ideals articulated in the Constitution, the Declaration of Independence, and the Emancipation Proclamation. The specific strand of black church tradition referred to in this essay represents a long stream of tradition in the African American community in which liberation and integration are inextricably linked. Theologically, Howard Thurman labeled this quest "the search for common ground"; and Martin Luther King called it "the search for the beloved community." Lawrence Jones contends that "ever since blacks have been in America, they have been in search of the 'beloved community,'" a community that is grounded in an unshakable confidence in a theology of history. Jones observes that African American churches sought to actualize on earth the vision of the "beloved community" embodied in the Declaration of Independence and the Bible (Lawrence N. Jones, "Black Christians in Antebellum America: In Quest of the Beloved Community," *Journal of Religious Thought* 12, no. 2 [1985] 12). See also Vincent Harding, *There Is a River: The Black Struggle for Freedom in America* (New York: Harcourt Brace Jovanovich, 1981), 42–43; James Melvin Washington, *Frustrated Fellowship: The Black Baptist Quest for Social Power* (Macon, Ga: Mercer Press, 1986).

The approaches to the problem of community in American society by the illustrious exemplars in this tradition clearly constitute an analysis of the broader problematic of religion, race, and culture. The black church tradition, at its best, is an argument about the meaning and destiny of American democratic dogma. Alasdair MacIntyre has suggested that "a living tradition . . . is an historically extended, socially embodied argument, and an argument precisely in part about the goods which constitute that tradition" (Alasdair MacIntyre, *After Virtue: A Study in Moral Theory* [Notre Dame: University of Notre Dame Press, 1981], 222). James M. Washington placed the black church protest struggle for equality within "the American dissenting tradition." This tradition, according to Washington, included "abolitionists and many other varieties of social reformers. Many Americans do not understand or have forgotten how indebted we are to the stubborn tradition of loyal opposition in American history. The opposition's determination to put righteousness, conscience, and morality before social and political expediency helped to shape some of our most fundamental values and institutions" (*A Testament of Hope: The Essential Writings of Martin Luther King Jr.* [San Francisco: Harper and Row, 1986], xi). See also Cornel West, "The Prophetic Tradition in Afro-America," in *Prophetic Fragments:*

Illuminations of the Crisis in American Religion and Culture (Grand Rapids: Eerd-mans, 1988), 38–49.

4 Stephen L. Carter, *Civility: Manners, Morals, and the Etiquette of Democracy* (New York: Basic Books, 1998).

5 Council on Civil Society, *A Call to Civil Society: Why Democracy Needs Moral Truths* (New York: Institute for American Values, 1998).

6 Edward Shils, *The Virtue of Civility: Selected Essays on Liberalism, Tradition, and Civil Society*, ed. Steven Grosby (Indianapolis: The Liberty Fund, 1997).

7 For an excellent summary of the Aristotelian philosophical inheritance of civility and its modern theoretical history, see Lawrence Cahoone, "Civic Meetings, Cultural Meanings," in Leroy S. Royner, ed., *Civility* (Notre Dame: University of Notre Dame Press, 2000), 40–48.

8 James Schmidt, "Is Civility a Virtue?" in Rouner, ed., *Civility*, 17–19.

9 Amitai Etizioni's definition of civility is helpful. "The term "civility" has been used in different ways, most commonly it has referred to the need to deliberate in a civil manner about the issues society faces, and to sustain intermediary bodies that stand between the individual and the state." *The New Golden Rule* (New York: Basic Books, 1996), 95–96.

10 Robert D. Putnam's *Bowling Alone: The Collapse and Revival of American Community* (New York: Simon and Schuster, 2000) is one example of the ongoing public debate on the significance of civil discourse and social networking that is part of a larger conversation about the need to recapture, reappropriate, and sustain the habits and practices essential for the survival of an American ethos of generalized reciprocity and mutual obligation. See especially Putnam's discussion of the significance of social capital as both a bonding and bridging social phenomenon and its relationship to civic infrastructures that build community. *Bonding* refers to the ways in which social capital tends to reinforce exclusive identities and homogeneous groups. *Bridging* refers to ways in which social capital tends to produce broader and more inclusive group behavior and to encourage reciprocity (22–24).

11 Robert Wuthnow, *Christianity and Civil Society: The Contemporary Debate* (Harrisburg, Pa: Trinity Press International, 1996).

12 Michael Walzer, "The Idea of Civil Society," *Dissent* (spring 1991). Quoted from Wuthnow, *Christianity and Civil Society.*

13 Robert D. Putnam, *Bowling Alone*, 19.

14 Gunnar Myrdal, *An American Dilemma: The Negro Problem and American Democracy* (New York: Harper and Brothers, 1944).

15 Harold Cruse, *The Crisis of the Negro Intellectual: The Failure of Black Leadership;* Kevin K. Gaines, *Uplifting the Race: Black Leadership, Politics, and Culture in the Twentieth Century* (Chapel Hill: University of North Carolina Press, 1996), 5.

Darlene Clark Hine, "Rape and the Inner Lives of Black Women in the Middle West: Preliminary Thoughts on the Culture of Dissemblance," in *Unequal Sisters: A Multicultural Reader in U.S. Women's History,* ed. Ellen DuBois and Vicki L. Ruiz (New York: Routledge, 1990), 292–97; and Joy James, *Transcending the Talented Tenth: Black Leaders and American Intellectuals* (New York: Routledge, 1997). See Carl P. Henry, *Culture and African-American Politics* (Bloomington: Indiana University Press, 1990), 10–11, especially Henry's critique of Cruse's dilemma-oriented polemic, which leaves unresolved the ideological premise that black elites must provide an adequate social theory based on living ingredients of African American history. The challenge for Cruse, as for other black elites, tends to be this unresolved problematic often couched in dilemmatic language.

16   Ralph Luker, *The Social Gospel in Black and White* (Chapel Hill: University of North Carolina Press, 1991); Sidney M. Wilhelm, *Who Needs the Negro?* (New York: Anchor Books, 1971); Benjamin Quarles, *The Negro in the Making of America* (New York: Collier Books, 1964).

17   Joy James, *Transcending the Talented Tenth;* Ralph Luker, *The Social Gospel in Black and White.*

18   Patricia A. Turner, *Ceramic Uncles and Celluloid Mammies: Black Images and Their Influence on Culture* (New York: Anchor Books, 1994), is an excellent resource for the significance of the black iconography and its impact on cultural and ideological sequences in black life and the larger society. Similarly, Spike Lee's film *Bamboozled* expresses some of the fundamental concerns of racial ideology and iconography and their impact on black life, culture, and the larger society.

19   Ronald Takaki describes the development of the dilemma in this manner: "The fusion of Protestant asceticism and republican theory provided the ideology for bourgeois acquisitiveness and modern capitalism in the United States. The seventeenth-century belief in the covenant of grace had made it possible for the Puritan to affirm God's omnipotence while he strived to demonstrate he had outward signs of salvation. This Protestant anxiety—the need to know how one had been predestined and to do good works and diligently follow one's calling—led ironically to the erosion of piety itself. Good works resulted often enough in worldly goods and a concern for the here rather than the hereafter. Eighteenth century republicanism accelerated this thrust toward commodity accumulation and the primacy of the marketplace, as it disintegrated the feudal order and freed men as individuals to prove their virtue in the pursuit of possessions" (Ronald Takaki, *Iron Cages: Race and Culture in Nineteenth-Century America* [New York: Oxford University Press, 1990], 11). While Takaki relies heavily on Max Weber's *Protestant Ethic and the Spirit of Capitalism,* it is helpful to compare his analysis with H. Mark Roelofs's concept of "The Protestant-Bourgeois Syndrome" where he argues that Martin Luther is preferred over John Calvin for the Protestant pole of this syndrome "because his type of

radical, evangelical pietism was much more influential in the development of American religious feeling than was Calvin's more doctrinal theology." For the political, bourgeois pole, Thomas Hobbes is representative of the modern mind. Jonathan Edwards and Benjamin Franklin are their American counterparts (Roelofs, *Ideology and Myth in American Politics: A Critique of a National Political Mind* [Boston: Little, Brown, and Company, 1976], 51). See also Vetterli and Bryner, *In Search of the Republic: Public Virtue and the Roots of American Government* (Totowa, N.J.: Rowman and Littlefield, 1987), 1–18; C. B. MacPherson, *The Political Theory of Possessive Individualism: Hobbes to Locke* (New York: Oxford University Press, 1962); and MacPherson, *The Life and Times of Liberal Democracy* (New York: Oxford University Press, 1977).

20 See Orlando Patterson, *Rituals of Blood: Consequences of Slavery in Two American Centuries* (New York: Basic Books, 1998), 169–232. See also Rene Girard, *The Scapegoat,* trans. Yvonne Freccero (Baltimore: The Johns Hopkins University Press, 1986); Theophus Smith, *Conjuring Culture: Biblical Formations of Black Culture* (New York: Oxford University Press, 1994).

21 Toni Morrison, *Beloved: A Novel* (New York: Knopf, 1987), 198–99.

22 Ronald Takaki uses the metaphor of "iron cages" to describe the historical entrapment of American culture by the ideology of race. Responding to Stanley Elkin's claim that enslaved Africans adopted a mode of behavior that he called the "Sambo type," i.e., "the slave was 'submissive,' 'docile,' 'happy,' 'conscious of his [her] own inferiority and proud of being owned and governed by a superior'," Takaki argues that "The image of the slave as Sambo helped to comfort the tortured consciences of many of the members of the ruling class. . . . But the slavemasters' need for a Sambo was more complex than the desire to defend the peculiar institution and to mitigate guilt: The image helped to assure them that the slave was contented and controlled. Surely a happy slave would not violently protest his bondage; surely he would not slit his master's throat at night. So slavemasters wanted to believe. Yet while they were comforted by the happy Sambo, they were also terrified by the specter of the rebellious 'savage' " (121).

23 James D. Anderson, *The Education of Blacks in the South, 1860–1935* (Chapel Hill: University of North Carolina Press, 1988), see especially chapter 3, "Education and the Race Problem in the New South: The Struggle for Ideological Hegemony," 79–109. See also Luker, *The Social Gospel in Black and White.*

24 W. E. B. DuBois, *The Souls of Black Folk* (New York: Bantam Books, 1989), 45–46.

25 Kevin Gaines, *Uplifting the Race,* 33.

26 "In pursuit of this goal, they collided with the South's landed upper-class whites and their allies, who depended for their wealth and power on large classes of illiterate, exploited agricultural laborers." James D. Anderson, *The Education of Blacks in the South, 1860–1935* (Chapel Hill: University of North Carolina Press, 1988), 80–81.

27 Ibid.

28   C. Eric Lincoln, *Race, Religion, and the Continuing American Dilemma* (New York: Hill and Wang, 1984; and Victor Anderson, *Beyond Ontological Blackness: An Essay on African-American Religious and Cultural Criticism* (New York: Continuum, 1995). See Cornel West's observations on *doubleness* in "Black Strivings" — specifically, its relationship to despair, destruction, death using Du Bois's metaphor (Henry L. Gates and Cornel West, *The Future of the Race* [New York: Knopf, 1996]); see also Robert Michael Franklin's discussion of "strenuous life" in *Liberating Voices: Human Fulfillment and Social Justice in African-American Thought* (Minneapolis: Fortress Press, 1990).

29   See Evelyn Brooks-Higginbotham's discussion of "The Politics of Respectability" as being the primary sociopolitical strategy for women of the Negro Club Movement. At stake for these black elites was the promotion of "manners and morals" as a campaign against pejorative images of black womanhood depicted as shameless, bestial, and sexually licentious. *Righteous Discontent* (Cambridge: Harvard University Press, 1993).

30   Gaines, *Uplifting the Race,* 35.

31   Ibid., 99.

32   According to James, "Given our two conceptions of political activity, we can see straightaway how, in the struggle against race, gender, and class oppression, this distinction emerges in the difference between the classical sociological model of the charismatic leader-intellectual and the leader-intellectual who is guided by a sense of vocation and public responsibility" (*Transcending the Talented Tenth,* xiv–xv).

33   Ibid., 40 ff; 54.

34   Ibid., 16–17.

35   Gaines, *Uplifting the Race,* 31.

36   Gayraud S. Wilmore, *Black Religion and Black Radicalism: An Examination of the Black Religious Experience in Religion* (New York: Anchor Press/Doubleday, 1973), 226; "Bush Meeting Focuses on Role of Religion," *New York Times,* 21 December 2000; Richard A. Oppel Jr. with Gustav Niebuhr, "Bush Meeting Focuses on Fole of Religion," *New York Times,* 21 December 2000, 37.

37   Edward L. Wheeler, *Uplifting the Race: The Black Minister in the New South: 1865–1902* (Lanham, Md: University Press of America, 1986).

38   See Gayraud S. Wilmore, *Black Religion and Black Radicalism,* and *Black Theology: A Documentary History,* ed. Gayraud S. Wilmore and James H. Cone (Maryknoll, N.Y.: Orbis Books, 1993).

39   Stephen L. Carter, *Civility,* 11.

40   For classical critiques of the suffering-servant ideology from black theologians, see James H. Cone, *God of the Oppressed* (New York: Seabury Press, 1975), 163–94; William R. Jones, *Is God a White Racist? A Preamble to Black Theology* (Boston: Beacon Press, [1973], 1998), 71–168.

41   James Schmidt, "Is Civility a Virtue?" 17–19.

42   Lawrence Cahoone, "Civic Meetings, Cultural Meanings," 46.

43   Higginbotham, *Righteous Discontent,* 187.

44   See Anthony Pinn, ed., *Making the Gospel Plain: The Writings of Bishop Reverdy C. Ransom* (Harrisburg, Pa.: Trinity Press International, 1999); Ralph Luker, *The Social Gospel in Black and White;* Mordecai Wyatt Johnson, "Faith of the American Negro," in *Cavalcade: Negro American Writing from 1760 to the Present* (Boston: Houghton Mifflin, 1971); Walter Earl Fluker and Catherine Tumber, eds., *A Strange Freedom: Howard Thurman on Religious Experience and Public Life* (Boston: Beacon Press, 1998).

45   Mordecai Wyatt Johnson, "Faith of the American Negro," 681.

46   See Jeffrey C. Goldfarb's excellent discussion in *Civility and Subversion: The Intellectual in Democratic Society* (Cambridge: Cambridge University Press, 1998). Although the example he cites is the disruptive public speech of Malcolm X, the civility practiced by King and the modern civil rights movement represents the epitome of civility as disruptive speech and action. In this sense, King is rightly depicted as a *bricoleur*. See Jeffrey Stout, *Ethics after Babel: The Languages of Morals and Their Discontents* (Boston: Beacon Press, 1988).

47   Stephen Carter, *Civility,* 28–32.

48   E. Franklin Frazier, "Inferiority Complex and Quest for Status," reprinted in Frazier, *On Race Relations: Selected Papers,* edited and with an introduction by G. Franklin Edwards (Chicago: University of Chicago Press, 1968), 254.

49   See James M. Washington, *Frustrated Fellowship: The Black Baptist Quest for Social Power* (Macon, Ga: Mercer University Press, 1986); see respective essays by Clarice J. Martin, Marcia C. Riggs, and Cheryl Townsend Gilkes in Walter Earl Fluker, ed., *The Stones That the Builders Rejected: The Development of Ethical Leadership from the Black Church Tradition* (Harrisburg, Pa: Trinity Press International, 1998); James H. Evans, *We Shall Be Changed: Social Problems and Theological Renewal* (Minneapolis: Fortress Press, 1997), 17–43.

50   R. Drew Smith, "The Public Influences of African-American Churches: Local, National, and Transnational Civic Engagement." Proposal to the Pew Charitable Trust, June 1998.

51   Cornel West, "Black Strivings in a Twilight Civilization," in Henry Louis Gates and Cornel West, *The Future of the Race,* 67–68. Emphasis added.

52   Fredrick C. Harris, *Something Within,* 81–85.

53   See Peter J. Paris's excellent essay "Moral Development for African-American Leadership," in *The Stones That the Builders Rejected,* 23–32; Alasdaire MacIntyre, *After Virtue.*

54   In a recent publication (*The Stones That the Builders Rejected*) I have outlined my thoughts on the need for the development of ethical leadership from the black

church tradition. There I suggested that the black church tradition serve as a locus of inquiry for the kinds of stringent intellectual and creative tasks involved in the development of ethical leadership for civic life. Because of its distinctive sociocultural location and long history of producing ethical leaders, despite inadequate material and social resources, the black church tradition is a prime candidate for offering direction for the development of ethical leaders for our national and global communities. *Ethical leadership* refers to the critical appropriation and embodiment of moral traditions that have historically shaped the character and shared meanings of a people (an *ethos*). Ethical leadership does not emerge from a historical vacuum but arises from the *lifeworlds* of particular traditions and speaks authoritatively and acts responsibly with the aim of serving the collective good. Ethical leaders are leaders whose characters have been shaped by the wisdom, habits, and practices of particular traditions, often more than one, yet they tend to be identified with a particular ethos and cultural narrative. Finally, ethical leadership asks the question of values in reference to ultimate concern.

55 Referencing Hegel's dialectic of recognition between the lord and bondsman, Patterson writes, "Confronted with the master's outrageous effort to deny him all dignity, the slave even more than the master came to know and desire passionately this very attribute. For dignity, like love, is one of the human qualities that are most intensely felt and understood when they are absent — or unrequited" (Orlando Patterson, *Slavery and Social Death: A Comparative Study* [Cambridge: Harvard University Press, 1982], 100).

56 Howard Thurman, "A Strange Freedom," in *A Strange Freedom*, ed. Walter Earl Fluker and Catherine Tumber, vii.

57 Martin Luther King Jr., "The Drum Major Instinct," in *A Knock at Midnight: Inspiration from Great Sermons of Reverend Martin Luther King Jr.*, ed. Clayborne Carson and Peter Holloran (New York: Time Warner Books, 1998).

58 Lawrence-Lightfoot notes that respect is often viewed as "a debt due people because of their attained or inherited position, age, gender, class, race, professional status, accomplishments, etc. Whether defined by rules of law, habits of culture, respect often implies required expressions of esteem, approbation, or submission. By contrast, I focus on the way respect creates symmetry, empathy, and connection in all kinds of relationships" (Sarah Lawrence-Lightfoot, *Respect: An Exploration* [Cambridge: Pereseus Books, 2000], 9–10).

59 James H. Evans, *We Shall Be Changed*.

60 While this formulation is problematic because it uses the metaphor of an autonomous self, which connotes a highly individualistic consciousness to address a sociohistorical phenomenon, I think it is still useful for our purposes.

61 Ibid., 29.

62 Hans A. Baer and Merrill Singer, *African-American Religion in the Twentieth Cen-*

tury: Varieties of Protest and Accommodation (Knoxville: University of Tennessee Press, 1992); Carter G. Woodson, *The History of the Negro Church* (Washington, D. C.: Associated Publishers, 1972); and E. Franklin Frazier, *The Negro Church in America* (New York: Schocken Books, 1969).

63 Orlando Patterson, *Rituals of Blood,* 7–8.

6

NO RESPECT OF PERSONS?

RELIGION, CHURCHES, AND GENDER ISSUES

IN THE AFRICAN AMERICAN COMMUNITY

Allison Calhoun-Brown

The apostle Peter may have truly "perceive[d] that God is no respecter of persons," but the translation of this fact into the Christian doctrine with regard to gender has been a slow, tedious, and often painful process.[1] Indeed, a number of studies have identified high levels of religiosity, orthodoxy, and evangelical and fundamentalist religious beliefs as important determinants of antifeminist issue positions.[2] This has made for a very tenuous relationship between gender equality and conservative Christianity. The tenuous nature of this relationship is exacerbated in the African American religious community. Not only do African Americans exhibit higher levels of religiosity and a greater acceptance of fundamentalist and evangelical doctrines,[3] the political socialization that occurs in many African American churches tends to emphasize racial unity at the expense of gender concerns.[4] This lack of concern toward gender issues has prompted criticism by black feminists through womanist theology.[5] Their critique is that:

> Shaped by the Black Power/civil rights movement out of which it emerged, Black theology focused only on one dimension of Black oppression — white racism. Its failure to utilize Black women's experience further prevented it from developing an adequate analysis of Black oppression. It did not address the multiple social burdens, that is, racism, sexism, classism and heterosexism, which beset Black men and women. Consequently, it presented an image of God and Christ that was impotent in the fight for Black freedom. A Black God, one concerned only with the battle against

racism, could not sustain and liberate the entire black community. This God could not affirm and empower Black women as they confronted sexism.[6]

Critical of both the sexism in black theology and the racism in feminist theology, womanist theology "holds that full human liberation cannot be achieved simply by the elimination of any one form of oppression."[7] Cone observes that even black churches have fallen short in the fight for full human liberation: "Because the Black Church has a long history of struggle against racism, it should be in the vanguard of the struggle against Black women's oppression. But unfortunately, the Black church is one of the most sexist institutions in the black community and Black male ministers often appeal to the Bible to justify the subordinate role defined for women."[8] From this perspective, there is not much basis for predicting a positive relationship between religion and liberal positions on gender issues in the African American community.

However, contrary to these concerns, empirical research reveals that religion does not have a markedly negative influence on feminist issues among blacks. In fact, Wilcox and Thomas found that some of the religious variables that are strongly associated with antifeminism among whites actually increase support for organized feminism among African Americans.[9] Wilcox found that religion promotes support for collective action among African Americans that, in turn, translates into support for collective action in matters of gender equity.[10] Rather than black consciousness detracting from gender consciousness, it may indeed serve to enhance it. Explaining how this might happen, Wilcox and Thomas suggest that because religious messages heard in African American churches stress racial and political equality, they may somehow communicate a need for gender equality as well.[11] This of course conflicts directly with the critique of black churches and black theology by the womanist perspective. Moreover, I found that there is considerable variation among black churches with regard to degree of political orientation. Surprisingly, political announcements were heard in only 35 percent of black churches, and only attendance at these churches contributed to increases in black consciousness and political efficacy.[12]

In light of the womanist critique and the variation that exists in black churches, this essay will examine whether the political messages conveyed in black churches enhance or detract from a concern for gender equity among African Americans. By examining this issue one can gain a better understanding of the role churches play in political socialization as well as leverage on the more general question of how race, religion, and gender interact.

Religion and Gender Issues in the Black Community

The vast majority of studies of the relationship between gender and religion have focused on conservative white Christians. Though a sizable minority may embrace feminist ideas,[13] most research reveals that white evangelical women who attend church frequently or hold orthodox beliefs tend to be less feminist in orientation.[14] However, the research on blacks concerning gender issues reveals a very complicated relationship. Religiosity has smaller effects on the gender attitudes of black religious women than on white religious women.[15] Still, religiosity and orthodoxy decreased support for abortion,[16] but church attendance increased support for the Equal Rights Amendment.[17] Wilcox and Thomas found that while religious involvement and orthodoxy were negative predictors of support for abortion, they were often positively associated with support for gender equality and feminist organizations.[18]

The limited research on blacks seems to indicate that different components of religiosity have varying effects on gender attitudes. The multidimensionality of religion as a concept should not be underappreciated. This is especially true in the case of African Americans. Levin, Taylor, and Chatters observe that "a unidimensional model of religious involvement has promoted a view of African-Americans as a homogenous group, routinely religiously oriented with little if any variation in the form, intensity or pattern of religious involvement."[19] In recognition of the breadth of the concept, distinctions are often drawn between organizational, nonorganizational, and subjective religiosity.[20] Organizational religiosity reveals public institutional forms of religious involvement such as church membership, denomination, attendance, and participation in church activities. Nonorganizational religiosity refers to private informal types of religious involvement. Common measures include frequency of prayer and Bible reading. Subjective religiosity captures the attitudinal component of nonorganizational religion. It is often operationalized as the importance of religion to individuals or the level of guidance that it provides in their lives.

These are all important components of religiosity, but these measures alone may fail to capture an integral part of religious variation among African Americans. None of these measures assesses the political nature of the church a respondent attends. In light of the fact that "in the black community the church plays *the dominant role* in the socialization process," it is important to analyze whether these types of messages are being communicated.[21] As Wilcox and Thomas observe, "the political meaning of religious doctrine is partially contingent on the interpretive effort of religious elites."[22] These interpretive efforts are made at the congregational level by local pastors and ministers. This is why denomination alone is an insufficient operationalization of this element of organizational religiosity. While denominations certainly have different historical origins and sociopolitical bases and stances, ministers enjoy considerable autonomy. This is especially true in the black community, where the majority of blacks are Baptists. As a denomination the Baptist church has almost no hierarchical authority structure.[23] The independence of each church and pastor cannot be challenged by any denominational authority. Moreover, it is important to examine the political nature of the congregation a respondent attends because research reveals that the political nature of churches is relevant to increasing racial identification, consciousness, and political participation.[24] Therefore, given the socialization role of black churches, if one is concerned that racial identification and consciousness detract from gender identification and gender issue concerns, one must give special attention to the political nature of churches.

Data and Method

DATA

To examine the relationship between religion and gender issues in the African American community, this study uses data from the National Black Politics Study (NBPS), conducted by the Center for the Study of Race, Politics, and Culture at the University of Chicago in 1993. The NBPS is a national cross-sectional survey that yields a sample of 1205 adult African American respondents.[25]

DEPENDENT VARIABLES: GENDER ISSUES

One of the principal benefits of using the NBPS is the nature of the gender issue questions it contains. What is particularly interesting in studying
the position of African Americans on gender issues is not just their positions on those issues solely but their positions on them relative to racial ones.
To the extent that sexism existed in the black community, feminist ideals
were often seen as undermining the cohesion blacks needed to secure racial
equality. Giddings explains that this was a concern for many black women.
"The thinking was that before they could gain rights as black women, the
rights of black men needed to be assured." She continues, "Unity was important as a bulwark against not just the society at large, but also the implicit
and explicit racism of white feminists."[26] Thus the feminist agenda was often
thought to conflict with the racial agenda. There are several such questions
in the NBPS that capture this dynamic. All respondents were asked whether
racism, poverty, and sexual discrimination must be addressed together by the
black community or whether blacks should emphasize the struggle around
race. They were asked whether black feminist groups help the black community by working to advance the position of black women or whether black
feminist groups divide the black community. Respondents gave their opinion
on whether black women should share equally in the political leadership of
the black community or whether black women should not undermine black
male political leadership. Finally, they responded to whether they thought
the problems of black men deserved special attention or whether the problems of black men and women deserved equal attention.[27]

In addition to these measures, the data set contains two questions traditionally used to evaluate gender attitudes. For many feminists the right to
an abortion symbolizes the complete sovereignty of a woman over her body.
From this perspective, the right to an abortion is the ultimate measure of respect for individual rights. In the NBPS respondents were asked their view
on abortion. Respondents were also asked whether they thought that black
churches should allow more women to become members of the clergy. Even
though black churches are characterized by predominantly female membership, Lincoln and Mamiya report that "fewer than 5 percent of clergy in historic black denominations are female."[28] Sexism denies black women equal
opportunity in the churches' major leadership roles.

Finally, gender identification and solidarity are integral parts of gender consciousness.[29] Two measures of gender identification are included in this study. The first is a measure of common fate. Female respondents were asked whether they felt that what happens to white women had something to do with what happens in their lives. The second is a measure of feminist identification. Respondents were asked whether or not they considered themselves feminists. All dependent variables are coded toward the feminist position. If a measure is dichotomous it is coded 1 for the feminist position and 0 otherwise.

INDEPENDENT VARIABLES: RELIGIOSITY

Reese and Brown note that hearing political messages in churches is especially important in shaping the political attitudes of African Americans.[30] However, I stress that "it is a mistake to assume that the majority of African-American churches are political environments."[31] It is important to capture the variation in the political nature of African American churches. There are six variables in the NBPS that measure the political activity of churches. Respondents were asked whether they heard any discussions about politics at their place of worship, whether they talked to people about political matters at church, whether a member of the clergy encouraged them to become more involved in politics, whether a political leader spoke at a regular religious service, whether a member of the clergy ever suggested voting for or against certain candidates, and whether a clergy member had suggested they take some political action such as writing a letter, attending a political meeting, going to a protest march or demonstration, or getting in contact with an elected official. In the multivariate analysis an additive index of these variables was created to aggregate the total political effect of the religious environment. This index ranging from 0 to 6 was highly reliable with an alpha coefficient of .76. Table 1 confirms that considerable variation exists among churches in the black community with regard to political orientation. The values are widely dispersed, as evidenced by the fact that the modal category contains only 20.2 percent of respondents.

In appreciation of the multidimensionality of religion the present study includes additional measures of organizational and subjective religiosity. Organizational religiosity reveals the public institutional forms of religious involvement. There are two additional measures of organizational religiosity in the NBPS. The first is a measure of the level of a respondent's church

TABLE 1 Variation in the Political Nature of Churches (Percentages)

	%	Frequency
0 (Not political)	16.4	147
1	10.3	93
2	12.8	115
3	13.5	121
4	17.0	153
5	20.2	182
6 (Very political)	9.8	88
TOTAL	100.0	N = 899

involvement. This measure was constructed from responses to a question about frequency of church attendance and about church participation on committees, projects, and meetings apart from worship services. The second measure of external religiosity operationalizes different denominational traditions. In view of the fact that denominations have different doctrinal teachings on gender as well as different traditions with regard to the treatment of women and their role in church leadership, it is important to take denominational context into account in examining the effect of religion on gender issues.[32]

Chronicling the history of black denominations[33] and the ordination of women, Lincoln and Mamiya explain that after considerable struggle, all black Methodist congregations allowed for the full ordination of women by 1955. Among black Baptist denominations, there is no specific policy against the ordination of women, but the general climate has not been supportive of women preaching or pastoring churches. The Church of God in Christ, the largest black Pentecostal denomination, has a firm policy against the full ordination of women as clergy.[34] Wilcox found that Pentecostal and Holiness churches impede the formation of gender consciousness.[35] Black Muslims also have such a policy against female clergy. Barbara Sizemore explains that Nation of Islam founder Elijah Muhammad openly stated that women were property. He is quoted as saying "the woman is man's field to produce his nation."[36] Although more than 80 percent of all black Christians attend church in predominantly black denominations, the vast majority of female clergy members are found in nontraditional or independent churches.[37] Catholics and other respondents who attend white denominations must also be looked at separately because these denominations have an entirely different history on both gender and racial concerns. Dummy variables were created for each of the preceding groups with white denominations being the comparison category.[38]

Subjective religiosity captures the attitudinal component of religion. Respondents were asked the amount of guidance they felt religion provided in their daily lives. Because conservative Christianity is associated with antifeminism, the expectation is that respondents who said that they received a lot of guidance from religion will be less supportive of feminist issue positions. Unfortunately, the NBPS contains no measure of nonorganizational religiosity, so the impact of frequency of prayer or Bible reading cannot be assessed using this data.

CONTROL VARIABLES

In analyzing the relationship between religiosity and gender issue positions it is important to consider the potentially confounding effects of several sociodemographic variables. Thus, this study controls for age, education, gender, income, and rural location. The expectation is that older respondents, the less educated, males, individuals with less income, and those who live in rural locations will be less feminist in orientation.[39]

Findings

Table 2 records the bivariate relationships between the political activities that take place in churches and gender issue positions. Although the zero-order correlations are relatively modest, the statistical significance of these relationships indicates that churches may indeed be potent environments for the communication of gender values. What is particularly interesting is that in almost all the statistically significant cases, political activity is associated with a respondent having a liberal gender issue position. This is somewhat unexpected given a traditional understanding of the effect of religion and churches on gender attitudes.

Table 3 begins to explore the relationship between religion and gender issue attitudes in more detail, using multivariate analysis. Multivariate analy-

TABLE 2 Zero Order Correlations, Political Church Variables, and Gender Issue Positions

	Political discussion at place of worship	Respondent talked politics at place of worship	Clergy talked about political involvement
Address all discrimination	.10**	.09*	.09*
Feminist help community	.03	.03	.10**
Black women leadership	.06	.05	−.01
Equality of problems between men and women	−.03	−.12***	−.05
Right to an abortion	.01	.04	.05
More female clergy	.06	.04	.04
Common fate with white women	.19***	.12**	.16***
Feminist identification	−.04	−.06	−.03

	Political leader spoke at service	Clergy suggested voting for or against candidate	Clergy encouraged marching, etc.
Address all discrimination	.09*	.01	.09*
Feminist help community	.08**	−.01	.06
Black women leadership	.01	.01	.07*
Equality of problems between men and women	−.04	−.00	−.05
Right to an abortion	.03	−.02	.07*
More female clergy	.06	.01	.07*
Common fate with white women	.07	.01	.10*
Feminist identification	−.01	−.05	−.01

*p<.05
**p<.005
***p<.0005

sis is important because only by controlling for several factors simultaneously can the true association between variables be clearly seen. Table 3 examines the issues that involve racial-gender tension. The womanist perspective might predict a strong negative relationship between the religious variables and these issues. However, this is not the case. Controlling for sociodemographic factors, religious guidance and religious participation have no statistically significant impact. Moreover, the effect of the aggregated indicator of political church activity on gender-racial issues is positive. The more political the church that respondents attend, the more likely they are to believe in the need to address racism, poverty, and sexual discrimination simultaneously instead of emphasizing the struggle around race. Attending political churches also enhances a belief that black feminist groups help the black community by working to advance the position of black women, as opposed to black feminist groups just dividing the black community. Still, political churches have no effect on the opinion that the problems of black men and women deserve equal attention or the perspective that black women should share equally in the political leadership of the African American community.

It is notable that political churches are only a positive factor on the issues that do not directly juxtapose men and women. The churches seem to be important in providing an abstract linkage for all oppression as well as in seeing a positive role for black feminists. However, when the issue comes down to black female leadership versus undermining black male leadership or "special attention to endangered black males" versus "equal attention for black men and women," political churches are noninfluential.

The only support for the womanist critique of religion on gender-racial issues in these data comes from the fact that Baptist identification is a negative predictor of a belief that all forms of discrimination should be addressed simultaneously. One might be tempted to conclude that this association is significant because of the important role that Baptist churches played in addressing racial discrimination during the civil rights movement. From the womanist perspective, their intense interest in challenging racial discrimination hinders them from challenging gender discrimination. However, only the most political Baptist churches involved themselves in the movement, and political activity is positively associated with addressing all discrimination simultaneously.[40] The negative sign of this variable (and all the denominational variables) indicates that this relationship more likely reflects the tra-

TABLE 3 Determinants of Racial-Gender Issue Positions: Logistic Regression Coefficients

	Address all discrimination		Feminist help	
	B	SE	B	SE
Political church	.11*	.04	.10*	.04
Religious participation	−.03	.09	−.14	.09
Religious guidance	−.08	.12	.11	.12
Baptist	−.75*	.37	.46	.31
Methodist	−.72	.46	.18	.39
Moslem	−.29	.68	.71	.61
Catholic	−.63	.49	1.00	.56
Pentecostal	−.41	.49	.21	.42
Constant (white denominations)	.06	.68	−.66	.64
Age	−.00	.01	−.00	.01
Education	.11**	.03	.06*	.03
Gender (female)	.32	.18	.34	.17
Location (rural)	−.13	.19	−.06	.18
−2 Log likelihood	837.4		884.1	
Cases predicted correctly	72.4%		67.7%	
	N = 750		N = 721	

	Black women leadership		Equality of problems	
	B	SE	B	SE
Political church	.06	.05	−.06	.04
Religious participation	−.16	.11	−.05	.08
Religious guidance	.03	.14	.09	.11
Baptist	.15	.34	.29	.28
Methodist	.22	.44	.28	.36
Moslem	.10	.72	.14	.52
Catholic	.40	.53	.24	.40
Pentecostal	.15	.48	−.58	.38
Constant (white denominations)	1.93*	.73	.43	.59

TABLE 3 *Continued*

	Black women leadership		Equality of problems	
	B	SE	B	SE
Age	−.02**	.01	.01**	.00
Education	.07*	.03	−.05	.03
Gender (female)	−.26	.21	−.06	.17
Location (rural)	−.36	.20	.19	.18
−2 Log likelihood	724.4		1036.4	
Cases predicted correctly	81.6%		61.0%	
	N = 794		N = 786	

*p<.05
**p<.005
***p<.0005

ditional nature and structure of Christian churches, which may make them somewhat reluctant to embrace gender issue concerns.

Education is the only consistently feminizing factor in these racial-gender issues. In three of the four cases, those with higher levels of education were more likely to be supportive of liberal gender positions. It is also interesting that age has an inconsistent effect on the two measures that juxtapose men and women. Older people tend to believe in the equality of the problems of black men and women. However, there is a negative relationship between age and a belief that black women should share equally in the political leadership of the black community.

The relationship between religion and the dependent variables that are traditional measures of gender attitudes highlights the multidimensionality of religion as a concept in the African American community. Table 4 underscores that differing components of religiosity have different effects. Political church is a strong positive predictor of the prochoice position. The more politically active the church the respondent attends, the more likely she or he is to support the abortion right. However, those who are very involved in church and those who get a lot of guidance from religion are more likely to be opposed to this option.

TABLE 4 Determinants of Attitudes Toward Abortion and Female Clergy

	Abortion regression coefficients		More female clergy logistic regression coefficients	
	B	SE	B	SE
Political church	.04*	.02	.11*	.05
Religious participation	−.14***	.04	−.36**	.11
Religious guidance	−.17**	.05	−.17	.15
Baptist	.26	.14	−.17	.34
Methodist	.33	.18	.55	.48
Moslem	.04	.26	−.47	.62
Catholic	.24	.19	−.27	.48
Pentecostal	−.04	.19	.22	.48
Constant (white denominations)	3.87***	.29	3.31***	.74
Age	−.01***	.00	−.02**	.01
Education	.03*	.01	.05	.03
Gender (female)	.21*	.07	−.15	.20
Location (rural)	−.30***	.08	−.26	.19

			−2 Log likelihood	765.5
	$R^2 = .12$		Cases predicted correctly	79.2%
	N = 797		N = 790	

*p<.05
**p<.005
***p<.0005

A similar relationship exists between the religious variables and attitude toward black churches allowing more women to become members of the clergy. The debate about the place of women in the leadership of churches symbolizes the fight for equality in the religious context. The more political the church a respondent attends, the more likely it is that he or she promotes gender diversity among the clergy. However, those who are heavily involved in church were less likely to approve of females as preachers. This is ironic because women are more likely to be very involved in churches.

After controlling for sociodemographic variables, no denominational distinction is meaningful for predicting positions on these traditional gender issues. The sociodemographic variables are particularly important determinants of abortion attitudes. They are not as useful in the female clergy model. Only age was statistically significant. All relationships are in the expected direction.

Finally, Table 5 reports the determinants of gender identification and solidarity. First, female respondents were asked whether or not what happens generally to white women had something to do with what happens in their lives. Similar common fate questions were asked about women in general, black women, and nonwhite women as well. The results for these measures are similar to the ones presented here (not shown). The choice was made to report the model of common fate with white women because it is the most extreme case. Given the challenge of racism, and different socioeconomic and historical circumstances, it would be most difficult for political churches to promote a common fate with white women. If such a fate is predicted by attending political churches, it suggests that these contexts may indeed enhance gender identification. Table 5 shows that there is a positive relationship between political churches and a belief in a common fate with white women.[41] After controlling for sociodemographic factors, only education and attending such churches were statistically significant predictors of this opinion.

However, attending politically active churches did nothing to enhance feminist identification. The fact that attending a political church has no impact on identification with the label "feminist" is interesting especially when one considers that attending such churches actually promotes most liberal gender issue positions. This suggests that in churches the label "feminist" may have a more negative connotation than many of the issues closely associated with it.

Discussion and Conclusion

Normally, research involving the study of religion and gender involves white conservative Christians; however, by analyzing this relationship among blacks, a number of things are learned about the role of churches in political socialization as well as the nature of racial and gender issue interaction in the African American community. First, African American churches are

TABLE 5 Determinants of Gender Identification and Solidarity: Logistic Regression Coefficients, Women Only

	Common fate with white women		Feminist identification	
	B	SE	B	SE
Political church	.13**	.05	−.03	.05
Religious participation	.12	.10	.16	.11
Religious guidance	−.01	.14	.05	.15
Baptist	−.40	.33	.27	.34
Methodist	−.33	.43	.76	.43
Moslem	.05	.91	.29	.91
Catholic	−.25	.49	.44**	.50
Pentecostal	−.27	.44	−.46	.53
Constant (white denominations)	−1.35	.74	−1.54*	.78
Age	−.01	.01	.01	.01
Education	.10**	.03	−.04	.03
Location (rural)	.27	.20	−.15	.21
−2 Log likelihood	693.6		636.5	
Cases predicted correctly	62.0%		67.0%	
	N = 533		N = 512	

*p<.05
**p<.005
***p<.0005

extremely important to political socialization. This point has been well demonstrated by others.[42] Still, this present research adds clarity to the point. Churches are important to political socialization. However, on gender issues, instead of having the conservatizing effect most often associated with them, black churches can promote gender equality as well. Moreover, in the African American community, the political nature of churches is the single greatest determinant of whether this occurs. Research on the impact of religion has usually focused on denomination or religious involvement, both of which can be influential. However, these data suggest that their impact on gender issues is smaller and often contrary to the effect of the political nature of the church. Appreciating the multidimensionality of religiosity among African Americans leads to a clearer understanding of the relationship between religion and gender issue positions among blacks.

Second, this research confirms Wilcox and Thomas's assertion that the political messages conveyed in black churches increase concern for gender equity among African Americans.[43] Even though the majority of black churches tend to be doctrinally conservative and led by men, if a person attends a church that is politically active, that person is more likely to hold liberal gender issue positions. This implies that in hearing the equality and empowerment messages of black churches people make not only racial but gender application as well. This is especially notable when one considers the structure and doctrine of churches as institutions often do not reinforce the acceptance of equal gender positions.

This is not to assert that the structure is inconsequential. Nor would I argue that African Americans have a tendency to separate doctrinal teaching from political positions. It is, in part, the male authority structure and conservative doctrines of black churches that have kept them from taking a leadership role on many contemporary "civil rights" issues such as gender equality and homosexual rights. It was not possible to test directly the effect of doctrine using these data.[44] Moreover, as it is reasonable to assume that the doctrinal teachings of many black churches are conservative on women's issues, it is also reasonable to assume that the doctrines and history of black churches reinforce the equality of all human beings. Perhaps the latter teachings are more salient. What this research reinforces is the complexity of the relationship between religion and politics.

Finally, womanist theology suggests that black churches have to some extent contributed to the subjugation of black women. Delores Williams contends that among the sins of black churches and black ministers is collusion with "the political forces oppressing black women."[45] However, these data provide no evidence that churches heavily involved in politics tend to work in any way to the detriment of feminist causes. In fact, Allen, Dawson, and Brown suggest that churches that have embraced liberation theology have the biggest impact politically.[46] Thus, one might expect that churches embracing liberation theology might be most supportive of liberal gender issue positions. This aspect could not be directly tested using these data. Still, the evidence is clear that highly political churches, most often associated with promoting racial politics, also promote feminist ideas.

This of course is not to say that sexism does not exist in black churches, even black political churches. Evidence to the contrary is overwhelming. Even this research shows that in cases where the agenda of black women is directly juxtaposed to the agenda of black men, political churches have no liberalizing effect. Moreover, it is important to note that there is a difference between holding liberal gender issue positions and having gender consciousness. Gender consciousness implies elements of system blame, power discontent, and collectivist orientation that could not be tested with these data.[47] Still, the point of this chapter is that messages of equality and empowerment are beneficial to gender issue concerns. They are beneficial even within the context of black churches frequently associated with promoting contrary gender issue ideals.

Notes

1 Acts 10:34, King James Version.
2 Clyde Wilcox, "Religious Orientations and Political Attitudes: Variations Within the New Christian Right," *American Politics Quarterly* 15 (1987): 274–96; C. Peek and S. Brown, "Sex Prejudice among White Protestants: Like or Unlike Ethnic Prejudice?" *Social Forces* 59 (1980): 169–85; Pamela J. Conover and Virginia Gray, *Feminism and the New Right* (New York: Praeger, 1983); D. Brady and K. Tedin, "Ladies in Pink, Religion, and Political Ideology in the Anti-ERA Movement," *Social Science Quarterly* 56 (1976): 564–75.
3 Clyde Wilcox, *God's Warriors: The Christian Right in the Twentieth Century* (Baltimore: The Johns Hopkins University Press, 1992).
4 Bettye Collier-Thomas, *Daughters of Thunder: Black Women Preachers and Their Sermons, 1850–1979* (San Francisco: Jossey-Bass Publishers, 1998); James Cones and Gayraud Wilmore, *Black Theology: A Documentary History,* 2d ed., volumes 1 and 2 (Maryknoll, N.Y.: Orbis Books, 1993); C. Eric Lincoln and Lawrence Mamiya, *The Black Church in the African-American Experience* (Durham: Duke University Press, 1990); Paula Giddings, *When and Where I Enter: The Impact of Black Women on Race and Sex in America* (New York: William Morrow, 1984).
5 Delores Williams, *Sisters in the Wilderness: The Challenge of Womanist God-Talk* (Maryknoll, N.Y.: Orbis Books, 1993); Jacquelyn Grant, *White Women's Christ and Black Woman's Jesus: Feminist Christology and Womanist Response* (Atlanta: Scholars Press, 1989); Katie G. Cannon, *Black Womanist Ethics* (Atlanta: Scholars Press, 1988).

6 Kelly Brown-Douglass, "Womanist Theology: What Is Its Relationship to Black Theology?" in *Black Theology: A Documentary History*, vol. 2, ed. James Cone and Gayraud Wilmore (Maryknoll, N.Y.: Orbis Books, 1993), 291.

7 Jacquelyn Grant, "Womanist Theology: Black Woman's Experience as a Source for Doing Theology," *Journal of the Interdenominational Theological Center* 13 (1986): 199.

8 Cone and Wilmore, *Black Theology*, 281.

9 Clyde Wilcox and Sue Thomas, "Religion and Feminist Attitudes among African American Women: A View for the Nation's Capitol," *Women and Politics* 12 (1992): 19–40.

10 Clyde Wilcox, "Black Women and Feminism," *Women and Politics* 10 (1990), 65–84; and Clyde Wilcox, "Race, Gender Role Attitudes, and Support for Feminism," *Western Politics Quarterly* 43 (1990): 113–23.

11 Wilcox and Thomas, "Religious and Feminist Attitudes among African American Women."

12 Allison Calhoun-Brown, "African-American Churches and Political Mobilization: The Psychological Impact of Organizational Resources," *Journal of Politics* 58 (1996): 935–53.

13 R. Booth Fowler, "The Feminist and Anti-Feminist Debate Within Evangelical Protestantism," *Women and Politics* 9 (1986): 27–50.

14 Clyde Wilcox "Feminism and Anti-Feminism among White Evangelical Women," *Western Politics Quarterly* 42 (1989): 147–60.

15 Clyde Wilcox, "Race, Gender Role Attitudes, and Support for Feminism," 113–23.

16 Clyde Wilcox, "Race Differences in Abortion Attitudes: Some Additional Evidence," *Public Opinion Quarterly* 54 (1990): 248–55.

17 Susan E. Marshall, "Equity Issues and Black White Differences in Women's ERA Support," *Social Science Quarterly* 71 (1990): 299–314.

18 Wilcox and Thomas, "Religion and Feminist Attitudes among African American Women."

19 Jeffrey Levin, Robert Taylor, and Linda Chatters, "A Multidimensional Measure of Religious Involvement for African-Americans," *Sociological Quarterly* 36 (1995): 167–68.

20 Gordon Allport, *The Individual and His Religion* (New York: Macmillan, 1950); David Leege and Lyman Kellstedt, *Rediscovering the Religious Factor in American Politics* (New York: M.E. Sharpe, 1993).

21 Hanes Walton, *Invisible Politics* (Albany: SUNY Press, 1985), 48.

22 Wilcox and Thomas, "Religion and Feminist Attitudes among African American Women," 34.

23 Lincoln and Mamiya, *The Black Church in the African-American Experience*.

24 Calhoun-Brown, "African-American Churches and Political Mobilization"; Laura

Reese and Ron Brown, "The Effect of Religious Messages on Racial Identity and System Blame Among African-Americans," *Journal of Politics* 57 (1995): 24–43.

25 The NBPS employed a multiple frame design comprising two subsamples of equal size. One sample used random digit dialing. The other sampled out of census tracts that were over 30 percent black. There were no appreciable differences between the subsamples. The response rate was 65 percent. To get an idea of the socio-demographic characteristics of the sample, it can be compared with the widely used 1984 National Black Election Study (NBES) conducted by the Institute of Social Research at the University of Michigan. The NBES was the first large-scale scientific survey of the political beliefs of African Americans exclusively. The principal investigators report that the two studies are very similar. However, respondents in the NBPS are slightly better educated and more urban than those interviewed for the NBES. See Final Report on the 1993–94 National Black Politics Study for further information.

26 Giddings, *When and Where I Enter,* 309, 310.

27 The exact wording of the gender-racial questions is as follows: "Please tell me what is most true for you . . . (a.) The problems of racism, poverty, and sexual discrimination are all linked together and must be addressed by the black community OR blacks should emphasize the struggle around race. (b.) Black feminist groups help the black community by working to advance the position of black women OR black feminist groups just divide the black community. (c.) Black women should share equally in the political leadership of the black community OR black women should not undermine black male political leadership. (d.) The problems of black men and women deserve equal attention OR black men are endangered and their problems deserve special attention." Unfortunately these variables were not correlated sufficiently to scale (alpha=.17). The low level of correlation indicates that while all of these questions measure some aspect of gender-racial tension, issues involving gender and race contain a complexity that is not adequately captured through simple aggregation.

28 Lincoln and Mamiya, *The Black Church in the African-American Experience,* 289.

29 Arthur Miller, Patricia Gurin, Gerald Gurin, and Oksana Malanchuk, "Group Consciousness and Political Participation," *American Journal of Political Science* 25 (1981): 494–511.

30 Reese and Brown, "The Effect of Religious Messages."

31 Calhoun-Brown, "African American Churches and Political Mobilization," 951.

32 Collier-Thomas, *Daughters of Thunder.*

33 Black denominations are those churches that are administratively independent of predominantly white denominations (Lincoln and Mamiya, *The Black Church in the African-American Experience*).

34 Ibid.

35 Clyde Wilcox, "Racial and Gender Consciousness among African-American Women: Sources and Consequences," *Women and Politics* 17 (1997): 73–94.

36 Barbara Sizemore, "Sexism and the Black Male," *Black Scholar* 4 (1973): 6.

37 Lincoln and Mamiya, *The Black Church in the African-American Experience,* 289.

38 These dummy variables were created from the combination of two questions: "What is your current religion or religious preference? — Protestant, Catholic, Islamic, Judaism, None, Other, Don't Know; and if Protestant, what church or denomination do you belong to? Baptist, African Methodist Episcopal, African Methodist Episcopal Zion, Church of God in Christ, National Baptist Convention, USA, National Baptist Convention of America, Progressive National Baptist Convention, Church of God, Nondenominational, Christian Methodist Episcopal, all other predominantly white Protestant groups, Interdenominational, Don't Know." Coding for the dummies is as follows: Baptist includes all Baptist classifications. Very few respondents actually identified a specific denomination. While there are certainly some Baptists who attend white denominations (i.e., Southern Baptists), the vast majority belong to black denominations. Methodist includes all Methodist denominations. Pentecostals include the Church of God and the Church of God in Christ. White denominations include interdenominational, nondenominational, and all other predominantly white Protestant groups. Catholics and Moslems are self-identified. There were no black Jews. Religious others and nones are excluded from this analysis because of missing correlations on the religiosity questions.

39 Some readers may be interested in the relationship between independent variables. Table 6 is a correlation matrix reporting their associations.

40 Lincoln and Mamiya record that the Progressive Baptist Convention was formed over a dispute within the National Baptist Convention about the propriety of church involvement in political and social action.

41 This finding differs from that of Wilcox, "Racial and Gender Consciousness among African-American Women." Using another data set, the National Black Election Study, he found political churches were negative predictors of a belief in a common fate with black women. In the NBPS political churches were significant positive predictors of the same position. This highlights the need for additional survey instruments and research into the attitudes and beliefs of African American women.

42 Walton, *Invisible Politics;* Fredrick Harris, "Something Within: Religion as a Mobilizer of African-American Political Activism," *Journal of Politics* 56 (1994): 42–68.

43 Wilcox and Thomas, "Religion and Feminist Attitudes among African American Women."

44 Neither the National Black Politics Study nor the National Black Election Study contained doctrinal questions. The impact of religious doctrine on the political behaviors of African Americans is an understudied area in this field.

45 Williams, *Sisters in the Wilderness,* 208.

TABLE 6 Correlation Matrix Independent Variables

	Political church	Age	Education	Gender	Rural	Religious involvement	Religious guidance	Baptist	Methodist	Moslem	Catholic	Pentecost.	White denom.
Political church	1.00												
Age	.03	1.00											
Education	.18***	-.13**	1.00										
Gender	-.04*	.06*	.02	1.00									
Rural	-.02	-.05	-.04	.03	1.00								
Religious involvement	.26**	.16***	.05	.15***	.09*	1.00							
Religious guidance	.11**	.12***	-.01	.12***	.04	.35***	1.00						
Baptist	.00	.03	-.08**	.02	.02	-.12***	-.04	1.00					
Methodist	.07*	.09***	.10***	.03	.04	.05	-.02	-.41**	1.00				
Moslem	.08*	-.07*	.02	-.09**	-.06*	.03	.06	-.13***	-.13***	1.00			
Catholic	-.08*	.02	.09***	-.00	-.07*	-.05	-.13***	-.25***	-.07*	-.04	1.00		
Pentecost.	.00	.00	-.02	.03	.03	.10**	.09**	-.23***	-.06*	-.02	0.07*	1.00	
White denom.	-.09*	.02	.00	.07**	-.00	.12***	.08	-.50***	-.12***	-.04	-.06*	.07	1.00

*p<.05
**p<.005
***p<.0005

46 Richard Allen, Michael Dawson, and Ronald Brown, "A Schema Based Approach to Modeling an African-American Racial Belief System," *American Political Science Review* 83 (1986): 421–41.

47 See Wilcox, "Racial and Gender Consciousness among African-American Women." It would be very helpful if survey instruments would standardize the questions used to measure racial and gender consciousness. Similarly worded questions for both blacks and women concerning racial or gender identification, power discontent, collectivist orientation, and system blame should be utilized. In this way very interesting comparisons could be made for black women concerning their relative levels of political consciousness on these important components of identity.

7

"DOING ALL THE GOOD WE CAN":

THE POLITICAL WITNESS OF AFRICAN AMERICAN

HOLINESS AND PENTECOSTAL CHURCHES IN

THE POST–CIVIL RIGHTS ERA

David D. Daniels III

In the period since the civil rights movement, black Pentecostalism has played an important role in reshaping the religious landscape and in generating new Christian political activists within the African American community. The growing political witness of black Pentecostal and Holiness churches during the post–civil rights era has built on the political involvements of key political activists within these churches during the early and mid-twentieth century. This recent activism has been encouraged as well by the prominence of the leaders participating in the civil rights movement, which served to legitimate (in unprecedented ways for black Pentecostal and Holiness leaders) the idea of Christian political activism.[1] Some degree of convincing was definitely required, given that while black Baptist and Methodist leaders debated political strategies for social change during the civil rights movement, many black Holiness and Pentecostal leaders were debating the appropriateness of clergy entering the political arena at all.

The scant historiography on the African American Holiness and Pentecostal movements in the post–civil rights era has tended to focus on the nonactivist majority. Arthur Paris's study of three African American Pentecostal congregations in Boston during the 1970s identified a quietistic posture toward the political order. Yet he discovered a high "level of political awareness" coupled with the absence of an "aggressive political self-consciousness." He argued that their personalist moral and social ethic translates "public issues into personal problems" and deprives them of a framework that makes political action religiously meaningful. Paris notes that the black Pentecostal "grammar of causation" precludes the human responsibility to make and change history. Research by Mark Chaves and Lynn M. Higgins, according to Fredrick C. Harris, indicates the reluctance of many African American Pentecostal churches to engage in civic activism in the post–civil rights era. Besides theological reasons, some studies demonstrate a correlation between the level of theological education among the clergy and the degree of commitment to Christian political activism, thus suggesting that the degree of commitment to Christian political activism increases as the level of theological education among the clergy increases. However, the general effect of the altering of the religious landscape by the growth of Pentecostalism during the post–civil rights era has been a lessening of the overall commitment to Christian political activism within the black church, since the average level of theological education among African American Holiness and Pentecostal clergy lags behind that attained by their counterparts within other black denominations.[2]

Consequently, a historical analysis of Christian political activism by African American Holiness and Pentecostal leaders could illuminate the contours and describe the character of their activism. Existing historiography on African American Holiness and Pentecostal political activists, such as that by Hans Baer and Robert Franklin, tends to classify their activism similarly to other black church activism as reformist, accommodationist, and pragmatic in their relationship to the dominant political order. Nevertheless, a discussion of the particularity of the Holiness and Pentecostal activism should provide additional insights into the nature and detail of this activism.[3]

This essay will focus on the minority for whom political activity has been part of their African American Holiness and Pentecostal identity, including those for whom political activity has served as a component of Christian ministry. I contend that the political activism of African American Holiness and Pentecostal churches in the post–civil rights era resembles, yet differs from, the political activism of the black church during this era. The difference lies in the way that the personalist moral and social ethic militates against the political activism within the African American Holiness and Pentecostal movement and in the way that these activists engage their activism theologically to sustain their political and ethical commitments. The essay consists of four sections. In the first, I describe the ecclesiastical landscape inhabited by African American Holiness and Pentecostal churches, and in the second I highlight the forebears of their Christian activism. I explore the contours of their Christian political witness in the third section, and in the fourth I discuss how the political activism promoted by them has been informed by various theological-political orientations held within their respective ranks.

The Ecclesiastical Landscape

The growth of black Pentecostalism began within urban centers during the Great Migration of the post–World War I era and has spread dramatically throughout urban and rural contexts across the country. Currently, the black denominations formed within the Pentecostal and Holiness traditions outnumber the denominations affiliated with black Baptist and Methodist denominations combined in terms of quantity, albeit not membership. By the 1980s, the Pentecostal and Holiness movement surpassed the black Methodist movement in church membership to become the second-largest religious tradition among African American Christians. Emblematic of their growth in membership and political capital is that within cities such as Los Angeles, Philadelphia, Detroit, Dallas, and Chicago, the largest African American congregations are Pentecostal. The African American Pentecostal and Holiness movements are a reservoir of organizational resources. Although there are more than a hundred denominations within this family of churches, the vast majority of the black Pentecostal-Holiness members belong to two denominations: the Church of God in Christ (cogic) and the Pentecostal Assemblies of the World. Also, since the 1960s, Pentecostalism has intersected with the major African American denominations to create a neo-Pentecostal movement with astonishing growth, especially among the African Methodist Episcopal Church and Baptist congregations. Black neo-Pentecostals both compete with and complement the classical African American Pentecostal and Holiness movements.

Despite the expansion of this ecclesiastical sector, the landscape of the African American Holiness and Pentecostal movement remains invisible to most Americans. There is little familiarity within *mainstream* America, for example, with the names of existing black Pentecostal and Holiness denominations—although, currently, the Church of God in Christ is emerging as the representative denomination. This obscures, however, the vitality and particularity of the Holiness and Pentecostal denominations that constitute the movement. While there is merit in suggesting that Holiness and Pentecostal churches operate in a shared religious orbit, distinctions between the two communions and within African American Pentecostalism also deserve scrutiny. Although many observers classify Holiness and Pentecostal together (with some using the category "Sanctified Church tradition"), most insiders of these movements make keen distinctions. Part of the difficulty in making fine distinctions, however, is that there are many African American Pentecostal churches that identify themselves as Holiness churches — thus combining the holiness tradition and Pentecostalism in their expression of the faith.

The holiness tradition focuses heavily on the personal Christian experience. It teaches that the Christian life is marked by two moments: justification and sanctification. Justification occurs when a believer first accepts Christ, and sanctification occurs when Christ changes the believer. The proponents of sanctification employed various images to describe the event: cleansing, empowerment, and habitation. Finally, there was a debate about whether sanctification was a recognizable experience analogous to conversion or a definitive commitment to a particular Christian lifestyle.[4] The Pentecostal tradition highlights the Pentecost event in Acts 2 as the pivotal experience in the Christian life. It defines this experience as the baptism of the Holy Spirit and describes the experience in terms of power or empowerment. While many Pentecostals recognize "speaking in tongues," or glossolalia, as the evidence of receiving this baptism, others characterize the experience in broader terms. What is key to many is that this Pentecostal baptism accompanies consistent Christian living.

A significant distinction among Pentecostals is their theology of God. The two theological camps are defined as trinitarian and apostolic ("oneness"). The trinitarian camp espouses the historic Christian theology of the communal or social nature of God. Apostolics believe that Jesus was the name of God and that while God expressed Godself in the form of the Father, Son, and Holy Spirit, these are expressions or "titles" of God, not distinct persons.

The demographics of the African American Holiness and Pentecostal movements create an interesting profile. Currently, the Holiness wing of Pentecostalism possesses a large segment of the movement, possibly 70 percent. In comparison with the non-Pentecostal Holiness movement, the

Pentecostal-Holiness wing outnumbers its non-Pentecostal Holiness counterparts more than ten to one. Consequently, the Pentecostal-Holiness wing
functions as the ecclesiastical norm for all Holiness churches from the sheer
force of its numbers and visibility. While the Church of God in Christ is
the most prominent denomination within the Pentecostal-Holiness wing,
the largest non-Pentecostal African American Holiness denomination is the
Church of Christ (Holiness). There are other African American Holiness adherents in the Church of God (Anderson) and the Church of the Nazarene.
Apostolics make up approximately 30 percent of all African American Pentecostals, with the Pentecostal Assemblies of the World possessing the largest
membership. Although African American Pentecostal congregations exist in
each of the fifty states within the Union, Apostolics tend to be more concentrated within the Midwestern and mid-Atlantic states. In contrast, the
Church of God in Christ is national in its membership, albeit with strong
concentrations in large states such as Texas, California, and Illinois.[5]

The ecclesiastical landscape of the African American Holiness and Pentecostal movement reveals a diverse religious movement. Yet the predomi-
nance of two major denominations — the Church of God in Christ and the
Pentecostal Assemblies of the World — demonstrates both the organizational
prowess of these two communions and the existence of a type of organizational unity that embraces the majority of African American Holiness and
Pentecostal adherents.

The Forebears of the Contemporary Political Witness

Political activity among African American Holiness and Pentecostal adherents began prior to the post–civil rights era. A minority within this community had participated in political activity since the 1890s. These activities
included the holiness AMEZ Bishop Alexander Waters' role in the founding of both the Afro-American League and the National Association for
the Advancement of Colored People. The pacifist campaign of the COGIC
Bishop Charles Harrison Mason during World War I was the first major
political activity of Pentecostal African Americans. E. R. Driver, a COGIC
pastor in Los Angeles, participated in the nationalist campaign of Marcus
Garvey and the Universal Negro Improvement Association along with other
African American Holiness and Pentecostal clergy from various denomina-

tions. These clergy included L. E. Hargrave, Sidney Solomon, Prince C. Allen, Stephen I. Lee, R. H. Parker, and Phillip Bishop. Robert C. Lawson, founder of the Church of Our Lord Jesus Christ, engaged the politics in Harlem between the two world wars. Arenia C. Mallory, a leader in the Church of God in Christ and an associate of Mary McLeod Bethune, was a member of Eleanor Roosevelt's Negro Women's Cabinet that advised the First Lady on issues from the black women's perspective. William Roberts, a COGIC bishop, participated in the political activism of the Fraternal Council of Negro Churches. In 1953 Lillian Brooks Coffey, the head of the international Women's Department of the Church of God in Christ, spearheaded the passing of a racial justice resolution at the denomination's Women Convention. The resolution espoused cooperation "with any and all organizations within the framework of our American government which is seeking justice, equality, and integration of all Americans into the democratic way of life."

In the 1950s, Smallwood Williams led a legal battle against segregated public schools in Washington, D.C., and J. O. Patterson Sr. participated in the local civil rights campaign in Memphis, Tennessee. During the 1960s, Arthur Brazier and Louis Henry Ford were active in the civil rights efforts in Chicago, while Ithiel Clemmons and Herbert Daughtry in New York City were similarly involved in civil rights campaigns. Charles Brewer and Talbert Swan were active in Connecticut and Massachusetts, respectively. Charles E. Blake participated in the march from Selma to Montgomery. On the national scene the most active persons were Addie Wyatt and Fannie Lou Hamer, both Holiness leaders.

Yet it is unclear to what degree an African American Holiness and Pentecostal political trajectory emerged that connected the first or second generation of political activity to the subsequent ones. Still, the existence of political activity within this movement demonstrates the capacity of the African American Holiness and Pentecostal traditions to sustain such activity.

The Contours of the Political Witness

At the advent of the post–civil rights era, the Church of God in Christ was among a cadre of African American Holiness and Pentecostal denominations that included within their doctrine and discipline themes related to the political role of the church in the society. In 1973 the General Assembly of the denomination authorized this political role. Included in the doctrine and discipline manual are social policy statements. While these statements focus heavily on the public nature of personal morality, they also offer a political vision. They express support of the prohibition of alcoholic production and sales, the repeal of legalized gambling, and the abolition of capital punishment. In addition these statements advocate a vision of economic and social equality and a concern for the poor. More than mere moral support for these causes, the manual promotes the public role of the church in securing social equality for all people, regardless of "race, creed, or national origins," through social justice movements and the use of Christian persuasion. While the Church of God in Christ officially espouses a political vision, this vision remains isolated from the Christian identity of the majority of the leaders and members within the denomination. Yet this theology offers sanction for the political witness of congregations and leaders within the Church of God in Christ.[6]

Clergy greatly inform the political witness of African American Holiness and Pentecostal churches. While various congregations and denominations implicitly and even explicitly espouse a political vision, for the most part this vision is crafted and projected by leaders. For the sake of categorization, the discussion here will present types of political activity practiced by African American Holiness and Pentecostal leaders. In order to provide specificity to the discussion, I will limit it to African American Pentecostals in Chicago and New York City. I will, however, make a few references to other cities. The focus on particular cities is also helpful because currently the absence of a national movement makes much of the activity local or statewide in nature. The types of political activity will be placed into two clusters, which are types that reflect different political realities rather than historical periods during the post–civil rights era.

The political realities defined by the passing of the 1965 Voting Rights Act changed the political landscape of African Americans and the American society. The new political landscape encompassed political contexts wherein African Americans functioned increasingly as insiders, and less as outsiders, relative to the political order. The presence of African Americans as political insiders on the municipal level was often associated with the rise of black mayors in major urban centers like Gary, Newark, Cleveland, Detroit, Washington, D. C., New Orleans, Atlanta, Los Angeles, Chicago, and New York

City. The election of L. Douglas Wilder as governor of Virginia as well as interracial coalitions resulting in his victory did signal the presence of African Americans as insiders on the state level, at least in Virginia. The presidential campaign of Jesse Jackson during the 1980s also created space for African Americans as insiders within the Democratic Party. Even though African Americans became political insiders within sectors of the political order during the post–civil rights era, insider status was not the only political approach pursued by African Americans, or by black Holiness and Pentecostal leaders in particular.

One cluster of political activism among African American Holiness and Pentecostal leaders highlights the political orientations of protest, accommodation, and cooperation. The restriction of the political space makes protest and accommodation the primary political options. African Americans as a group relate to the structures of political power basically as outsiders. The term "cooperationist" differentiates between the politics of black neoconservatives and liberals or neoliberals during the post–civil rights era, especially during the political realignment of the new conservatives under Ronald Reagan, the Moral Majority, and the Christian Coalition. The second cluster of political activism is within the new political arena where African Americans relate to the structures of political power as insiders — albeit within what is still contested and negotiated political space. Within urban contexts, the dividing line tended to be the election of the first African American mayor within the particular city.

The protest orientation is integral to the first cluster of political activity. Within the protest tradition resides the political orientation of Arthur Brazier, Leon Finney, Mrs. Willie Barrow, Mrs. Addie Wyatt, Herbert Daughtry, and Al Sharpton. Each of these leaders engaged in protest during the early years of the post–civil rights era prior to the election of black mayors Harold Washington and David Dinkins in Chicago and New York, respectively. Arthur Brazier, the Pentecostal Assemblies of the World (PAW) pastor and later bishop, and Leon Finney, a PAW pastor, were trained in community organizing and protest tactics by Saul Alinsky and the Industrial Areas League. The primary institutional base for Brazier and Finney was The Woodlawn Organization (TWO), a leading African American community organizing agency and later a community development agency. Under Brazier's leadership TWO provided significant opposition to the Richard J.

Daley administration in the civil rights and post–civil rights eras. They used protest effectively in the campaign to advance the political agenda of the people of Woodlawn. In the 1980s Brazier and others expanded their strategy to promote the revitalization of Woodlawn through housing development and through encouraging businesses to remain open in the community. Mrs. Willie Barrow, a Church of God (Anderson) clergywomen, served as an executive to the Rainbow/PUSH organization, embracing the protest tactics of Jesse Jackson, president of Rainbow/PUSH. Mrs. Addie Wyatt, also a Church of God (Anderson) clergywoman, was introduced to political activity through leadership positions, local and national, within the labor movement. In her various posts, Wyatt participated in the labor union's quest for advancing the agenda of working women and men and served as a leader in the various incarnations of the Rainbow/PUSH organization. Herbert Daughtry and Al Sharpton were key figures in protest activity within New York City. Daughtry served as one of the founders of black nationalist political groups such as the Black United Front and the African Christian People's Organization. Daughtry and Sharpton were the main fixtures of protest politics in New York during the post–civil rights era. Sharpton would later become a national figure (although transferring his church membership from Pentecostal to Baptist in the 1990s).[7]

For the most part, these leaders entered the political arena through their engagement of political trajectories outside of their religious movements. These political trajectories encompassed community organizing, labor, black nationalism, black theology, and black Christian ecumenism. Although some of these political elements have had noticeable footholds within black Holiness and Pentecostal activist circles, these elements operating within Holiness and Pentecostal churches need to intersect more effectively with other movements to generate a broader Christian political activism.

During the post–civil rights era, the agendas of the leaders listed above addressed a range of issues including: (1) increasing the percentage of African Americans in city jobs such as the police force, fire department, and as heads of municipal departments; (2) increasing cities' services in black communities; (3) revitalizing underclass neighborhoods; (4) improving public school education; and (5) ending police brutality. These agenda items often dovetailed with campaigns for black mayors. Most of the leaders believed that a black mayor would support their political vision for their cities and regions.

By the 1990s the protest orientation within the African American Holiness and Pentecostal movements found clear expression. According to the Lincoln-Mamiya study on COGIC political attitudes, the majority of the COGIC respondents supported civil rights protest, with a 78 percent positive response. Similarly, the ITC/Faith Factor Project 2000 Study of Black Churches found different results in its survey of COGIC clergy. Their study found a majority of COGIC clergy approved of civil rights protest. In both studies, however, the rate of approval within the COGIC samples was less than the overall black church samples. Nonetheless, COGIC's approval rate of civil rights protest is likely still higher than the majority of other African American Holiness and Pentecostal denominations.[8]

Although a sizable number of COGIC members support civil rights protests on the part of their clergy, the majority of black Pentecostal and Holiness church members tend more toward accommodationism and cooperationism than protest. With respect to accommodationism, within the post–civil rights era it has probably been the black neoconservatives who could most accurately be referred to as accommodationist. One such person within the Pentecostal and Holiness camps is Hiram Crawford, an independent Holiness pastor in Chicago who has embraced elements of the black neoconservative platform. He has supported the Pro-Life/Pro-Family coalition and has affiliated with the Illinois Right to Life and the Americans for Life. Crawford also participated in Jerry Falwell's Moral Majority and has supported Pat Robertson's Christian Coalition. Within Chicago politics, he has directly challenged those supporting the political agenda of Jesse Jackson.[9]

The cooperationist title is a potential fit for Louis Henry Ford, especially during the years prior to the Harold Washington administration. Ford carried over his political alliance with the Richard J. Daley machine during the civil rights era (based as it was on a patron-client political relationship) into the post–civil rights years, into which the senior Daley's administration extended. Ford contended that religious leaders must find productive ways to engage political power for the benefit of the people. This often put Ford in a fine political balancing act, especially when the movement for a black mayor of Chicago was gaining momentum throughout the late 1970s, a political outcome he did not perceive as feasible. Another candidate is Charles Brewer in New Haven, Connecticut, where he was among the black political religious elite of the city.[10]

The existence of politicoreligious leaders such as Ford and Brewer as co-operationists seems sensible emerging from a conservative movement such as black Pentecostalism. However, the existence of leaders such as Brazier, Wyatt, and Daughtry — cast by some as militants — is surprising. Both orientations broke the otherworldly posture of the African American Holiness and Pentecostal movement. The protest orientation revealed the revolutionary and countercultural tendencies within Pentecostalism that scholars such as James S. Tinney and Luther P. Gerlach and Virginia H. Hine analyzed in their studies. Recently, black Pentecostal activist Alexander D. Hurt has advocated a Pentecostal progressivism in which connections are made between "biblical faith and social change." These Pentecostal progressives recall the earlier American Progressive Era that produced a "new cadre of leaders" and a new discourse that would challenge "existing norms, change assumptions and life options, and chart a new course for humanity."[11]

The second cluster of political activity highlights the presence of African Americans as political insiders to the political structures. In this era a cadre of Holiness and Pentecostal leaders became insiders and they changed their way of relating to city government at least. While a few Holiness and Pentecostal African Americans continued to utilize protest or an accommodationist tradition, most adopted roles either as political party officials, political party activists, elected government officials, or as independent political activists and coalition-builders where they could promote their political vision from their own political location. For instance, Willie Barrow served as a member of the National Democratic Committee during the late twentieth century. Henry Louis Ford and others became loyal Democratic Party members.

Although African American Holiness and Pentecostal adherents joined the ranks of mayors and state legislators during the post–civil rights era, their proportion of black elected officials was significantly smaller than their proportion within black Christendom. Eugene Sawyer, a Church of God (Anderson) layperson, and James Hayes, a COGIC pastor, served as the mayors of Chicago and of Fairbanks, respectively. Among the ranks of current and former state senators are COGIC clergyman J. O. Patterson Jr. of Tennessee, COGIC evangelist Yvonne Miller of Virginia, and Bible Way pastor Darrell Jackson of South Carolina. Among the ranks of current and former state representatives are COGIC clergyperson Robert Harris of Utah, COGIC pastor

Joseph Clemmons of Connecticut, COGIC layperson Benjamin Swan of Massachusetts, Church of God (Anderson) clergywoman Triette Lipsey Reeves of Michigan, and COGIC laywoman Johnnie Morris-Tatum of Wisconsin.

While many Holiness and Pentecostal African Americans held different political roles and exercised political leadership through these roles, each honestly and accurately contended that their prophetic voice had precedence over all their political allegiances. This position also informed the role of independent political activist assumed by Arthur Brazier and Herbert Daughtry during the late twentieth century.

Although a change in the political landscape occurred, it was not always permanent. In Chicago Brazier, Wyatt, and Barrow entered a critical alliance with a white mayoral candidate who became Chicago's mayor, while in New York, with a different political climate, Daughtry (and, in certain ways, Sharpton) returned to protest politics. In the latter part of 2001, however, Sharpton announced that he had formed a committee to explore the feasibility of a Sharpton presidential candidacy in 2004.

The latest and most novel political development within the African American Holiness and Pentecostal movement is the formation of the Pan-African Charismatic Evangelical Congress (PACEC) by Charles E. Blake and Eugene Rivers. Blake is the pastor of the 18,000-member West Angeles Church of God in Christ in Los Angeles, and Eugene Rivers is the pastor of the Azusa Christian Community, cofounder of the Ten-Point Coalition, and a Church of God in Christ minister. As the first major black Pentecostal political activist organization, PACEC defines itself as a new post–civil rights movement that is committed to a multifaceted strategy of political action. This new strategy combines "protest and direct action" with influencing public policy, developing programs, and focusing on measurable results. PACEC stresses its political independence with a strong commitment to coalition-building.[12]

While the political roles of Holiness and Pentecostal African Americans vary, for the most part they all affirm a political vision of racial justice. The differences lie in whether racial justice is defined in liberal or nationalist terms. Arthur Brazier and Addie Wyatt would employ political liberalism, with a strong element of black self-determination, and Al Sharpton and Herbert Daughtry would employ a more nationalist framework. The goal of those with a liberal political vision is to create a "just" America, a new

America through a progressive political agenda and with a justice emphasis as a means of empowerment and liberation. While the liberal political vision offers little systematic differentiation from, or critique of, "the predominant culture" in terms of race, there is an explicit public concern with the urban situation, defined not exclusively in terms of race but in terms of conditions and issues that affect everyone, especially African Americans. Their political agenda emerges from these commitments. The goal of those with a nationalist political vision is for African Americans to be at the forefront of social and economic progress in order to usher in a more just and democratic society. These nationalists supply harsh critiques of the racism and the racial realities of the United States, regularly sounding those critiques through social protest. They craft their political agenda in light of the racial regime.

Theological Issues and Political Christian Witness

The theological perspectives of African American Holiness and Pentecostal tradition inform their political activism. Their political perspectives relish political outcomes where God's intervention can be seen as miraculous and against political wisdom. Their framework is structured by a deliverance motif employed to demonstrate the reality and power of God over against the political prowess or connivance of the opponents.[13] The central theme of this political perspective is that "God can supernaturally intervene" in the political arena. A historical example of how this has been employed by black Holiness and Pentecostal leaders is their use of such language to describe the initial victories of Harold Washington and Carol Moseley Braun.

These African American Holiness and Pentecostal political perspectives reflect a world that stresses God's agency, the reality of satanic activity within human affairs, and the limits of human agency. In this world the supernatural outweighs the influence of the political. Even when human agency is highlighted, the person is seen as acting only because God has prompted him or her to do so. A large spiritual drama serves as the backdrop to the political arena, then, with political actors committing good deeds in response to divine influence and bad deeds in response to satanic influence.[14] The devaluing of human agency in the African American Holiness and Pentecostal narrative and analysis is in tension with political tactics and strategy. Even among the most pragmatic black Holiness and Pentecostal churchpersons—for example, those who acknowledge the strategic individual and collective agency of civil rights and black power movement activists—the political pragmatism must still incorporate a strong sense of divine agency.

In a way, the political arena becomes a place where African American Holiness and Pentecostal Christians learn to engage in a bicultural or bilingual context. In this context they learn to move between worlds, religious and political. Bicultural refers to being able to operate in religious and political realms. Bilingual refers to the ability to speak two languages: religious and political. What is central is that they hold both of these worlds simultaneously without conflating, integrating, or blending them. The switch in discourse, languages, or cultures profoundly shapes political activity. For instance, individuals could espouse theological perspectives that are individualistic and conservative at the same time, promoting political perspectives that are communitarian, radical, or liberal. This is not deemed contradictory or inconsistent because the community values the bicultural character of its political and religious life.[15]

This is evidenced in the Church of God in Christ's 1973 doctrine and discipline manual, which expressed theological themes such as creation, the Church, and the kingdom of God to support political activism. Their theology of creation espoused the "brotherhood of man" and "the godly purpose" of humankind. The theology of the Church stressed the role of the church in securing social justice and equality. And the theology of the kingdom of God highlighted the dual loci of the kingdom: earth and heaven. These themes supplied theological rationale for COGIC's involvement in the political order. While their theology acknowledged that the government was a "God-given institution for the benefit" of humanity, Christians were to engage in civil obedience, on the one hand, but recognize the primacy of the Christian conscience in relationship to the government, on the other hand—even to the point of civil disobedience at times.[16]

A leader within black Pentecostalism, James Forbes (who now pastors the Baptist/UCC affiliated Riverside Church in New York), has suggested a corporate model of religious transformation to augment the personal model of religious transformation that has dominated black Pentecostal discourse. Forbes's theological objective shifts the focus from personal issues to social problems within Pentecostal rhetoric in order to promote the Pentecostal engagement of the political order as well as nurture church-based political activism among black Pentecostals. Forbes recommends a new motif within Pentecostal pneumatology wherein Pentecostals recognize the movement of the Holy Spirit "in the shadows of sacred places and in the structures of secular institutions." Forbes argues for the theological liberation of the Holy Spirit from the ecclesial arena and the theological acknowledgment of the Holy Spirit within political and economic sectors. In classic Pentecostal form, Forbes affirms human and divine agency: "Where there exists community strife, ignorance and war, we [the church] will offer peace and wisdom as gifts of God through both human effort and divine intervention."[17]

Another Pentecostal pastor, Herbert Daughtry, has proposed another alternative to Pentecostal tendencies toward a personalist moral ethic. Daughtry, like Forbes, sees institutional domains as contexts where spirit-led transformation occurs. Daughtry approaches this out of both reformist and revolutionary objectives—viewing some institutions as capable of being reformed, while others require replacement by new structures. Daughtry derives commitments for restructuring the social order in Jesus Christ—whom he views as a revolutionary who confronted and shattered "religious and social and political systems." Daughtry clearly states that the historical Jesus shunned violence, but he notes the role of violence in the activity of the eschatological Jesus. He notes the inauguration of a new order in Jesus requires the overturning of the old order and the introduction of the primacy of justice and righteousness.[18]

Important perspectives on the parallels between spiritual and political dimensions have also been provided by Robert Franklin, a COGIC clergyperson and social ethicist, and by Cheryl Sanders, a Church of God (Anderson) pastor and social ethicist. Franklin advocates a prophetic radicalism that embraces the liberation framework. Employing themes of God as liberator and judge, he promotes a democratic socialist vision. He seeks more than a "fair distribution of goods such as education, housing, health, and jobs." Social justice is the goal of his Christian political activism. Social justice will be achieved through "a radical restructuring of the free-market capitalist economy," thus undermining the "political and corporate status quo." He identifies protest as a relevant strategy in conjunction with negotiation. Sanders proposes an ethics of empowerment, substituting an empowerment model for the liberation/oppression framework. She defines empowerment ethics as the "norms, principles, and ethos ascribed to individuals and groups engaged in the task of liberating others by empowering them to act." She draws greatly on the African American Holiness and Pentecostal experience to inform her outline of "a holistic vision of African-American moral progress." Her aim is to fortify the "sacrificial struggle" of "empowered individuals who [will] maintain creative partnerships with the oppressed and who identify unambiguously with the best interests of the oppressed group."[19]

These various perspectives have provided options within African American Holiness and Pentecostal thought for alternatives to the personalist moral and social ethic. These alternatives have created theological space within the African American Holiness and Pentecostal traditions for new ways of thinking about and acting on their political concerns.

Conclusion

During the post–civil rights era, a new religious and political landscape has emerged that African American Holiness and Pentecostal movements have contributed to in important ways. Leaders from these movement have risen to prominence within certain political arenas. Although very few of these leaders have attained national stature, their engagement of city- and state-wide politics has been significant in key places. Their accommodationist, cooperationist, and protest strategies have, at points, reinforced existing governmental and nongovernmental political structures and have helped develop new institutions such as the Black United Front and the African People's Christian Organization. The formation of Pentecostal and Holiness activist organizations such as the Pentecostal Coalition for Human Rights and the Pan-African Charismatic Evangelical Congress demonstrates the organizational capabilities of this movement.

Critical to the sustaining of Christian political activism within these Holiness and Pentecostal movements is the strengthening of the activist trajectories within them. The emergence of theological perspectives with grammars of causation that accent the role of human agency in making and changing history might supply the intellectual apparatus necessary to fortify activism among Pentecostal and Holiness churches, and beyond. By promoting a corporate moral and social ethic that highlights the systematic rather than individualistic nature of public issues, a politically and spiritually conscious movement may evolve that builds on the ecclesiastical dynamism of Pentecostal and Holiness churches and on political instincts among this growing family of churches that were not adequately connected to civil rights movement politics.

Notes

1   Robert Michael Franklin, " 'My Soul Says Yes': The Urban Ministry of the Church of God in Christ," in *Church, Cities, and Human Community: Urban Ministry in the United States 1945–1985,* ed. Clifford J. Green (Grand Rapids: William B. Eerdmans Publishing Company, 1996), 92; Clarence Taylor, *The Black Churches of Brooklyn* (New York: Columbia University Press, 1994), 192–93.

2   Arthur E. Paris, *Black Pentecostalism: Southern Religion in an Urban World* (Amherst: University of Massachusetts Press, 1982), 134–35, 132; also see Hans A. Baer, "The Socio-Political Development of the Church of God in Christ," in *African-Americans in the South: Issues in Race, Class, and Gender,* ed. Hans A. Baer and Yvonne Jones (Athens: University of Georgia Press, 1992), 111–22; Robert M. Franklin, *Another Day's Journey: Black Churches Confronting the American Crisis* (Minneapolis: Fortress Press, 1977); and Gayraud Wilmore, *Black Religion and Black Radicalism: An Interpretation of the Religious History of African-Americans* (Maryknoll, N.Y.: Orbis Press, 1998), 255–61, 274; Fredrick C. Harris, *Something Within: Religion in African-American Political Activism* (New York: Oxford University Press, 1999), 182; Mark Chaves and Lynn M. Higgins, "Comparing the Community Involvement of Black and White Congregations," *Journal for the Scientific Study of Religion* 31, no. 4: 425–40, cited in Harris, 182.

3   Baer, "The Socio-Political Development of the Church of God in Christ," 121; Franklin, *Another Day's Journey,* 44–45.

4   See David D. Daniels III, "The Cultural Renewal of Slave Religion: Charles Price Jones and the Emergence of the Holiness Movement in Mississippi" (Ph.D. diss., Union Theological Seminary, New York, 1992), 142–98.

5   The sanctified church thesis is promoted by Cheryl J. Sanders in her book *Saints in Exile: The Holiness-Pentecostal Experience in African-American Religion and Culture* (New York: Oxford University Press, 1996); on the membership statistics, see Wardell J. Payne, ed., *Directory of African-American Religious Bodies* (Washington, D.C.: Howard University Press, 1991).

6 *Official Manual with the Doctrines and Discipline of the Church of God in Christ* (Memphis: Board of Publication of the Church of God in Christ, 1973), 131–36, 137, 141–42.

7 Arthur M. Brazier, *Black Self-Determination: The Story of the Woodlawn Organization* (Grand Rapids: William B. Eerdmans Publishing Company, 1969); Addie Wyatt, "The Role of Women in the Harold Washington Story," in *The Black Church and the Harold Washington Story*, ed. Henry L. Young (Bristol, Indiana: Wyndham Hall Press, 1988), 95–103; on Daughtry and Sharpton, see Taylor, *The Black Churches of Brooklyn*, 191–200, 209–34.

8 C. Eric Lincoln and Lawrence H. Mamiya, *The Black Church in the African-American Experience* (Durham: Duke University Press, 1990), 224; COGIC Churches, ITC/ FaithFactor Project 2000 Study of Black Churches (Atlanta: ITC/FaithFactor Project 2000, 2001), 7.

9 Matthew Price, fieldnotes on Israel Church, Religion in Urban American Program, cited in David Daniels, "Chatham and Greater Grand Crossing: The Dominance of Religion and Race," in *Final Research Report of the Religion in Urban American Program* (Chicago: Office of Social Science Research, University of Illinois at Chicago, 1995), 199.

10 On Ford, see Robert Michael Franklin, "'My Soul Says Yes,'" 77–96; on Brewer, see Yohura Williams, *Black Politics, White Power* (Dover: Delaware State University, Brandywine Press, 2000).

11 Luther P. Gerlach and Virginia H. Hine, *People, Power, Change: Movements of Social Transformation* (Indianapolis: Bobbs-Merrill Company, 1970); James S. Tinney, "A Theoretical and Historical Comparison of Black Political and Religious Movements" (Ph.D. diss., Howard University, 1978); Alexander D. Hurt, "Pentecostal Progressive," in *The American Prospect* (9 April 2001).

12 Valerie G. Lowe, "Standing on Holy Ground," *Charisma and Christian Life* 23, no. 9 (April 1998): 38–39, 46, 114–15; Dan Kennedy, "Eugene River's Moment," *Phoenix* (2001), www.bostonphoenix.com/boston/news, 26 June 2001.

13 Ray Allen, *Singing in the Spirit: African-American Sacred Quartets in New York City* (Philadelphia: University of Pennsylvania Press, 1991), 117; Mary McClinton Fulkerson, *Changing the Subject: Women's Discourses and Feminist Theology* (Minneapolis: Fortress Press, 1994), 264, 257.

14 Peter D. Goldsmith, *When I Rise Cryin' Holy: African-American Denominationalism on the Georgia Coast* (New York: AMS Press, 1989), 111.

15 Morton Marks, "Uncovering Ritual Structures on Afro-American Music," in *Religious Movements in Contemporary America*, ed. Irving I. Zaretsky and Mark P. Leone (Princeton: Princeton University Press, 1974), 64.

16 *Official Manual*, 137 and 142.

17   James A. Forbes Jr., "Shall We Call This Dream Progressive Pentecostalism," *Spirit: A Journal of Issues Incident to Black Pentecostalism* 1, no. 1 (1977): 13–14.

18   Herbert Daughtry Sr., *My Beloved Community: Sermons, Speeches, and Lectures* (Trenton: Africa World Press, Inc., 2001), 24, 26, 29, 151–52.

19   Robert M. Franklin, *Another Day's Journey,* 107, 45–46; Sanders, *Saints in Exile,* 1, 4, 5, 8, 118.

8

BLYDEN'S GHOST:

AFRICAN AMERICAN CHRISTIANITY

AND RACIAL REPUBLICANISM

C. R. D. Halisi

It has become axiomatic to refer to Benedict Anderson's observation that nations are not merely the products of given sociopolitical conditions, including language, race, religion, and other factors; nations everywhere were, to some extent, imagined into existence by visionary nationalist thinkers. By emphasizing the imagined or subjective dimension of nationalism, scholars have come to better appreciate the significance of self-representation as an important dimension of the nationalist project. It is now more widely accepted that some nationalisms can be likened to unrequited loves—the nation never gets married to a state or marries into a multiethnic nation-state that suppresses its people's desire for autonomy. Yet even in such circumstances, nationalism as an intellectual impulse can, nonetheless, remain a protean contributor to thought and culture. As we will see in what follows, the latter observation has certainly been true of the African American nationalist tradition.

Partha Chatterjee reminds students of anticolonial nationalism that the history of Western nationalism does not fit all parts of the world in some modular fashion. Were this to be overlooked, then, says Chatterjee, "even our imaginations must remain for ever colonized."[1] In Asia and Africa, for example, the claims of nationalism as a purely political movement may have been taken too literally and seriously. Chatterjee makes his argument against the overdetermination of political nationalism thus:

> . . . anticolonial nationalism creates its own domain of sovereignty within the colonial society well before it begins its political battle. It does this by

dividing the world of social institutions and practices into two domains—
the material and the spiritual. The material is the domain of the "outside,"
of the economy and of statecraft, of science and technology, a domain
where the West had proved its superiority and the East had succumbed. . . .
The spiritual, on the other hand, is an "inner" domain bearing the essential
marks of cultural identity.[2]

In the African American experience, the idea of cultural nationalism as
inner, spiritual domain is provocative, especially given the pan-African pro-
clivities of black nationalist thought. Black Christian nationalism laid the
foundation for its secular counterpart and, as a result, salvation and self-
governance are interconnected themes in African American religious history.
As Gayraud Wilmore rightly contends, "the emergence of black nationalism
in America and Africa cannot be understood apart from the zeal of believers
to Christianize the land of their ancestors and to open up an administrative and communications network between churches for the promotion of
Christian missions in both Africa and the Caribbean."[3] Given the complex
relationship between religion and race, ministers such as Alexander Crummell, Edward Blyden, and Henry McNeal Turner stand out as pioneers of
both pan-racial identity and church history. As Wilmore suggests, the initial African American nationalist vision encompassed freedom, modernity,
solidarity, and intercourse shared among all people of African descent. Just
as religious and secular nationalisms were intertwined, so, too, were ideas of
freedom and self-governance in Africa, the Caribbean, and/or America.

Perhaps due to its perpetual gestation as imagined community, African
American nationalism has encompassed a diverse range of thinkers and activists. For example, black Christian nationalists are intent on transforming the
African American church into an institution compatible with some visions of
racial nationality; they have, at times, been supported and opposed by other
religious nationalists who want to replace Christianity's influence in black
communities with an African-centered alternative that may include black
Islam. One of the more idiosyncratic aspects of the African American nationalist tradition is the prominence of a racialized version of Islam that some
view as a theology or eschatology of black liberation. Pan-racial (previously
pan-Negro) nationalists are devoted to the spiritual and material upliftment
of African people worldwide; they have always been active in black churches,

served as missionaries, and established secular community organizations for racial advancement. By contrast, nonracial pan-African radicals reject an exclusive emphasis on racial identity, preferring class-based ideologies instead. Advocates of black republican thought insist that genuine freedom and development will come only with the advent of self-sustaining republics on the African continent or an African American cultural "nation within a nation." In search of this ideal, they have relocated to independent African nations, laid plans to recapture America's black belt states, founded independent schools, and established autonomous Yoruba communities. Likewise, pan-Africanists have championed a variety of transcontinental commitments that include, among others, lobbies for constructive support of independent African nations, political parties committed to Nkrumah's ideal of a United States of Africa, and mobilization of people and resources to help defeat South African apartheid. Moreover, the strands of thought that comprise this rich panoply of approaches usually overlap — a tendency readily seen in the interviews with black Christian nationalists in this chapter.

Today the vast majority of black nationalists are cultural nationalists — they do not advocate a return to Africa but rather seek to construct and preserve black institutions as bulwarks against full integration into American society. However, it can be argued that Blyden and other nineteenth-century nationalist thinkers, who were willing to contemplate African emigration as a solution to American race relations, articulated a set of core values that continue to inform present-day discourse on the nature of black political participation; this is so even when these solidaristic values are not configured by a conscious nationalist ideology. Imagined communities are utopias until transformed into institutions and, even then, utopian conceptions of community remain an important source of legitimacy. The vision of a racially homogeneous republic — modern, autonomous, unified, participatory, and nurtured by spiritual institutions consistent with the republican mission — constitutes the dominant, often unconscious utopian vision at the heart of black nationalist thought.

The extent to which the uniquely communitarian characteristics of the black church reflect African cultural survivals or derive from a distinctly African American pedigree has long been a source of controversy among scholars and intellectuals. Conceived as the medium for redressing ethical as well as social deficiencies (i.e., health, education, joblessness, food, clothing, burial grounds, civil liberties, and civil rights), black religion became the organizational principle for national community life. Joseph Washington cogently summarizes the black church as a national, cultural institution:

> Black religion is a civil as well as a civilizing religion. . . . The function of religion in matters of public regard is not an issue unique to black Americans, but it raises a distinctive and in many ways decisive issue for black religion. . . . Religious variations and institutions were not only the first creations of the black community, but they are as well its only nearly universal and definitely national organ.[4]

The long struggle for racial equality in America has given the civil dimension of black religion a special significance to nationalists and nonnationalists alike. Black nationalists, both Christian and secular, tend to view political participation through the prism of "racial-nationality," and this can engender a sense of black republican, civic identity. Irrespective of its civil rights activism and standing as the most authentic African American institution, the black church, according to both secular and religious nationalists, can be found wanting in the area of political participation. Given the extent of its community involvement, what, then, are the foundations of nationalist criticism? In large measure, the nationalist critique is rooted in a continued commitment to the precepts of racial-nationality—best exemplified by the thought of Edward Blyden. In other words, nationalist criticisms of church participation are framed by black republican values and assumptions regarding the nature of political obligation; these values often function as an alternative to the hegemonic nonracial liberalism of American public life.

Given these assertions regarding nationalism as an intellectual and political construction, this essay has three parts with specific goals. First, it reconstructs Blydenite nationalism as a prototype of black republican thought on religion and politics. Fortified by serious scholarship on ancient civilizations in Africa, Asia, and the Middle East as well as highly informed insight into the intellectual currents of his era, Blyden provides us with an exceptionally useful grounding for many of the fundamental values of contemporary black nationalism. Second, interviews conducted with a select group of black Christian nationalists are used to highlight contemporary criticism of the African American church as a political force in black communities. In conclusion, I consider convergence and contention in contemporary black Christian nationalist thought.

Blyden's Republican Ideals: Christianity and Islam

Indeed, the most prescient critique of African American Protestantism, and the Christian church in general, can be rightly claimed by Edward Wilmot Blyden—the St. Thomas–born Liberian pioneer, linguist, theologian, scholar, minister, educator, politician, diplomat, and public intellectual—who, during the nineteenth century, anticipated the essential tenets of black nationalism. Casely Hayford contends that Blyden stands out even when compared with powerful personalities such as Crummell, Booker T. Washington, or W. E. B. Du Bois. Blyden's immense reputation among all thinking Africans, according to Hayford, "rests . . . upon the general work he has done for the race as a whole."[5] An internationally active public intellectual for well over fifty years, Blyden left to posterity a large corpus of high-quality commentary concerning black humanity. Hollis Lynch, a fellow West Indian and sympathetic biographer, characterizes Blyden's writings as a "curious blend of propaganda and scholarship, of the messianic, the mystical and metaphysical with the historical and sociological."[6] Despite this admixture of influences, Lynch is quick to concede that Blyden's use of historiography, anthropology, and sociology was as sophisticated as any of his time.

At the core of Blydenite nationalism were several interrelated concepts including racial environmentalism, organic black unity, providential design of races and nationalities, as well as a belief in innate racial capacities. These were ideas that Blyden gleaned from a wide range of sources in numerous languages, transforming them into an arsenal of arguments to support claims of African dignity and equality. Blyden and many of his black nationalist contemporaries clung to the view that each race had a distinct mission; they nevertheless refused to use black nationalism as a vehicle to articulate racial superiority. Blyden did, however, call on African people to reap the benefits of nationalism, as were Americans, Germans, Italians, Slavs, and many others. To his way of thinking, "nationality is an ordinance of nature . . . the heart of every true Negro yearns after a distinct and separate nationality."[7]

While mostly discredited in our time, many Blydenesque assumptions continue to influence the way black nationalists view the political dimension of African American religion. Although his teachings are less well known than those of Marcus Garvey, Malcolm X, Louis Farrakhan, Cheik Antia Diop, Leopold Senghor, Steve Biko, Molefe Asante, or Maulana Ron Karenga, Blyden presaged ideas associated with all of these thinkers — Islamic and cultural black nationalism, Negritude, Black Consciousness, Afrocentrism, as well as those forms of racial nationalism inspired by Egyptian antiquity. Each one of these formulations has found secular and theological expression in contemporary black nationalist thought and practice. In addition, the study of Blyden's intellectual legacy has provided an interesting point of convergence for students of African American Christianity and black nationalism. For example, Albert Raboteau refers to Blyden's and Crummell's largely unanswered call for "African-Americans to abandon the American wilderness for an African Zion."[8] St. Clair Drake believes that had it not been for Blyden, "Ethopianism might have remained merely an escapist myth-system based on Biblical proof-texts and confined to the circle of Negro church people."[9]

Although an ordained Presbyterian minister for most of his life, Blyden was a powerful critic of the practices of the Christian church in Africa, especially its complicity in slavery, racial domination, and cultural imperialism. He surmised that wherever European Christians went "their aim was to realise the Kingdom of God in civil institutions of men, and to confine it by a system of caste to their own people."[10] As a black Christian, Blyden believed in the superiority of Jesus' teachings. Nevertheless, a lifelong opposition to the racism of white Christian communities informed his unceasing effort to formulate a "total philosophy of Africanness."[11] A critique of white Christian racism was central to the basic precepts of Blydenite pan-Africanism. Blyden contended that black evangelism could provide a counterpoint to white Christian influence in Africa. Furthermore, he was deeply skeptical about the prospects of black religious or civic institutions that were not based on African soil. Throughout his life, Blyden cautioned African Americans against the belief that their racial destiny was to be found in a multiracial America. As he saw it, "we should not content ourselves with living among other races, simply by their permission and endurance . . . we should build Negro states."[12] A resident of Liberia or Sierra Leone his entire adult life, Blyden refused to contemplate a liberal-integrationist foundation for black progress, and this may well have allowed him to articulate a more coherent nationalist perspective on black civil religion, nationality, and black republican citizenship. "It is painful," he remarked, "in America to see the efforts which are made by Negroes to secure outward conformity to the appearance of the dominant race."[13] In essence, Blyden thought of race, nationality, and religion as inseparable. By focusing on this early black Christian nationalist, we are reminded of the degree to which, in the African American experience, the projects of spiritual uplift and political liberation, including racial nationalism, have been in a dialectical relationship with one another. Blyden, and many of his black Christian nationalist colleagues, including the influential Episcopal minister Alexander Crummell, felt that nationality, citizenship, and peoplehood had to be organized through an overarching pan-racial identity. Lynch captures the significance of this original form of race-conscious internationalism when, in the subtitle of his seminal biography, he refers to Blyden as a "Pan-Negro Patriot."

As a racial partisan, Blyden judged all religious movements by their impact on African people, and he aptly titled his best-known collection of essays *Christianity, Islam, and the Negro Race* (1887). Christianity, he believed, had been travestied and diluted "to suit the 'peculiar institution' by which millions of human beings were converted into 'chattles.'"[14] Blyden felt that white Christians were too quick to characterize Islam as pagan, despite its shared origins with their own religious faith. Comparisons of the African activities of these two religious movements led Blyden to the controversial contention that Islam would prepare the way for a version of Christianity suited to African conditions. In purely political terms, Blyden saw in Islam the paradigm for a black republicanism that wedded racial nationality and civil religion. According to V. Y. Mudimbe, there are three main considerations at the core of Blyden's political philosophy—the organized community under Muslim leadership, the concept of an African nation, and the unity of the African continent.[15]

What most impressed Blyden about Islam was that "it claims as adherents the only people who have any form of civil polity or bond of social organization."[16] Consequently, he concluded that Islam was far less destructive of indigenous African civic life, which it had, most often, managed to morally improve. For Blyden, the black republican ideal was expressed through institution building, and this became his litmus test for genuine nationalist commitment. He specifically called on African peoples to build a wide array of institutions, including states, churches, governments, schools, presses, and laws.[17] Independent institutions, nationalists have long argued, allow for autonomous forms of black participation. Blyden believed that being in control of a weak African state held advantages over those enjoyed by Negroes in America who were "the passive spectators of the deeds of foreign race."[18] For example, Liberians were represented in forums of world power despite the insignificance of their nation.[19] Thus, from a black nationalist perspective, participation must, of necessity, be linked to independent black institutions whose attributes were often conceived in metaphysical as well as political terms. For Blyden, the soul force of a race found expression in its institutions. Races breathe their God-given genius into a unique institutional life, and this fact made institutions nontransferable from one race of people to another. "To kill those institutions is to kill the soul — a terrible homicide."[20]

In this respect, Blyden contrasted what he perceived as the autonomy of Islamic institutions in Africa with the dependency of Christian republics. In his opinion, Christianity had nothing to compare with the vibrant Islamic commercial centers of West and Central Africa, nor, in general, was it able to accommodate the degree of African agency that Blyden associated with Islam. He notes that

> Haiti and Liberia, so-called Negro Republics, are merely struggling for existence, and hold their own by the tolerance of the civilized powers . . . there are numerous Negro Mohammedan communities and states in Africa which are self-reliant, productive, independent, and dominant, supporting without the countenance or patronage of the parent country, Arabia, whence they derived them, their political, literary, and ecclesiastical institutions.[21]

Anticipating black nationalist organizations like the Nation of Islam (NOI) by nearly a century, Blyden argued that Christianity arrested the development of African peoples, while the impact of Islam had proved to be far more salutary.[22] Although some of its claims are clearly questionable, Blyden's interpretation of Islam contributed to the religion's influence with African Americans — today the largest single ethnic group among the Muslim community in North America. Blyden was a sophisticated scholar of Islamic theology and history and, perhaps, even a Muslim convert in his later years. Based on his personal experiences with black converts to Islam, he drew a sharp distinction between imitation of an alien religion and true discipleship. This dichotomy led him to the view that "the Mohammedan Negro is a much better Mohammedan than the Christian Negro is a Christian, because the Muslim Negro, as a learner, is a disciple, not an imitator."[23]

Though much taken with Muslim racial tolerance and political civility, Blyden did not see Islam as a theological alternative to Christianity. Indeed, he augured that Islam could pave the way for a genuinely African Christianity. He captures this vision of a religious convergence where Islam was preliminary and preparatory and Muhammad would prove to be a servant of Christ thus:

> The "Dark Continent" will no longer be a name of reproach for this vast peninsula, for there shall be no darkness here. Where the light from the Cross ceases to stream upon the gloom, there the beams of the Crescent will give illumination; and as the glorious orb of Christianity rises, the twilight of Islam will be lost in the greater light of the Sun of Righteousness. Then Isaac and Ishmael will be united, and rejoice together in the faith of their common progenitor.[24]

As Blyden predicted, the most compelling aspects of Islam and Christianity would eventually interface to create a new vision of religion for African Americans.[25] Therefore, Ben Chavis, the former head of the NAACP and a Christian clergyman, tapped into a very old nationalist tradition when, upon his conversion to the Nation of Islam, he stood before his black Muslim brethren with the Bible in one hand and Qur'an in the other and stated, "I find no theological contradiction between being a black Christian and a black Muslim."[26]

In his *Islam in the African-American Experience,* Richard Brent Turner insists that Blyden's "Pan-African internationalist perspective was very important because African-American Muslims in the Twentieth century would use it to globalize their religious political discourse."[27] Nonetheless, he does not believe that Blyden provided an adequate or accurate account of racial prejudice among Muslims and unwittingly constructed "the first myth of a race-blind Islam."[28] Given that Islam, when compared to European colonialism, allowed Africans to maintain a degree of political and cultural autonomy, Turner finds Blyden's extrapolation understandable.[29] However, Blyden reminded both Muslims and Christians—and this was emblematic of his African-centered outlook—that Africa incubated both religions in their infancy.[30] Yet he felt that Muslims, and especially the Prophet Muhammad himself, were far more willing than Christians to acknowledge Africa's contribution. Although Muslims were not free of racism or trading African slaves, Blyden held to the view that they had done far more than Christians to address racial distinctions among Islam's faithful and its social practices were more consistent with autonomous African civic and commercial development. Blyden may well have mistaken African "syncretisms" associated with West African Islam for Islam in its entirety. Turner contends that in Blydenite pan-Africanism "the black Muslim community model was the global tradeoff for the racism and slavery of Islam."[31]

Uppermost for Blyden was Islam's ability to accommodate African cultural nationalism and black republican aspiration. The first wave of powerful West African empires purposely assembled mixed forms of Islamic governance willing to accommodate African traditional religion and customary law.[32] Turner perceptively observes that, "on the eve of modernity, Islam in West Africa was destined for radical changes, although its themes of racial and cultural particularism, signification and jihad were destined to live on as the paradigm endemic to global Islam, and would later be utilized by black Muslims in America."[33] As organizations like the Moorish Science Temple and the Nation of Islam made clear, aspects of Islamic doctrine could be easily transformed into cultural nationalism, black liberation theology, or an eschatology based on the damnation of white people — all only remotely associated with established Islam. It is important, however, to recognize in these new doctrines that both Islam and Christianity are subsumed within cultural nationalist frameworks that often reflect the primacy of African traditions. In short, Blyden used Islam and Christianity, at one time or another, to express a black nationalist project or agenda.

Compared with Crummell and most other of his contemporaries, Blyden developed a far more respectful view of African tradition and its moral foundations. In 1892 Blyden announced that he was now teaching that Mohammedanism was the form of Christianity best adapted to the Negro race.[34] While noting his contradictory defense of both a strong African civilization and European imperialism, Tunde Adeleke does not include Blyden in his sarcastic characterization of men like Delany, Crummell, and McNeal Turner as "UnAfrican-Americans" — the title of his book.[35] In his 1881 Inaugural Address as president of Liberia College, Blyden warned his audience that Africans would never advance as long as they employed the methods of a foreign race. He declared, "we must study our brethren in the interior, who know better than we do the laws of growth for the race."[36]

By relating race development, cultural nationalism, and institution building, Blyden paved the way for future generations of black nationalist thinkers who would similarly transform strategies inspired by the struggle for independence on the continent into cultural nationalist precepts relevant to Africans in the Diaspora, and vice versa. Given that he called on Africans to return to their ancestral land, Blyden would not be sanguine about cultural nationalism or the idea of an African Diaspora—to the extent that these identities legitimated a continued black presence outside of Africa. Nevertheless, as Lamin Sanneh has recently shown, Blyden was part of a larger vanguard of men and women who returned home, especially to West Africa, from the African Diaspora with aspirations for economic development, racial equality, and political progress; many of the ideas they brought with them flew in the face of traditional structures of power and, thus, contributed to the evolution and character of modern African nationalism.[37]

Black Christian Nationalism Today

Based on several in-depth interviews with black religious nationalists, in this section I discuss themes in contemporary Christian nationalism, many of which mirror concerns similar to those of Blyden. The primary voices in this conversation are those of Reverend Jeremiah Wright, Elder M. Andrew Robinson-Gaither, Reverend Dr. Richard Byrd, Amina Thomas, and Naima Olugbala-Knox. I also refer to Conrad Worrill and Reverend Al Sampson.[38]

THE CALL

Reverend Dr. Richard Byrd is an ordained and licensed minister of the Unity Churches centered in Lees Summit, Missouri, outside Kansas City. As of 1991, the teachings of his KRST Unity Center for African Spirituality in Los Angeles were based on the Kemetic Text. Reverend Byrd's transition to Kemetic theology was not a part of his training as a Unity minister. He made the discovery through "prayer, meditation and asking Spirit for direction, in response to the crisis of our people as well as to a vision and a mission given to me." What was revealed to him was the fact that the New Thought doctrine of the Unity Church was fundamentally African spiritual teachings. He believes that, in several important respects, it was easier for him, as a Unity minister, to embrace an African-centered theology because "we don't hold up Jesus as God, or our Savior . . . God no more speaks through him than he does through us. When we look at our ancient African story, it is the same story that Unity tells." For example, says Byrd, the emblem of Unity, the Winged Globe, is directly from Egypt. Moreover, the founders of Unity acknowledge that it is from Egypt. However, they came along at the time of the revisionist theory of Egypt that purposely obscured its African origins. The founders of Unity would probably not have claimed it if they had known that it represented a black civilization. Still, the whole of New Thought is nothing more than ancient African spiritual teachings.

Despite his revelation, Reverend Byrd did not have the kind of information that he felt he needed on ancient African spirituality. However, during the weekend of his revelation, he heard Leonard Jefferies on the Pacifica radio station in Los Angeles and soon discovered that the Association for the Study of Classical African Civilizations (ASCAC) conference was meeting in town that very weekend. "Although I did not know anything about ASCAC, I came back with seven or eight books and I started devouring them. While I did not hear a direct affirmation of my own revelation at the conference, I knew from what I had heard that Spirit had directed me correctly. So, we started teaching."

Elder M. Andrew Robinson-Gaither of Faith United Methodist Church of Los Angeles has sought to bring to his congregation "a sense of black nationalism in the context of who they are as Christians." He goes on to say that "we have initially approached this concept through the Bible and changing our visual understanding of the Bible—that is we see the biblical people as people who look like us. And that liberates us to embrace a concept of black nationalism." Originally from Baltimore with an undergraduate degree in urban planning from Morehouse College in Atlanta and a masters of divinity from the Claremont School of Theology in California, Elder Robinson-Gaither describes himself as someone who spent a great deal of time running away from being called to the ministry. For a time, he was a graduate student at Claremont and affiliated with Wesley United Methodist Church in Los Angeles, at the time pastored by Reverend Sylvester Gillespie. Gillespie helped Robinson-Gaither come to grips with his call to the ministry. However, it was not until his graduate school days that Elder Robinson-Gaither came to fully appreciate the importance of an African-centered perspective. His goal is a theology that combines spiritual and self-liberation. Moreover, he strongly believes that had he not had a period of learning and reflection at Claremont, "I would not have been comfortable embracing liberation theology or black theology." Due to his divinity school experience, he says, "I am able to articulate why I reached a nationalist position." When first making his transition, Robinson-Gaither turned to local black nationalists like Maulana Ron Karenga for advice. In the end, however, his primary inspiration came from Reverend George Augustus Stallings of Washington, D.C. Stallings broke with the Roman Catholic Church in 1989 and founded the African-American Catholic Congregation that combines Catholic rites and African-centered worship. Robinson-Gaither says, "I came from a Pentecostal background with a strong spiritual foundation but a weak understanding of the social gospel. Therefore, I did not know how to move my people toward some kind of black enlightenment. At the time, George Stallings was wrestling with the Roman Catholic Church with respect to an Afrocentric agenda." A friend familiar with Stallings's ministry suggested that Robinson-Gaither go to Washington, D.C. to talk with him. He did, and the two of them communicate to this day. Says Robinson-Gaither, "we even toyed with the idea of a national organization that brings the church together with what we are comfortable with in black nationalism."

Reverend Jeremiah Wright denies the need for any "call to nationalism." His way of dealing with the origins of blackness in Christianity places him in a unique position to formulate a black Christian critique of nationalist criticism; this will be dealt with below. Reverend Wright believes that "when you find out how Africans practiced the faith in the New World as well as the fact that there were African Christians before slavery, there is no way you can come away not being African-centered. There is no need to inject anything. The Christian story cannot be separated from the African story."

He argues that his understanding grows out of the way he was raised. "My daddy was a student of Carter G. Woodson. I have been reading African/African-American history since I was ten or eleven years old." Consequently, recounts Wright, "I was having a serious problem with what I was hearing in church, in school, and at Virginia Union Seminary." When he got out of the service, he transferred to Howard and studied under Sterling Brown,

Arthur Davis, John Lovell, Chancellor Williams, and William Neal Hansberry. Wright believes that there is no way you can read J. A. Rodgers, John Henrik Clarke, Chancellor Williams, W. E. B. Du Bois, and slave narratives or hear work songs and spirituals without the black experience becoming part of your understanding of the Christian faith. "I don't need H. Rap Brown or Maulana Karenga; all what they are saying is very new when compared to older traditions of black nationalist thought."

Black ministers willing to make a connection between nationalism and black identity often attract former nationalists back to church and, more specifically, to their congregations. For example, Reverend Jeremiah Wright claims a strong nationalist membership at Trinity in Chicago. In Los Angeles, Reverend Frank M. Reid III, the pastor of Ward AME until the early 1980s, had a major impact on black nationalists who wanted to reconnect with the church. C. Eric Lincoln and Lawrence Mamiya describe Reid as "one of the more vocal black clergy in the political affairs of Southern California, supporting black nationalists and being involved in police-community relations issues."[39]

Both Amina Thomas and Naima Olugbala-Knox attribute their smooth transition back to the Christian fold to Reverend Reid, whom they remember as having been greatly influenced by Albert Cleage's *Black Christian Nationalism.* Reid had a close relationship with black nationalists in Los Angeles. Naima and Amina were both impressed by Reid's blend of theology and nationalism as well as how comfortable he seemed to be with nationalist issues and causes. Both Naima and Amina agree that there was also a generational affinity. Much their own age, Reid was, in their eyes, a young man seeking the truth of the connection between race and spirituality, as were they. For Naima, Reverend Reid represented a turning point at a time when she had not gone back to church but felt that she wanted to. Naima was working with the New African People's Organization (NAPO) and other black nationalist groupings close to the Republic of New Africa. One Sunday, along with Chokwe Lumumba, Mukungu, and several of their friends from the Pan-Africanist Congress of Azania (South Africa), Naima attended Ward AME. On this occasion, Reid turned the podium over to the nationalists and made a thousand-dollar contribution from his own pocket to the struggle in South Africa. "That," says Naima, "was an amazing day . . . I joined Ward the next year along with a whole bunch of other NAPO people." Amina, a former U.S.

activist, also became a member of Ward AME and recalls having been exposed to the black consciousness sermons of Reverend Wright through Reid and his ministry.

With respect to worship, Naima notes that nationalists, who had experienced a certain kind of African-centered form of religious expression whether grounded in Akan, Yoruba, or other belief systems, had been taught to deal with their spirituality in an African context. They took those experiences with them when they rejoined the church. "At Ward, Reverend Reid allowed you to freely express your African self in worship. We felt we had been turned loose to be free Africans and to worship as we pleased."

IMPLEMENTATION AND RESISTANCE

In the implementation of African-centered Christianity, Robinson-Gaither decided that he had to first confront the Eurocentric aesthetic that dominated Faith United Methodist Church. When he arrived, the church was considered a "transitional" church — a white church in the process of becoming black. Although the so-called transition began in 1971, it was still incomplete when he became pastor in 1986. In other words, "everything was conducted as if this was still an Anglo church." Robinson-Gaither felt that the removal of the church's white religious aesthetic was crucial to making his congregation "know that liberation is in you and in a God that looks like you." For example, we took down the Eurocentric windows and all the white images of Christ. However, this turned out to be a ten-year process, as part of the congregation resisted the changes. "Many of the older members of the church did not come around until other folk outside the church began to affirm the aesthetic changes." With respect to religious teachings, Robinson-Gaither brought in Cain Hope Felder, a scholar of the Old Testament from Howard University and a contributor to the *African Heritage Bible*. "Cain came and spent some time with us in order to help acclimate our people to placing the biblical story in an African context."

When Reverend Byrd introduced African spiritual teachings to his Unity congregation in 1991, the church tore up. A prominent member of the board of directors came to him and said "he could not serve with a Minister that wore an African hat." When Reverend Byrd called a board of directors meeting to deal with what the board member had said, he found that the others held similar views of his hat and African spirituality. Reverend Byrd promptly resigned. However, two respected elders came to him and insisted that he stay and fight for his position. He admits that, at the time, he really did not know a lot about African spiritual teachings, given that he had just been exposed. Even at that early stage, he recognized, "you have to listen to your elders if you are going to be of an African expression." Finally, the congregation voted to continue Reverend Byrd's ministry and the board of directors resigned.

However, Byrd would have to survive two more rebellions, and he was constantly questioned about the direction in which he was trying to take the church. He was unsure himself; he only knew that African spirituality and the needs of the black community had to be the focus of his mission. He also surmised that those in the congregation who were in interracial marriages (or whose children were) had the most difficulty with the changes. When Reverend Byrd hung a beautiful African tapestry as a backdrop for the altar, he discovered that "one of my board members, a beautiful black woman with a daughter married to an Italian, got headaches severe enough to warrant her leaving the church."

Rather than make an abrupt change in the conduct of worship, Reverend Byrd decided on a two-tiered strategy. In 1993 he initiated a night service called the "Center for African Spirituality" while continuing with Unity theology at the usual morning service. In the evening, he began to invite high-profile black nationalists from around the country. Those who he thought would be too much for the moderate morning service he confined to the Center of African Spirituality. On the other hand, those nationalists considered to have crossover appeal were allowed to participate in the morning service. In this way, Reverend Byrd gradually integrated the two services over time.

Since his church was only ten years old when he became its pastor, Reverend Wright feels fortunate not to have inherited a church that consisted of a group of "Negroes who have wanted to be white for fifty years." When he came to Trinity, he recalls, there were three people over sixty. He did face some problems because his congregation wanted to be a black church that represented the black community. However, "saying that intellectually, theologically, and cognitively, you want to be a black church is very different than experiencing that existentially. So when the music changed and the socioeconomic level changed because we started welcoming everybody, twenty-two of my original eighty-seven members left because they just could not handle it." In 1981, without any coaxing from him, Reverend Wright's congregation adopted a black value system that was unrelated to Maulana Karenga's Kawaida system. The system adopted by Trinity was based on the dual commitment to God and the black community. According to Reverend Wright, value number eight was especially interesting in that it disavowed the very notion of a black middle class and drew a distinction between the pursuit of a better income and a middle-class status and mentality. As Reverend Wright puts it, "Karl Marx was not talking about black people."

ON CHURCH PARTICIPATION

The nationalist critique functions at two levels. The grand critique has to do with the nature of the church as an institution. As Conrad Worrill, a well-known Chicago nationalist, puts it, "you cannot make a white institution black. Black people are Baptist because white people were Baptist, not out of any innovation on their part." Although acknowledging that Christianity is older than European hegemony in the religion, many nationalists point to the Council of Nicaea in A.D. 325 as the watershed for its co-optation by Europeans. Here, we need only remember Blyden's observation that "since Christianity left the place of its birth it has seemed to be the property exclusively of the European branch of the human family."[40] Therefore, those nationalists concerned with the subject are fond of drawing a distinction between "religion" and "spirituality." Thus, black nationalists tend to link their grand critique, based on the racial character of black institutions, to a more pedestrian criticism of the church as civic participant. To borrow Fred Harris's antinomy, nationalists are able to reject the idea of black religion as inspiration and offer a race-based argument for Christianity as an opiate of black people.[41]

Reverend Al Sampson of Fernwood United Methodist Church in Chicago believes that there are three types of African American churches. The entertainment church has no concern whatsoever with community transformation. The containment church, where a modern-day "talented tenth" gathers to worship, completely ignores its responsibility to the black community. In contrast, the Martin Luther King church, says Sampson, "stands, as King did, for taking the church out of the church and into the community, but when King was assassinated, the church left the community and went back to church." Sampson strongly identifies with the King church.

Rejecting the idea that a black or liberation theology can resolve the "national question" in Christianity, Reverend Byrd contends that it does not make a difference whether "Jesus is an African or a Chinaman . . . you still have a dependent religion based on a slave tradition that places the power for your life in the hands of someone outside yourself." For Reverend Byrd, a failure to reinterpret the Eurocentric foundations of theology simply means that dependency remains the core subtext of an ostensibly black institution where "so much energy is put into wrong ideas." When confronted with the argument that Africans in America transformed Christianity, Byrd has a simple answer: "That's hokum!" He reasons that while Africans may have transformed Christian music and the style of worship, this resulted in a worse trap, given that black people's natural spirituality was perverted. The power to emote got confused with the genuinely transformative nature of African spirituality. "We think we have experienced a change when all we've done is emoted." Since it makes black Christians complacent and freezes them in place, Reverend Byrd believes that there is a direct relation between a theology of dependency and a lack of civic participation. Byrd's interpretation of the way whites deal with institutionalized religion and participation is absolutely Blydenesque. "White people have no problem with going to church on Sunday and doing their hour or two, at the maximum, and getting up on Sunday afternoon and taking care of business. They are able to compartmentalize and this allows them to engage in destruction, war, and calamity the rest of the week." Byrd is deeply concerned by the condition of the black community, especially with respect to the number of young black men in prison and the cocaine epidemic. He concludes, "Christian ministers are caught in a framework that makes it impossible for them to be involved with a truly revolutionary transformation in our community."

Elder Robinson-Gaither works closely with Reverend Byrd in Los Angeles Metropolitan Churches (LAM) and the October 22nd Coalition that fights police brutality and the criminalization of a generation of black youth. Byrd is the cofounder of LAM and Robinson-Gaither the faith coordinator for the October 22nd Coalition. He readily admits that for most of his black clergy colleagues, "nationalism is just not where they see themselves. . . . In this city, black nationalism is a minority position embraced mostly by Richard Byrd and myself." However, Robinson-Gaither believes that the late Reverend Cleage and his Church of the Black Madonna "laid the foundation for unifying the church and nationalism." One of the things Robinson-Gaither feels that nationalism has given him is "the ability to embrace issues that are not safe issues." He thinks that the black clergy tends to grab onto far too many safe issues. "For example, AIDS is not a safe issue." Robinson-Gaither is a strong proponent of women's and gay rights. Indeed, one strand of black nationalism he rejected early on was African tradition as a justification for male chauvinism. While the black clergy and nationalists may disagree on many issues, Robinson-Gaither believes that they nonetheless share a deep homophobia. Departing from their practices in the sixties, he notes that some local nationalist groups, such as the Organization U.S., have placed women in major positions of authority. "Oddly, now that women are poised to as-sume pastoral leadership, it is the women sitting in the pews who do not want women in the pulpit. However with respect to gays, the black church community finds a drug addict more acceptable than a homosexual."

Despite their charisma and large followings, Robinson-Gaither considers ministers like Reverends Wright of Chicago and Reid of Baltimore to belong to a safe stream of nationalism. He places himself, Stallings, and Byrd in a more genuine nationalist tradition. In his estimation, these two streams are distinguished by the kinds of political issues to which the ministers relate and the centrality of black struggle in the devotional life of the church. In his own case, he hosted the families and lawyers of the black youth who attacked Reginald Denny during the 1992 disturbances in Los Angeles and honors Malcolm X's birthday at the devotional hour. Even in the case of a church like Reverend Cecil Murray's First AME in Los Angeles, Robinson-Gaither would argue that its nationalist potential is hamstrung by the middle-class aspira-tions of its congregation. He considers his church to be the seat of grassroots activism in the city. For example, Geronimo ji Jaga came to Faith United after his release from prison; he was at odds with First AME because Julius But-ler—the black man who conspired with white authorities to send Geronimo to jail—was a member.

According to Robinson-Gaither, the wealthiest and most powerful churches in Los Angeles—West Angeles, First AME, Greater Bethany, and Faithful Central—derive a portion of their income from large corporations, and they are, therefore, prevented from being socially prophetic, for that would jeopardize revenue. While they do not place their activities within the framework of any nationalist agenda, most of the large churches are engaged in affordable housing and other development projects. With respect to the need for the black church to engage in economic development, the Los Angeles civil unrest of 1992 was a turning point for Robinson-Gaither. After the uprising, it was apparent that black people had been left out of the recovery. At the same time, the unrest gave him the best opportunity to use his church as a bully pulpit. While most of his social gospel instincts are left-liberal, Robinson-Gaither is a Blydenite in a very basic sense. "I have embraced a segregationist model of community development. I do not want to integrate. When we were segregated, we had money in the black community; we had legitimate, lucrative black businesses, despite the existence of illegal activities like numbers running. The money stayed in our community and supported businesses and churches. I consider myself a realist and I know folk do not like to hear me to say this." Interestingly, Naima remembers the Church of God in Christ as having had serious community outreach that fed the hungry and ministered in the Mission District of Los Angeles. Robinson-Gaither, on the other hand, attributes innovations in faith-based services to the more nationalistic and nonmainstream religious movements from Daddy Grace to the Black Panther Party.

CHRISTIANITY AND ISLAM

Naima says, "Think about how far our understanding of Islam has come over the last thirty years or so. When Muhammad Ali came out and said that he would not go to Vietnam, my mother's generation assumed that it was the result of his being a Muslim. They never thought that he might be using Islam to express his blackness." Naima has vivid memories of the relationship between Reverend Reid and Minister Louis Farrakhan of the Nation of Islam (NOI). "Farrakhan had a real bad position on Jesus Christ and it was Reid who helped him to reevaluate it." The Muslims had always maintained that Jesus was not the Son of God but rather a prophet like John or Paul. They often went so far as to suggest that Jesus was merely a disciple of Master W. D. Fard Muhammad, the same man who converted Elijah Muhammad to Islam. Naima could see that the joint statements issued by Reid and Farrakhan were politically worded, but for her "the bottom line was that black Muslims would not teach against Jesus; this was important for me as a young black nationalist trying to reconnect with the church." Nor was the relationship between black ministers and Farrakhan a one-way street. Reverends Wright and Reid, recalls Naima, incorporated features of the NOI such as a prison ministry and a Band of Men inspired by the Fruit of Islam.

At one time or another, Robinson-Gaither has housed the activities of three of the six or so factions of the NOI and feels that he has a good relationship with the movement. Despite the past, he does not believe that the NOI in any way seeks to discredit the black clergy. If anything, "Farrakhan has tried to encourage black clergy to work with the Nation of Islam." Various NOI groups have asked Robinson-Gaither to collaborate with them on economic development ventures. In his assessment, the NOI is far more respecting of black clergy than the other way around. "Based upon my relationship with the Muslims in Los Angeles, they have a great respect for the Christian churches, but the black churches do not have any respect for them." Moreover, he does not think that the Muslims have an incentive to attack Jesus. After all, they are trying to attract people who are leaving the church and this, he finds, to be another two-way street. "Many of the men who have been attracted to the ministry at my church were, at one time, a part of the Nation or some other Islamic group."

Robinson-Gaither is convinced that the wedding of nationalism and religion is the deciding factor in the NOI's appeal in the inner city. He does not believe that the NOI really has a spiritual agenda or, for that matter, a coherent theology based on God-consciousness. The Nation's emphasis on proper male-female relationships and how the Muslim family should operate within the NOI, in Robinson-Gaither's estimation, comes closest to approximating an indigenous black theology. On reflection, many of his congregants who have been members of the NOI conclude that the experience was more social than spiritual.

Still, there is a fear of Muslims among black clergy. Some of it has to do with the belief that Islamic movements are taking black men from churches. Says Robinson-Gaither, "The men are not coming back; many find the discipline and regimentation in the NOI very attractive." He goes on to relate an interesting experience. "Awhile back, there were a series of advertisements on the radio announcing Muslim Awareness Workshops which were associated with powerful churches like West Angeles and Faithful Central. Word has it that some conservative white faith group from Orange County handsomely sponsored these ads. I consider Muslims as my brothers and sisters and believe that they should be allowed to express their faith in the manner they see fit. I immediately called West Angeles and let them know how divisive I thought the ads were."

While Wright and Robinson-Gaither disagree over how much credit the Muslims should be given for the Million Man March, they agree that Farrakhan's appeal derives from his image as a "truth teller" who does not fear the white establishment. From their respective points of view, Farrakhan's nationalism benefits the black clergy; he makes the extreme case, allowing black ministers not to have to. In Wright's words, "We need someone who can scare white folks into paying attention and who pulls the cover off of hypocrisy, racism, and white supremacy." With respect to the Million Man March, Robinson-Gaither argues that, at least among average black men, it showed that the NOI had serious credibility. Reverend Wright simply says, "Do your math! If the Muslims can only claim a national membership of 40,000, the other 960,000 black men at the March had to be Christians." Wright has a working relationship with the NOI and other groups in Chicago and was a member of a delegation of black leaders who attended the 1984 Libyan Peace Conference where Farrakhan spoke on topics ranging from Black Muslim mythology to Yakub and the Mothership. Wright and other black nationalists in attendance were surprised to find that Farrakhan's speech and his brand of Islam infuriated Muslim leftists and fundamentalists assembled in Tripoli.

Both a Pentecostal minister and scholar, Louis DeCaro contends that Farrakhan longs for the very thing he can never possess—the mantle of the black church. "He may win the hearts of individual Christian pastors and may even enjoy the arm's-length favor of many Christian people, but like Simon Magus of old, he is caught in the galling trick bag of his own religious legacy."[42]

CRITIQUING THE CRITIQUE

Of the Christian nationalists I spoke with, Reverend Jeremiah Wright is best placed to offer, and does, the most systematic critique of the nationalist position on the church. Chicago, his home base, boasts the largest and most well-organized black nationalist community in the country. In addition, it is evident from his conversation and insights that Wright is a scholar of black history and religion and he has given considerable thought to the relationship between black nationalism and Christianity. He begins by stating that he has "never met a black nationalist who has a personal relationship with Christ.

Christianity has to do with devotional life, religious language, and a personal relationship with the Lord." Reverend Wright goes on to say that he is familiar with two types of nationalists: secular problack nationalists who have no real spiritual commitment and the Kemetic nationalists, like J. Carruthers (of Chicago), who actually organize African-centered worship services.

Wright has three fundamental political criticisms of black nationalists. First, while they cannot stand to be lumped together, they refuse to make distinctions when it comes to the different political positions among black clergy. They conveniently harp on conservatives and so-called Uncle Toms associated with the church but choose to ignore the fact that the entire black abolitionist tradition — including Denmark Vesey, Gabriel Prosser, Nat Turner, Harriet Tubman, and Frederick Douglass — were all ministers. Second, black nationalists constantly attack the church for its lack of participation. Yet whenever they get into political trouble or need support and/or troops, they come running to the black clergy. He asks rhetorically, "How many followers do black nationalists really have?" Third, for all their talk about "institution-building," nationalists have few institutions that can be compared to the black church or its community development programs on a national scale. However, Wright is well aware that, despite their lack of accomplishment, nationalists have a peculiar kind of legitimacy in black communities that reminds one of an Irish adage — "a nationalist may live a life of relative obscurity and poverty, but you would not know that by the people who turn out for his/her funeral."

Reverend Wright recognizes that one of the problems the average member of the black clergy faces in dealings with black nationalists is that the former are often not well trained in the ways theology relates to the black experience. Many members of the clergy are self-proclaimed bishops or apostles. "These ministers have never heard of the *Negative Confessions,* the *Egyptian Book of the Dead,* or Chancellor Williams." According to Wright, the average black minister cannot hold his own against black nationalist critiques of the church, which are grounded in African/African-American literature, religion, and history. While he feels that a new generation of clergy is being better trained at seminaries like Howard, the Interdenominational Theological Center (ITC), Morehouse, Virginia Union, Shaw, and Payne, Wright insists that too many black ministers only know the Bible and are not conversant with its African context.

Although clearly influenced by currents in African nationalism and pan-Africanism, Wright is primarily an African American nationalist. He believes that giving up your African American identity is like allowing an airline to take your carry-on luggage. Wright asserts that when black nationalists try to "leap back through West Africa to Egypt," they betray something valuable in their African American identity. Indeed, similar to Wright, Wilson J. Moses, the accomplished scholar of nineteenth-century black nationalism, confesses that he does not share the current obsession with Egypt.[43] Moses believes that the idea of Afrocentrism is broader, and far more complex, than Egypto-centrism — an exclusive focus on whether Egypt was a black civilization and harbinger of all others.

Central to his defense against criticisms by Kemetic or Egyptocentric theologians, Wright refuses to concede that African American Christianity has been racially corrupted. Black nationalists are so angry at whites, and the lies they have told about Christianity, that they do not engage in an in-depth study of Christianity before slavery. When Wright reflects on the use of Islam to criticize Christianity, the influence of Chancellor Williams, who was his professor at Howard, is evident. "We always concentrate on the Atlantic Slave Trade and forget how mean Muslim slavery was. If Muslims had not sent black slaves as a gift to Prince Henry of Portugal, the Europeans might have never got in on the slave trade." Wright refuses to countenance any moralizing from black Muslims on the issue of slavery. Although he is a knowledgeable admirer of Blyden, Wright does not understand how he downplayed Muslim slavery or converted to Islam in old age. Much like Richard Brent Turner, Wright does not accept Blyden's construction of a color-blind Islam, but he does admire the farsightedness of Blyden's nationalism. Wright carefully constructs an argument designed to undermine the popular historiography that supports black nationalist criticisms of the church. Nor is Wright above a humorous moral dig at his numerous black nationalist friends. With specific nationalists in mind, he retorts, "Most of their former wives attend Trinity now. Some have to talk to their daughters and sons through me when they are not speaking. I don't want to hear all this nationalist rhetoric about African-centered family values."

Conclusion: Convergence and Contention

Few, if any, black secular nationalists harbor hopes of supplanting the un-questioned cultural hegemony of the church in African American communi-ties. As evident from our interviews, black Christian nationalists recognize, despite the comingling of race conscious and religious sentiments in black churches, that theirs is a minority position. Secular nationalist critics external to the church may be vulnerable to the countercriticisms so aptly put forward by Reverend Wright in his "critique of the critique." However, Wright and the other Christian nationalists share a disquiet regarding the black church as a prophetic voice and an institution for community renewal and trans-formation—values central to the church's own traditions and sense of mis-sion. In Wilmore's forceful words, "Black pride and power, black nationalism and Pan-Africanism have had no past without the black church and black religion, and without them they may well have no enduring future."[44] With respect to challenges currently facing black communities, Mark Chapman believes that, at least in African American religious thought, Christianity re-mains on trial and divided.[45]

At any given time, institutions have to adapt to social movements and on many occasions become conduits for currents of political change. The rise of social movements and shifts in black mass attitudes have had a great im-pact on the church as an institution. Over time, this has created both conten-tion and convergence between religion and nationalism. All of the Christian nationalists interviewed wanted the black church to better reflect cultural values that speak to the African American heritage, social crises in black com-munities, and issues of esteem associated with being black in America. For Reverend Jeremiah Wright's congregation, this meant the development of a black-conscious value system; Robinson-Gaither introduced his congre-gation to the *African Heritage Bible* and struggled with them about remov-ing the omnipresent white aesthetic that dominated the sanctuary. Reverend Byrd took even more drastic measures. Given their past or present involve-ment with nonreligious pan-African nationalist movements, Byrd, Amina Thomas, and Naima Olugbala-Knox were in search of a deeper synthesis of spirituality and explicit nationalist politics. A good deal of the conversation between black nationalists and their Christian sisters and brothers is essentially about comprehending the nature of change—most often by looking through the lens of the past.

However, as Fred Harris astutely observes, "the exclusion of African Americans from the nation's civic and social life with the onset of Jim Crow cemented a racialized public sphere."[46] In our day, black clerics, who are viewed as indigenous leaders and, consequently, wooed by political entrepreneurs, have become the most crucial connection between the establishment (black or white) and a *black counterpublic* consisting of religious institutions, social movements, civil rights organizations, black magazines and newspapers, Masonic groups, social clubs, and many other black institutions.[47] Today as in the past—even if not under the threat of legal segregation—the black clergy and black nationalists inhabit a separate racial sphere—a world of "spatial separations built on pre-established social demarcations between blacks and whites."[48] Harris is right in his observation that "when mobilized, individuals do not detach themselves from their cultural milieu."[49] With respect to political participation, a black "public sphere" can be imagined from the vantage point of pluralism or separatism—as a national African American community or as a black nation within a white one. These contrasting ways to imagine black public life have always cut across the black political spectrum and continue to shape patterns of ideological contention and convergence in black politics.

From Blyden to Garvey to the Nation of Islam, most nationalist movements have infused a religious or spiritual agenda—primarily Christian although not exclusively—into their programs. All of the nationalists interviewed for this chapter, whether critical of the movement or not, utilized the NOI as a means of holding up a mirror to some failure of the black church. The relationship between nationalism and the church has always had a symbiotic dimension. Richard Burkett dissuades us of the view that there was an unbridgeable chasm between the clergy and black nationalists during Garvey's time or, for that matter, any other.[50] Garvey considered the Universal Improvement Association (UNIA) to be essentially a religious organization and did not think that, "anyone who gets up to attack religion will get the sympathy of this house."[51] The relationship was reciprocal. "Every independent Black denomination with a membership of more than twenty-five thousand in 1920 had clergymen who were actively working on behalf of the UNIA, as did many of the smaller independent Black denominations."[52] Set in this historical context, Robinson-Gaither's observation that many of the men in his inner-city Los Angeles congregation are former Muslims should come as no surprise. Indeed, Black Muslims may be more comfortable with Byrd and Robinson-Gaither because they cling to the separatist tradition of Albert Cleage. Cleage could not have made the Christian nationalist position any clearer. "Black Christian Nationalism joins this select company of Black men who have realized that integration is death and separatism is life."[53] As he saw it, a black theology that did not emphasize the "black nation" was in fact courting genocide.[54] Elijah Muhammad, in his characteristically direct style, reduces black republicanism to a basic principle, "love your own kind."[55] In the 1960s, Maulana Ron Karenga, a leading cultural nationalist, identified four basic contradictions of the black church—a false feeling of power, a faulty concept of black people, incessant internal conflicts, and lack of a viable political structure.[56]

Therefore today, as in the past, the dynamics of racial-nationality play themselves out in the overall social, intellectual, and spiritual life of most black religious institutions. And for many, black congregants and clergy alike, liberal strategies rooted in appeals to moral conscience and liberal democracy are necessary but insufficient as a foundation for black church action. Black republicans, including members of the clergy, insist that the mode of black political participation *should* be dictated by a conception of the African American people as a "cultural nation." Thus, religion, per se, is not the central difference between nationalists and the mainstream of the black clergy but rather how religious institutions relate to the construction of "racial-nationality."

Herein, I have maintained that the black republicanism of Blyden and other nineteenth-century thinkers informs present-day black nationalist critiques of the African American church. Black republicanism connotes a form of collective political identity, a sense of peoplehood based on racial sentiments. However, "republicanism, unlike nationalism, is an idea about the form and nature of government as opposed to the liberation of a people from alien rule or the exercise of national power."[57] The intermingling of these two imagined communities—Christian and nationalist—will continue to converge and contend as well as to connect and reconnect the themes of salvation and self-governance in African American political and religious culture.

Notes

1 Partha Chatterjee, *The Nation and Its Fragments: Colonial and Postcolonial Histories* (Princeton: Princeton University Press), 5.

2 Ibid., 6.

3 Gayraud S. Wilmore, *Black Religion and Black Radicalism: An Interpretation of the Religious History of the Afro-American People,* 2d ed. (New York: Orbis Books, 1983), 100.

4 Joseph R. Washington Jr., ed., *Black Religion and Public Policy: Ethical and Historical Perspectives* (A personally revised and published collection of the papers from the conference on "Black Religion and Public Policy" sponsored by the Afro-American Studies Program at the University of Pennsylvania, March 1978): iii–iv.

5 In Hollis R. Lynch, *Edward Wilmot Blyden: Pan-Negro Patriot, 1832–1912* (London: Oxford University Press, 1970), 241.

6 Ibid., 81.

7 Ibid., 30.

8 Albert Raboteau, *A Fire in the Bones: Reflections on African-American Religious History* (Boston: Beacon Press, 1995), 35.

9 St. Clair Drake, *The Redemption of Africa and Black Religion* (Chicago: Third World Press, 1970), 54.

10 Kola Adelaja, "Nineteenth-Century Social Thought: Blyden's Ideas on Religion," in Onigu Otite, ed., *Themes in African Political and Social Thought* (Enugu, Nigeria: Fourth Dimension Publishers: 1978), 187.

11 Robert W. July, *The Origins of Modern African Political Thought: Its Development in West Africa During the Nineteenth and Twentieth Centuries* (New York: Frederick A. Praeger, 1967), 210.

12 Quoted in V. Y. Mudimbe, *The Invention of Africa: Gnosis, Philosophy, and the Order of Knowledge* (Bloomington: Indiana University Press, 1988), 106.

13 Edward Wilmot Blyden, *Christianity, Islam, and the Negro Race* (Chicago: Aldine Publishing Company, 1969), 77.

14 Blyden, *Christianity,* 32.

15 Mudimbe, *Invention of Africa,* 114.

16 Blyden, *Christianity,* 6.

17 Lynch, *Blyden,* 30.

18 Blyden, *Christianity,* 75.

19 Mudimbe, *Invention of Africa,* 106.

20 July, *Origins of Modern African Thought,* 214.

21 Blyden, *Christianity,* 10.

22 Lynch, *Blyden,* 55.

23 Blyden, *Christianity*, 37.

24 Blyden, *Christianity*, 24

25 Richard Brent Turner, *Islam in the African-American Experience* (Bloomington: Indiana University Press, 1997), 53.

26 Louis A. DeCaro Jr., *Malcolm and the Cross* (New York: New York University Press, 1998), 4

27 Turner, *Islam*, 52.

28 Ibid., 55.

29 Ibid., 52.

30 Ibid., 13.

31 Ibid., 55.

32 Ibid., 19.

33 Ibid., 21.

34 July, *Origins of Modern African Thought*, 227.

35 Tunde Adeleke, *UnAfrican Americans: Nineteeth-Century Black Nationalists and the Civilizing Mission* (Lexington: University of Kentucky Press, 1998), 13.

36 Blyden, *Christianity*, 77–78.

37 See Lamin Sanneh, *Abolitionist Abroad: American Blacks and the Making of Modern West Africa* (Cambridge: Harvard University Press, 1999).

38 Jeremiah Wright, 2000, telephone interview by author, Los Angeles, 26 April 2000. M. Andrew Robinson-Gaither, interview by author, Los Angeles, 4 April 2000. Richard Byrd, interview by author, Los Angeles, 27 February 2000. Amina Thomas and Naima Olugbala-Knox, interview by author, Altadena, California, 26 February 2000. I also refer to Conrad Worrill and Reverend Al Sampson, with whom I had long telephone conversations between 2 and 3 May 2000 on this subject. Reverend Wright is the minister of Trinity Unity Church of Christ in Chicago. Reverend Dr. Byrd is the senior minister at the KRST Center of African Spirituality in Los Angeles. Amina Thomas is a former member of U.S. Organization, an itinerant deacon for AME Church, and will soon be an ordained elder. Naima Olugbala-Knox is the cofounder of Omoyale Ujamaa—Northwest Community School, a former member of the Republic of New Africa, and an ordained elder in the AME Church.

39 C. Eric Lincoln and Lawrence H. Mamiya, *The Black Church in the African-American Experience* (Durham, N.C.: Duke University Press, 1990), 387.

40 Blyden, *Christianity*, 241.

41 Fredrick C. Harris, *Something Within: Religion in African-American Political Activism* (New York: Oxford University Press, 1999), 5–7.

42 DeCaro, *Malcolm and the Cross*, 5.

43 Wilson J. Moses, *Afrotopia: The Roots of African-American Popular History* (Cambridge: Cambridge University Press, 1998), 1.

44   Wilmore, *Black Religion,* x.

45   See Mark L. Chapman, *Christianity on Trial: African-American Religious Thought Before and After Black Power* (Maryknoll, N.Y.: Orbis Books, 1996), chapters 1 and 2.

46   Harris, *Something Within,* 9.

47   Ibid.

48   R. Drew Smith, "Black Religious Nationalism and the Politics of Transcendence," *Journal of the American Academy of Religion* 66, no. 3 (1998): 535.

49   Harris, *Something Within,* 136.

50   See his *Black Redemption: Churchmen Speak for the Garvey Movement* (Philadelphia: Temple University Press, 1978).

51   Robert A. Hill, introduction to *Marcus Garvey: Life and Lessons,* ed. Robert A. Hill and Barbara Bair (Berkeley: University of California Press, 1987), xxxvii.

52   Drake, introduction, *The Redemption of Africa and Black Religion,* xvii.

53   Albert B. Cleage Jr., *Black Christian Nationalism: New Directions for the Black Church* (New York: William Morrow Company, 1972), 12.

54   Ibid., xvii.

55   Chapman, *Christianity on Trial,* 53.

56   "Kawaida Doctrine Book" (personal papers).

57   Richard L. Sklar, foreword to *Black Political Thought in the Making of South African Democracy* by C. R. D. Halisi (Bloomington: Indiana University Press, 1999), xi.

PART III

Black Churches and "Faith-Based Initiatives"

9

DOING SOMETHING IN JESUS' NAME:

BLACK CHURCHES AND COMMUNITY

DEVELOPMENT CORPORATIONS

Michael Leo Owens

A critique of black churches is that they are detached from the secular problems of urban blacks.[1] During the 1960s, sociologist Kenneth Clarke observed that one could "regard the church as basically irrelevant to the hard and difficult realities of race."[2] Three decades later, sociologists C. Eric Lincoln and Lawrence Mamiya noted that there is still "a sector of black churches and clergy who stress an otherwordly, pie-in-the-sky attitude toward everyday social and political problems"—a sector that does little to address the social needs and political interests of urban blacks.[3] However, there are many activist black churches concerned with the temporal problems and secular concerns of their communities, and they are committed to translating their concerns into action.

Although black churches cannot do everything to reverse the negative conditions in urban black neighborhoods, they can, to quote a worshiper at Ebenezer Missionary Baptist Church in Flushing, New York, "do something in Jesus' name that would make a difference and bring glory to God."[4] The "something" many activist black churches, independently and collectively, have done in the name of their Lord is engage in community development, which is a process that unites the efforts of citizens with those of governmental authorities and private institutions to improve the physical, economic, and social conditions of communities, to integrate neighborhoods into the life of cities, and to enable them to contribute fully to the progress of cities.[5]

Community development corporations (CDCs) are often essential to successful community development, and black churches across the country have experimented with them to revitalize their geographic communities, both urban and rural, as well as reinvigorate the faith communities that gather inside their edifices. CDCs are tax-exempt, not-for-profit organizations covered by Section 501(c)(3) of the Internal Revenue Code. Specifically, they are neighborhood-based, nonprofit corporations existing to meet the values, needs, and interests of an identifiable constituency through the provision of goods and services that contribute to its general welfare.[6] CDCs associated with black churches may be nonprofit subsidiaries that individual black churches charter by self-initiative or nonprofit ecumenical institutions black churches create through collective action. Presently, black church-associated CDCs, regardless of type, are among the most recognized CDCs in urban America.[7] Examples include the Renaissance Development Corporation of First AME Church in Los Angeles and REACH, Inc. of the Twelfth Street Missionary Baptist Church in Detroit.

The use of CDCs by black churches exhibits their "flexibility in adopting new approaches to the exigencies of the times."[8] It also demonstrates their desire to increase the production and reliability of their service to black communities, along with the efficiency and effectiveness of their ministries. Black churches are looking to solve, or at least manage well, the social problems that have increased in Afro-America due to the macroeconomic, demographic, moral, and political changes that social scientists believe negatively affect black communities, while manifesting fully their Afro-Christian faith tradition by serving the needy, and perhaps in the process saving souls.[9] Nevertheless, the use of CDCs by black churches reveals their understanding of the interdependence of the public sector and civil society, especially the third sector. Since the 1960s, the public sector routinely relied on public-nonprofit partnerships to address collective problems. According to Stephen Monsma, by the 1990s these partnerships had both survived and prospered, with church-associated nonprofit organizations participating in and benefiting from them.[10]

From the perspective of black churches, the advantages of chartering CDCs include risk management, efficiency, institutionalization, access to public/nonprofit funds, "spiritual integrity," and focused purpose, while deflecting the proselytizing critique and confirming the churches' commitment to their neighborhoods.[11] From the perspective of the communities served by CDCs

associated with black churches, the advantages include the presence of indigenous incubators for socioeconomic change; access to new financial and
human capital; a heightened sensitivity to neighborhood needs; and new
needed services and programs.[12]

Black church-associated CDCs have "created some of the most persis-
tent and innovative community development programs in [cities]; they have
organized significant resources for the benefit of the poor; and they have
contributed to the national dialogue about faith-based development."[13] In
some cities, black church-associated CDCs—not electoral participation—
are a preeminent means by which urban blacks alter the physical and economic conditions of their communities.[14] Policymakers revere them, cele-
brating their activities and achievements in the areas of affordable housing
production, social services delivery, and innovative job creation.[15] Scholars
identify them as forces for positive change in the opportunity structures of
black neighborhoods.[16] In short, black church-associated CDCs are meaningful civic and social institutions, which one scholar calls "rising stars" in the
urban policy arena.[17]

This chapter considers the role of black church-associated CDCs as civic
and social institutions in urban black neighborhoods. It is based on surveys
and face-to-face key informant interviews with directors and staff of nine
black church-associated CDCs, along with an in-person survey of pastors of
ten activist black churches that have or support CDCs in New York City, which
arguably has the greatest concentration of black church-associated CDCs.[18]
Focusing on the works of black church-associated CDCs since the Reagan era,
this chapter overviews the origins, organizational types, interactions with
government, and the programs of black church-associated CDCs to improve
the physical conditions and socioeconomic opportunity structure in urban
black neighborhoods. In doing so, it demonstrates that black churches that
use CDCs routinely engage government not as an adversary but as an ally.
This is because the process of community development requires partnerships
between self-initiative and the dominant institutions of civil society and the
states. Nevertheless, such partnerships may have a deleterious effect on black
electoral participation in cities.

Reagan and Faith-Based Self-Initiative

Throughout the 1980s, the Reagan Administration made the work of bettering the life-chances of blacks eking out lives in inner-city neighborhoods tough. Federal government assistance to poor citizens grew modestly, while social and human services grants to city governments and community groups declined. This period in American history witnessed the "first reductions of consequence in grants-in-aid to expenditures since the 1940s."[19] A 1989 survey of city financial officers found that 86 percent reported that their city governments received less federal aid than they did at the start of the 1980s.[20] More than one-third of their city governments eliminated various municipal services and cut municipal workforces as a consequence of federal urban divestment. One observer described the actions of the federal government as "savaging housing and neighborhood programs designed to help cities and their poor."[21]

In New York City, while the Reagan reductions in federal aid took effect, conditions in urban black neighborhoods worsened. Unemployment rose to record levels. Homelessness became visible. The crack trade grew deadly, as the underground economy boomed and gangs fought for control of street corners. Segments of the black middle class and working class fled to the suburbs. Yet activist black churches remained in the city's distressed black neighborhoods and stood with their residents to face the consequences of cuts in federal funding and services. As community-based institutions distressed by the physical and socioeconomic conditions in the city's black neighborhoods, these churches developed new programs to address social needs in their neighborhoods.

The churches that stood with their communities rooted themselves in a liberal exegesis of the New Testament. Reverend Dr. William Augustus Jones of Bethany Baptist Church in Bedford-Stuyvesant writes in *God in the Ghetto* about the biblical influences on the activism of his church and his peers: "Jesus prayed as a priest that His Church would be prophetic. His petition made no room for a wordless witness. Believers are in the world and of the Church. Monasticism and asceticism are not presented in the Gospel narratives as models of Christian witness." Furthermore, the expectations of their congregants and community's residents spurred the churches to act. Reverend Gary Simpson of Concord Baptist Church of Christ in Bedford-

Stuyvesant observes: "Folks in the neighborhood expect[ed] much more from a local black church than a rousing sermon and a firm handshake from the pastor on the way out."[22]

The times, too, required the churches to change and experiment, for the pursuit of dramatic reductions in the breadth and depth of social, physical, and economic problems in black neighborhoods demanded broader definitions of ministry and missions. For some activist black churches in the city, the CDC accommodated their needs and provided a practical institution for neighborhood-based development. An informant of the Faith Center for Community Development comments:

> Back in the eighties, the Reagan-Bush years, government pulled out very extensively in giving money to the communities in need, and you know who lived in those communities. [Interviewer: No. Who?] You're funny. All right, I'll say it—blacks. Anyway, those pullbacks hurt our communities. The programs that were in place just couldn't continue to meet the need. Reaganomics caught up with us and it was a stretch for black people. I mean federal housing dollars ceased to come into the city. I'm exaggerating, but you know what I mean. Then crack [cocaine] restructured reality. Remember the violence? Remember the border babies? It was horrible. It really was. That encouraged the increase in our churches and other religious institutions stepping up their actions and activities in the whole process of black neighborhood redevelopment. It is a cause for why black churches like Allen, Bridge Street, Canaan, and all the others with CDCs have CDCs.[23]

From 1980 to 1995, nine black church-associated CDCs appeared among four majority-black neighborhoods in four of the city's five boroughs (map 1)—Harlem (Manhattan), South Jamaica (Queens), Bedford-Stuyvesant (Brooklyn), and Morrisania (Bronx). Among the earliest were CDCs rooted in ecumenism and collective action.

By 1999, thirteen years was the median age of the black church-associated CDCs. Staff size varied, ranging from a minimum of two full-time staff to a maximum of fifty-two, with a median staff size of thirteen. Together, the nine black church-associated CDCs employed 189 full-time workers, and another 55 part-time workers. Their executive directors were all black, with women heading 56 percent of them. Similarly, the majority (69 percent) of their full-time staff was female. The median annual budget of the nine black

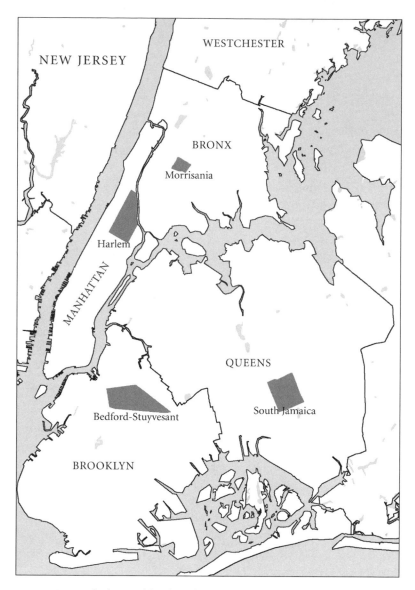

MAP 1 Four Black Neighborhoods with Church-Associated CDCs in
New York City. *Source:* Michael Leo Ownes, "Pulpits and Policy: The
Politics of Black Church–Based Community Development in New York
City, 1980–2000," Ph.D. diss., State University of New York at
Albany, 2001.

church-associated CDCs was \$550,000, with a low of \$150,000 and a high of \$5,000,000.

ALLIANCE-BASED BLACK CHURCH-ASSOCIATED CDCS

Historically, urban black clergy have used informal ministerial alliances or conferences as venues for discussion, civic action, and political engagement.[24] In New York City, from the late 1970s and to middle 1980s, multiple ministerial alliances such as the Metropolitan Ministers Conference and the African People's Christian Organization appeared in the city's black neighborhoods.[25] Black clergy used them to decide how their churches could collaborate to identify common problems, publicize neighborhood needs, and mobilize their communities for political action. Some used their ministerial alliances to assume broader missions, create bureaucracies, and perform roles that went beyond providing venues for black clergy to vent their concerns and improvise community-based responses. These alliances served as staging areas for the development of formal nonprofit institutions such as CDCs.

As of 1999, 249 churches were allied through four black church-associated CDCs that appeared in Harlem, Bedford-Stuyvesant, Morrisania, and South Jamaica between 1980 and 1987: Association of Brooklyn Clergy for Community Development, Bronx Shepherds Restoration Corporation, Harlem Congregations for Community Improvement, and Southeast Queens Clergy for Community Empowerment (table 1). These alliance-based black church-associated CDCs grew from the decade-long efforts by their sponsoring churches to work collectively to achieve improvements in their neighborhoods.[26]

Black clergy and their churches allied with others to charter CDCs because the alliance-based CDC afforded individual churches the opportunity to engage in levels of community outreach previously not feasible. From the beginning, the use of alliance-based black church-associated CDCs, according to Reverend Alan Watkins, formerly of the Faith Center for Community Economic Development and Chase Bank Community Foundation, allowed individual churches and other sectarian institutions, especially those with small to medium congregations, to build capacity collectively and reduce their overhead costs of community outreach.[27] Alliance-based CDCs provided churches with limited resources (e.g., volunteers, money, and political con-

TABLE 1 Alliance-Based Black Church-Associated CDCs

Community Development Corporation	Community	Year founded
Association of Brooklyn Clergy for Community Development	Bedford-Stuyvesant	1987
Bronx Shepherds Restoration Corporation	Morrisania	1980
Harlem Congregations for Community Improvement	Central Harlem	1986
Southeast Queens Clergy for Community Empowerment	South Jamaica	1986
Mean age		1985

Source: Owens, "Pulpits and Policy," Ph.D. diss.

nections) with what Mark Weinheimer describes as "strength in numbers, enabling member units to contribute skills and assets and to leverage the interests of other institutions" such as the city housing agencies and banks.[28]

The number of churches initially supporting the four alliance-based CDCs varied. Clergy alliances with memberships of more than twenty churches chartered two of them. In the case of Harlem Congregations for Community Improvement, its original membership consisted of forty churches. As for the initial memberships of the Southeast Queens Clergy for Community Empowerment and Bronx Shepherds Restoration Corporation, they numbered thirty-six and thirty, respectively. By 1999, the memberships of the three alliance-based black church-associated CDCs consisted of ninety congregations, eighty-five congregations, and forty-four congregations, respectively. The remaining alliance-based CDC, the Association of Brooklyn Clergy for Community Development, grew, too, from fifteen congregations to its current thirty.

Originally, the membership of the clergy associations that sponsored the four alliance-based CDCs consisted solely of black churches from the eight historically black denominations. For example, the original name of the Harlem Congregations for Community Improvement was Harlem Churches for Community Improvement. All of the alliance-based CDCs now, however, count black churches from other denominations and nonblack churches, as well as other religious institutions, as members. For instance, among the members of the Harlem Congregations for Community Improvement, Southeast Queens Clergy for Community Empowerment, Association of Brooklyn Clergy for Community Development, and Bronx Shepherds Restoration Corporation, 37 percent, 45 percent, 50 percent, and 57 percent, respectively, are nonblack churches. Episcopalians, Presbyterians, Roman Catholics, Lutherans, nondenominational Evangelical Christians, and Muslims all belong to Harlem Congregations for Community Improvement and Southeast Queens Clergy for Community Empowerment.

Other factors producing increased memberships in the alliance-based CDCs were the reputation and credibility of their organizations in relation to other community-based groups operating in their neighborhoods. For example, all of the alliance-based CDCs collaborated with the New York City Department of Housing Preservation and Development to increase affordable housing production in their neighborhoods. Their involvement with the public sector produced 2,903 new units of housing. As the alliance-based CDCs demonstrated that they could be catalysts for public and private investment in their communities, other churches, including some that had once questioned the utility of church-based collective action, joined the clergy alliances to lend their moral support for the work of the CDCs. The improved reputations and legitimacy the alliance-based black church-associated CDCs gained in their neighborhoods, rooted in their ability to work with other groups and deliver on their promises, turned some bystanders into participants and converted some opponents into allies.

INDEPENDENT BLACK CHURCH-ASSOCIATED CDCS
The formation of alliance-based black church-associated CDCs suggests that the black churches in the four neighborhoods maintained an appreciation for collective action. It also counters the stereotype held by elites and grassroots observers that black churches scrimmage over turf and compete for resources and prestige. Nevertheless, not all black churches favoring the CDC model to address problems in their neighborhoods allied with nearby churches to charter CDCs. Five activist black churches with relatively large congregations independently chartered CDCs as corporate nonprofit subsidiaries of their churches: Abyssinian Baptist Church, Allen African Methodist Episcopal Church, Bridge Street African Wesleyan Methodist Episcopal Church,

TABLE 2 Independent Black Church-Associated CDCs

Community Development Corporation	Community	Year founded
Abyssinian Development Corporation	Central Harlem	1989
Allen Neighborhood Preservation and Development Corporation	South Jamaica	1980
Bridge Street Development Corporation	Bedford-Stuyvesant	1995
Canaan Housing Development Corporation	Central Harlem	1980
Concord Community Development Corporation	Bedford-Stuyvesant	1994
Mean age		1988

Source: Owens, "Pulpits and Policy," Ph.D. diss.

Canaan Baptist Church of Christ, and Concord Baptist Church of Christ (table 2).[29]

The five churches displayed pragmatism in chartering independent black church-associated CDCs. Alliance-based CDCs might work well. This explains why Allen AME and Canaan Baptist assisted in the formation and early work of the alliance-based black church-associated CDCs in their neighborhoods. In South Jamaica, Allen AME gave technical assistance to the Southeast Queens Clergy for Community Empowerment. In Harlem, Canaan Baptist joined other black churches as the original chartering members of Harlem Congregations for Community Improvement, and it continues as a sponsoring member. However, both churches also decided that independent black church-associated CDCs were necessary for their churches to be influential in their immediate communities. This is because the success of alliance-based CDCs would be a function of their concentrated efforts.

To be effective, alliance-based CDCs have to focus on a particular area at a particular time. An alliance-based CDC like the Association of Brooklyn Clergy for Community Development (ABCCD) might have thirty member churches from the Bedford-Stuyvesant neighborhood in Brooklyn. For it to make a noticeable and substantive difference, it would have to concentrate its activities in a specific section of the community. The blocks of a few sponsoring churches would benefit immediately. Correspondingly, the blocks of most of the churches would receive little, if any, of the attention and services of the alliance-based CDC. Churches like Concord or Bridge Street could wait for ABCCD to focus on the problems of its immediate neighborhood or they could, as they did, develop their own CDCs in the interim.

The Works of Black Church-Associated CDCs

Generally, the practice of neighborhood revitalization via church-associated CDCs, as Alvin Mares observes, "enable[s] congregants to express their faith in a tangible and fulfilling way, in addition to giving congregants access to people who may not be willing to come to weekend church worship."[30] The actions of the black church-associated CDCs are suggestive of Jesus' emphasis in Luke 7:21–22, where He does not speak of the capacities of God to induce converts but demonstrates them: "In that same hour, he cured many of their infirmities and plagues, and of evil spirits; and unto many that were blind he gave sight. Then Jesus answering said unto them, Go your way, and tell John what things ye have seen and heard; how that the blind see, the lame walk, the lepers are cleansed, the deaf hear, the dead are raised, to the poor the gospel is preached." Through their deeds, not their words, black church-associated CDCs preach the gospel of their God.

The work of black church-associated CDCs to address physical and socio-economic problems assists their churches in manifesting their God's requirement that His followers care for the "least of these." Their prime objectives are to broaden and to better the socioeconomic opportunity structure of their neighborhoods. There are four chief program areas the black church-associated CDCs in New York City have worked in over the last twenty years. Housing and social services are the primary areas for a majority of them, while a minority attend to economic development and education.[31] This is not surprising; CDCs, be they associated with churches or operating as secular organizations, focus most of their attention and energies on housing development.[32]

HOUSING

The black church-associated CDCs engage mainly in housing-related activities. Housing is the only program area in which all nine CDCs are active. Eight of the black church-associated CDCs have participated in the development of

4,442 units of housing, including limited-equity cooperatives, condominiums, owner-occupied row houses with attached rental units, and multistoried rental apartments. Occupants range from low-income single mothers to moderate-income couples without children to middle-income two-parent families. Low- and moderate-income rental housing is the most common form of housing the black church-associated CDCs have developed, comprising 59 percent of their total units. Formerly homeless individuals and families occupy 5 to 10 percent of these rental units. Units in attached two-family houses, with an owner-occupied unit and one to three rental units, comprise 31 percent of housing the black church-associated CDCs sponsored or developed over the same period. Moderate- and middle-income owner-occupied-only housing comprises the remaining 9 percent of the housing associated with the black church-associated CDCs.

Since their creation, the black church-associated CDCs have been advocates for their neighborhoods. Whether it was raising public concern for speculation and gentrification or private responses to housing abandonment, these CDCs, particularly the alliance-based CDCs, communicated the claims of their communities to governmental and nongovernmental institutions to reform housing policies and practices. The black church-associated CDCs also formulated independent plans for housing renewal in their neighborhoods that they used to educate policymakers about neighborhood conditions and prospects for renewal. For example, Harlem Congregations for Community Improvement devised the Bradhurst Plan, which became the blueprint for a comprehensive community initiative in the CDC's neighborhood and a strategic plan that has guided public sector investment in the community for the last fifteen years. The city government committed more than $10 million from its capital budget to execute the plan's agenda for the development of 2,000 units of housing in the neighborhood.

The black church-associated CDCs have also been housing-related service providers. For example, they offer homeownership counseling. They convene neighborhood residents, banks, and housing agencies at workshops to discuss the process of homeownership. During these events, the CDCs educate prospective buyers and advertise homes they have developed or sponsored. The CDCs also provide residents with daily opportunities to learn about purchasing homes from the CDC or other housing developers in their neighborhoods. Professional staff is available to meet with residents about the homeownership process, including identifying lenders and lawyers, cleaning credit records and histories, and obtaining financing. Allen Neighborhood Preservation and Development Corporation even provides office space on its premises to a bank loan officer.

SOCIAL SERVICES

While it may not be the largest program area for all, six of the black church-associated CDCs offer services to address social and health-related problems in their neighborhoods. An informant of Harlem Congregations for Community Improvement observes: "People think real estate is our largest division; it's not, [health and human] services is."[33] Some social services they provide are disease screenings (e.g., cancer, sickle-cell anemia, hypertension, and diabetes); immunizations; funeral assistance; and public benefits counseling. Prevention, testing, and management of HIV/AIDS, as well as family mentoring and family skills development; food and clothing, mental and physical health, and domestic violence referrals; homeless shelter placement; childcare; and crisis management are other services the black church-associated CDCs offer their communities. They do so freely. Attendants of the churches associated with the CDCs, as well as congregants of other churches and other religious institutions, along with theists and atheists in their neighborhoods, may receive services equally and without or at little cost.

The black church-associated CDCs operate their own social service programs on site at their headquarters, in satellite offices in the rental properties they have developed, and at community fairs and workshops. For example, the Southeast Queens Clergy for Community Empowerment provides HIV prevention and education services on its premises, along with a set of outreach and case management services to individuals and families experiencing crises. However, black church-associated CDCs also collaborate with other organizations to deliver services in their neighborhoods. The Harlem Congregations for Community Improvement works with the Balm in Gilead, a national nonprofit organization that educates black clergy and their congregants through seminars, concerts, and workshops about HIV/AIDS in their communities and how they can assist those infected with, and affected by, the disease. The Southeast Queens Clergy for Community Empowerment has assisted more than twenty private and public social and health services agencies to provide services to its neighborhood residents. Agencies include the New

York Council on Adoptable Children, the AIDS Center of Queens County, Mary Immaculate Catholic Medical Center, Visiting Nurse Service, and the New York City Department of Health.

Black church-associated CDCs also manage space for other agencies to deliver neighborhood-based services. For instance, the New York City Human Resources Administration contracts with the Allen Neighborhood Preservation and Development Corporation to operate its South Jamaica Multi-Service Center. Professional social services agencies such as the Jamaica Service Program for Older Adults, South Queens Community Health Center, National Council of Negro Women, and South Jamaica Center for Children and Parents operate on the premises of the Multi-Service Center, which doubles as the headquarters for the CDC. The agencies, not the CDC, dispense information and provide services such as GED preparation, parenting skills for teenage mothers, nutrition counseling, and elder referral services to neighborhood residents.

ECONOMIC DEVELOPMENT

Few black church-associated CDCs engage in economic development. Three of the CDCs — Harlem Congregations for Community Improvement, Abyssinian Development Corporation, and Bridge Street Development Corporation — routinely develop commercial properties, encourage private commercial investment, and foster entrepreneurship in their neighborhoods. This is not to say that the black churches affiliated with the remaining CDCs do not understand the importance of economic development or discourage it in their neighborhoods.

First, many activist black churches themselves engage in economic development through their churches directly or by entities other than CDCs, especially credit unions. Five of the most historically activist black churches in the city — Abyssinian Baptist Church, Allen African Methodist Episcopal Church, Bridge Street African Wesleyan Methodist Episcopal Church, Canaan Baptist Church of Christ, and Concord Baptist Church of Christ — operate federal credit unions.[34] The mean date of incorporation for their credit unions is 1961, with the oldest and youngest of the credit unions being the Abyssinian Baptist Church Federal Credit Union (1940) and the Bridge Street AMWE Church Federal Credit Union (1983). The combined membership of the five credit unions is 4,573, with collective assets of $6,754,734 and outstanding loans of $1,062,342. In terms of assets, the largest of the five credit unions is the Concord Baptist Federal Credit Union (CBFCU), with $4,312,530. Chartered in 1957, it has a membership of 1,035 and outstanding loans of $275,525.

Second, CDCs are often just one of a set of nonprofit, even for-profit, subsidiaries of activist black churches in New York City. For example, in addition to its CDC, Allen African Methodist Episcopal Church operates the Allen AME Housing Corporation, which, despite its name, focuses on commercial strip revitalization proximate to the $26 million edifice of the church. As of 1998, it managed twenty-five church-owned commercial properties and earned $364,771 in rental income.[35] One of the two profit-making subsidiaries of the church is the Allen Transportation Corporation, a charter bus company that owns and operates a fleet of four motor coaches and arranges travel tours. In 1998 the corporation, which employs ten neighborhood residents full-time, grossed $850,698, up from $350,903 in 1992.[36]

Third, black church-associated CDCs may focus less on economic development because they are still establishing a successful record for housing development to serve as a gateway to economic development. Generally, according to Sarah Stoutland, developing affordable housing and rebuilding neighborhood housing markets provides CDCs with a foundation for pursuing successful economic development programs in the future.[37] Furthermore, the black church-associated CDCs focus on housing because there tend to be more external resources for housing development and (perhaps because of welfare reform and "charitable choice") social services delivery than neighborhood-based economic development in New York City. In the case of affordable housing production, there is a diversity of material resources, well-funded programs, and financial intermediaries and technical assistance organizations for building it successfully in New York.[38]

The black church-associated CDCs that engage in economic development rely on partnerships with other institutions in and beyond their neighborhoods. Some of their collaborations are small-scale. For example, in partnership with the Small Business Development Center of the City University of New York, Harlem Congregations for Community Improvement surveys economic needs and activities along commercial strips in its neighborhood and operates a program to assist local entrepreneurs in expanding their markets and modernizing their enterprises. Some partnerships of the black church-associated CDCs, however, are large-scale. The Abyssinian Development Corporation is perhaps the exemplar of how the black church-associated CDCs promote economic development through partnerships.

In 1990, Abyssinian Development Corporation established the Central Harlem Local Development Corporation (CHLDC) to improve the economy of Central Harlem. Among its initiatives, the CHLDC provides $5,000 to $25,000 loans to small businesses for working capital, inventory purchases, and expansion and renovation costs. It also provides $700 micro-enterprise grants for the start-up of new neighborhood-based businesses, especially by poor nonwhite women with children who receive public assistance. During the late 1990s, the Abyssinian Development Corporation, in conjunction with the Community Association of the East Harlem Triangle and the New York City Economic Development Corporation, developed the property for a 50,000-square-foot, $16 million, 24-hour Harlem Pathmark Super Center and a branch of Chase Manhattan Bank. It secured financing from a range of sources including Chase Community Development Corporation, EAB Community Development Bank, Local Initiatives Support Corporation, U.S. Department of Health and Human Services, and the Empire State Development Corporation.[39] Located on land that was a city-owned parking lot, the center, Harlem's first supermarket, employs 250 workers, of which 75 percent are neighborhood residents.

Along with the supermarket, the Abyssinian Development Corporation partnered with the Local Initiatives Support Corporation and Deutsche Bank to identify investors and open a Sterling Optical franchise.[40] As facilitator and limited-equity investor, the Abyssinian Development Corporation recruited entrepreneurs to co-own the Sterling Optical franchise with it. After structuring the partnership, Abyssinian Development Corporation monitors the franchise in accordance with presigned first-source hiring agreements that mandate the employment of Central Harlem residents. However, Abyssinian Development Corporation does not maintain any control over the operation of the franchise.[41]

In 2000, in partnership with the state government and Forest City Ratner Companies, one of the largest for-profit real estate developers in New York City, Abyssinian Development Corporation broke ground on the Harlem Center, an $85 million retail, office, hotel, and conference complex on property owned by New York State. It is expected to employ 825 permanent full-time workers and require the employment of 2,100 temporary construction workers. It will complement the $66 million, 275,000-square-foot, 500-employee Harlem USA Retail and Entertainment Complex, which the Abyssinian Development Corporation, in conjunction with the federal Upper Manhattan Empowerment Zone, was instrumental in developing. Karen Phillips, president of the Abyssinian Development Corporation, told the *New York Post:* "We will have stores that people go down to 86th Street for, but they leave their money down on 86th Street. Now they'll keep their money in Harlem and bring more money to Harlem."[42]

The Unseen Hand of the State

Self-help is central to community development. It is, according to Donald Littrell and Daryl Hobbs, "based on the premise that people can, will, and should collaborate to solve community problems. . . . It embodies the notion that a community can achieve greater self-determination within constraints imposed by the larger political economy in which it is embedded."[43]

Public institutional action, too, is essential to community development. Public policies regulate redevelopment. Public resources provide for direct redevelopment or leverage to encourage private institutional support and investment. Accordingly, community development requires citizens to influence the formulation of public policies, the implementation of programs, and the distribution of resources to benefit their communities. Moreover, it requires them to share in the production and delivery of public services, deliberately coproducing public programs and leveraging public and private resources to improve socioeconomic conditions (human, physical, and commercial) for the benefit of the current residents of targeted low- and moderate-income areas through neighborhood-based service programs.

In accordance with the definition of community development, the work of the black church-associated CDCs has relied greatly on indigenous self-initiative, at least in the design and operation of their programs. That is to say, much of the vision and action on behalf of the four black neighborhoods in New York City has come from the minds and hands of black people from the target neighborhoods. For instance, four of the nine executive directors of the black church-associated CDCs live in the neighborhoods their CDCs service, while a majority (75 percent) of their staff resides in them. However, the physical and material resources have come from outside the neighborhoods; philanthropy from the black congregants of their sponsor churches underwrites little, if any, of the achievements of black church-associated CDCs in New York City. No black church-associated CDC receives the bulk, or even a significant minority, of its administrative and programmatic resources from its affiliated churches. This was not always so.

Initially, the resources, financial and otherwise, of black churches underwrote the programs and activities of the black church-associated CDCs. Churches contributed all or a majority of the funds for the nine black church-associated CDCs in their formative stages. In particular, the five independent black church-associated CDCs were dependent almost completely on the resources of their chartering churches, particularly volunteers and church subsidies of money, office space, and equipment. However, as the visions and development agendas of the churches for their geographic communities outscaled their contributions, and as their staffs became more professional, the churches required their CDCs to seek, find, and follow "an avenue of funding beyond Sunday collections."[44] Fortunately for the CDCs, at least the majority of them, there was an extant avenue — government.

That black church-associated CDCs would look to the state is not surprising. Since the eras of urban renewal and the War on Poverty, government had assisted activist black churches in achieving civic purposes. Such churches had benefited from public policies that channeled funds into their neighborhoods for neighborhood revitalizations. For example, black churches across the country entered into partnerships with the federal government to use public dollars to sponsor the development of rental housing for moderate-income blacks via the Federal Home Administration 221(d)3 program.[45] Three decades later, the CDCs associated with black churches in New York City continued the practice of seeking and obtaining the substantive resources of government, as well as those of private sources external to their neighborhoods, for the development, support, and expansion of sacred-civic purposes such as housing production.

The substantive resources the public sector provided the black church-associated CDCs include money, land, buildings, technical assistance, and infrastructure, which the CDCs use to underwrite affordable housing development in their neighborhoods. Table 3 shows that the substantive resources

TABLE 3 Sources of Support for Black Church-Associated CDCs, 1980–1999

Community Development Corporations	Banks	Intermediaries	Churches	Federal government	State government	Local government	Corporations	Foundations	TOTAL
			Percent of Total CDC Support*						
Alliance-Based									
Assn. of Brooklyn Clergy for Community Development	5	5	—	5	15	70	—	—	100
Bronx Shepherds Restoration Corp.	15	5	—	10	20	45	—	5	100
Harlem Congregations for Community Improvement	10	20	—	15	10	35	5	5	100
South Jamaica Clergy for Community Empowerment	10	5	—	10	15	55	—	5	100
Independent									
Abyssinian Development Corp.	20	15	—	5	10	45	5	5	100
Allen Neighborhood Preservation and Development Corp.	—	—	—	—	10	85	5	—	100
Bridge Street Development Corp.	10	10	—	5	5	60	10	—	100
Canaan Housing Development Corp.	5	10	—	30	10	40	5	—	100
Concord Community Development Corp.	—	5	—	5	5	5	5	75	100

*Estimated proportional shares of support, inclusive of grants, donations, contracts, fees-for-services, loans, land, buildings, technical assistance, and infrastructure.
Source: Owens, "Pulpits and Policy," Ph.D. diss.

of the city government, in particular, are critical to black church-associated CDCs.

Money, in the forms of grants, contracts, subsidies, loans, and fees for services, is a chief substantive resource that government provides the black church-associated CDCs. Among the significant financial resources are Community Development Block Grants (CDBG) and HOME Investment Partnership (HOME) funds. CDBG and HOME Investment Partnership programs provide flexible grants from the federal government to state and local governments for housing construction and rehabilitation. HOME mandates that municipalities allocate a minimum of fifteen percent of their HOME funds to housing developed, sponsored, or owned by nonprofit housing organizations such as black church-associated CDCs. Both CDBG and HOME give wide discretion to local governments in formulating their responses to housing problems, which allows the black church-associated CDCs to develop a mix of housing types to meet the diverse needs of their communities. Increasingly, however, an important source of funding for black church-associated CDCs developed and sponsored in New York City is the federal Low-Income Housing Tax Credit (LIHTC) program. According to LIHTC program guidelines, private investors who provide black church-associated CDCs equity capital for new construction or the cost of substantially rehabilitated affordable housing units may receive an annual federal income tax credit of 9 percent for ten years. Tax credits go solely toward the proportion of units occupied by low-income households, as defined by the federal government. The LIHTC is introducing new, and sometimes very large, sums of private, corporate dollars into the majority-black neighborhoods of New York City served by black church-associated CDCs.

In addition to money, nonfinancial resources of government are equally important to the programming of the black church-associated CDCs, especially in the area of housing development. For example, the city government has conveyed in rem property (i.e., public-owned property acquired from private owners through tax foreclosure proceedings) to the black church-associated CDCs to develop affordable housing throughout their neighborhoods. Although there are no public data on the value of the properties the city government supplied to the housing initiatives of the black church-associated CDCs, a former city housing commissioner estimated the value at "anywhere from $20 million to $30 million, speaking conservatively, mind you."[46] The works of the black church-associated CDCs also benefit from other public resources, namely, infrastructure upgrades, tax abatements, mortgage insurance, loan guarantees, and technical assistance.

In seeking and obtaining public resources, the black church-associated CDCs sought to unite the historic efforts of the black faith sector with the resources of the public sector to improve the physical, economic, and social conditions of African American communities, to integrate black neighborhoods into the life of majority-white cities, and to enable them to contribute fully to the progress of cities. In short, neighborhood development by the black church-associated CDCs was unthinkable *without* government action. The black church-associated CDCs could look to the public sector because they were fiscally autonomous of their churches and not pervasively sectarian (i.e., religious education, worship, and proselytism are absent from their activities). The transfer of public resources, monetary and nonmonetary, to black church-associated CDCs, or any other religious-associated nonprofit organization, did not conflict with convention regarding church-state separation.[47] In fact, many of the community development policies of government encouraged religious organizations, albeit through nonprofit affiliates and subsidiaries, to seek and obtain public resources.

The Politics of Black Church-Associated CDCs

The functions of black church-associated CDCs are manifold. They have production functions that yield affordable housing, jobs, and businesses. They also have financial functions, namely, offering their churches an indirect means of securing public funding. Furthermore, they can serve spiritual functions such as allowing their staff to exercise their faith. However, they may also have political functions. Perhaps they promote neighborhood problems to political elites and identify policy alternatives for addressing them. This was an expectation that political scientists during the 1970s had of CDCs generally. Reginald Earl Gilliam, for example, expected that CDCs operating in majority-black neighborhoods would, aside from providing necessary services and fostering redevelopment, function as interest groups.[48] That is, CDCs would be instruments of political development, providing their neighborhoods with supplemental or alternative ways of biasing public agendas, decisions, and implementation.

In the case of the black church-associated CDCs that emerged in New York City during the 1980s and 1990s, their histories show that they were interest groups at their creation. From their inception, they made claims on public institutions, as well as private ones. Whether, in the words of their directors, to "put out the fires in the South Bronx," to "shelter the needy, sick, and shut-out," or "give folk a chance they never had," the black church-associated CDCs pressed public and private elites to attend to the concerns of their neighborhoods and redirect resources to them. In many instances, elites were responsive to the claims of the black church-associated CDCs, awarding them resources to build their capacities as developers, reduce neighborhood deficits, and establish reputations as neighborhood representatives. By the end of the 1990s, due to what Richard P. Nathan terms the "nonprofitization of community development services,"[49] the black church-associated CDCs were key members of a community development microregime in New York City, deriving benefits (i.e., money, land, and discretion) that allowed them to maintain their programs, as well as develop new ones.[50]

As interest groups, the black church-associated CDCs engage in interest-group pressure tactics to influence policymaking processes in New York City. A majority of the black church-associated CDCs, however, practice fewer modes of pressure than are available to them. Of twenty possible modes of pressure across the four forms of pressure (i.e., advocacy, community organizing, protest, and voter assistance), five or more of the black church-associated CDCs engage in nine pressure modes (see figure 1). Aside from practicing less than half of the pressure modes at their disposal, the black church-associated CDCs generally employ just two of the four forms of pressure; they choose advocacy and community organizing over protest and voter assistance to influence policymaking processes. Specifically, 88 percent of the pressure modes the black church-associated CDCs use involve advocacy (44 percent) and community organizing (44 percent).

Generally, the black church-associated CDCs have not adopted *political development*—the purposive use of various forms of political action to address collective problems in a neighborhood for the benefit of its current residents by influencing the political process of cities and affecting urban governance—as a core program area for their organizations.[51] Instead, they have left political development to the black clergy, along with other community-based leaders. The clergy are expected to make claims on the public sector

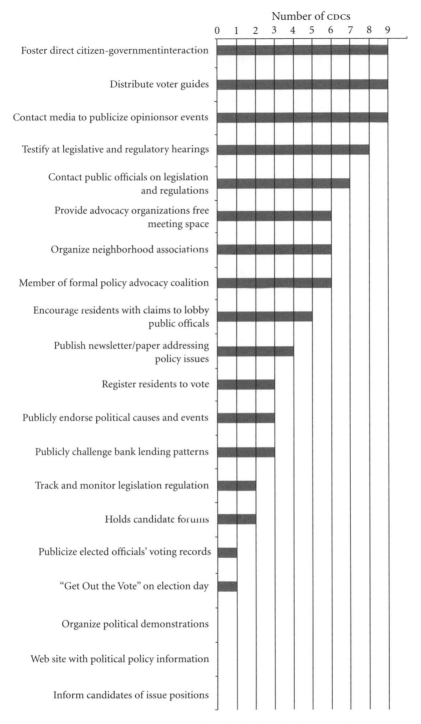

FIGURE 1 Interest Group Pressure by Black Church-Associated Community Development Corporations. *Source:* Owens, "Pulpits and Policy," Ph.D. diss.

and agitate for social and economic reform in their communities.[52] As a representative of Bronx Shepherds Restoration Corporation commented, "Our churches can tread the political water better than us, without facing the wrath of the powers that be."[53] Others echo the sentiment. In the words of an informant from the Southeast Queens Clergy for Community Empowerment, "the pastors know how to do it best; we're developers, not politicians. We simply focus on the needs and get to work addressing them."[54]

The black church-associated CDCs may overlook political development because they are subsidiaries of churches with activist black pastors. For example, the Allen Neighborhood Preservation and Development Corporation can pay less attention to politics because the pastor of its church, Reverend Floyd Flake, a former member of the U.S. House of Representatives, is a political insider, one who deliberately attempts to influence privately the decisions and actions of policymakers. While he may not take to the streets, Reverend Flake makes telephone calls to and meets behind closed doors with influential allies to negotiate political change or manage conflict.[55] He also is quick to voice his views through established organs such as the opinion pages of the press and to participate in political processes like public hearings. He has access to policymakers and often receives a broad hearing of his claims for particular political reforms.

Flake also uses electoral politics to advance the interests of his church and neighborhood, readily exchanging his political support for elected officials for patronage to his church and community. During the late 1970s and early 1980s, Flake backed Democratic and Republican incumbents, including New York City Mayor Edward I. Koch and U.S. Senator Alfonse D'Amato, for reelection, which yielded government contracts, grants, and land to Allen AME Church and its subsidiary corporations. For instance, the political support of Flake enabled Allen AME Church to secure a loan from the U.S. Department of Housing and Urban Development to build a $10 million affordable housing complex for senior citizens.

Generally, the pastors of churches associated with the nine CDCs are forthright concerning vexing social issues. Outspoken on public issues, the pastors appear not to fear retribution from the elected class of the city, particularly the mayor, if they protest or make disparaging comments. On *Like It Is,* a New York–based public affairs show, for instance, Reverend Butts of Abyssinian Baptist Church in Harlem clarified a public statement he made regarding racism in City Hall, particularly on the part of Mayor Rudolph Giuliani: "The mayor does not like black people and has no regard for the black community. I [have been] asked was I calling the mayor a racist. I thought long and hard about what I was saying and then I said yes."[56] Such public candidness by the pastors about policymakers and their actions comes with political costs to the black church-associated CDCs. For instance, following the statements about the Giuliani Administration, the mayor opposed a $49 million mall for Harlem that Butts supported and the Abyssinian Development Corporation would have developed.[57]

Other pastors and their CDCs have been punished for condemning the mayor or opposing city policies. "As many units of housing my church has completed in partnership with the city government," notes one Harlem pastor, "we've lost out due to my politics and big mouth."[58] An example of such a loss is the absence of her CDC among the participants in a recent and large commercial redevelopment project that New York City initiated in her neighborhood. The Alliance for Neighborhood Commerce, Homeownership, and Revitalization (ANCHOR), a program of the New York City Department of Housing and Preservation Development, funnels a minimum of $100 million into the West 116th Street corridor of Central Harlem, where the church is located. While the church has been the partner with New York City on other development projects in the neighborhood, the housing department selected a rival religious institution, a mosque no less, as the community sponsor for the ANCHOR project, consisting of the development of 96,000 square feet of retail space, 778 mixed-income housing units, and approximately 117 permanent jobs for neighborhood residents.[59]

Conclusion

Activist black churches have addressed neighborhood problems at the levels of the individual and the collective through "social enterprises" — nonprofit organizations dedicated to improving the social conditions in their neighborhoods by targeting the disadvantaged and distributing goods and services to supplement those of public agencies and private markets — and community development.[60] This chapter used New York City to illustrate the point. It showed that activist black churches, collectively and independently, may use and have used CDCs to improve the social, physical, and economic conditions of urban black neighborhoods. By creating church-associated CDCs, activist black churches are providing their communities with a set of new and enduring institutions for identifying neighborhood-based problems and formulating initiatives to reform them. They also provide their neighborhoods with black-controlled institutions that function as conduits for substantive resources (e.g., money and property) from institutions external to their communities. In doing so, they bring greater public and private resources to bear on poverty and weak economies that can result in new housing, social services, and jobs. However, an emphasis on community development by black churches, especially when placed in the hands of CDCs, may not be enough to revitalize most black neighborhoods.

Some directors say that they would like to see their black church-associated CDCs and others do more political development than they do. A CDC director in Brooklyn provides a coherent statement of this perspective.

> Community development corporations can play roles in providing space for [political] training to take place, to help identify those persons in their communities that's been working with them and who should be trained for office, and community development corporation can come together as a whole, because we can't do it separately, to develop some kind of training institute, whether it's structured or unstructured, that will go to all of the houses of worship and to our civic organizations and to our nonprofit organizations and say "Show me your brightest and best." Then let's train them to run for office and put together coalitions to support them as they run. I mean there are things we can do to start teaching our people what the electoral process is, without telling them who to vote for. But, we can at least tell them what is going on. We can at least start some kind of institutional structure, whether that's formal or informal, that identifies folk, that brings them along, and begins the training process. We're gonna get hit between the eyes and we're not ready.[61]

Other directors of black church-associated CDCs seem unwilling to go as far as establishing political recruitment and training organizations. Still, most agree that their institutions could do a better job of informing community residents and other stakeholders about the policymaking process and the need to track the decisions of their elected and appointed representatives. One contends:

We need to reengage the black community into public policy. We need to not only involve ourselves in public policy but educate our people in relationship to how public policy is developed and implemented, how it impacts our communities, and how we can impact public policy. I'm not as interested in elected officials as I am in helping our community understand the dynamics of accountability of their elected [and appointed] officials.[62]

Another notes: "We can do more. In order to rise to a new level of political sophistication we must begin to monitor our elected officials, from their votes to their attendance, as well as where their campaign money comes from."[63] The opinions and attitudes of the directors allow one to infer that it is possible for black church-associated CDCs to be stronger, effective *political* institutions in policymaking. The potential or capacity for action and the will for it, however, will ultimately influence the realization of the possible in the political sphere by black church-associated CDCs in urban America.

Notes

A 2000 Ford Foundation Minority Doctoral Dissertation Fellowship and a 1999 United States Department of Housing and Urban Development Doctoral Dissertation Research Grant (#H-21182SG) supported this research. The findings and statements contained here do not necessarily represent those of the Ford Foundation and the United States Department of Housing and Urban Development.

1   See, for example, Hans Baer and Merrill Singer, *African-American Religion in the Twentieth Century: Varieties of Protest and Accommodation* (Knoxville: University of Tennessee Press, 1992); Cathy J. Cohen, *The Boundaries of Blackness: AIDS and the Breakdown of Black Politics* (Chicago: University of Chicago Press, 1999); and Adolph Reed Jr., *The Jesse Jackson Phenomenon: The Crisis of Purpose in Afro-American Politics* (New Haven: Yale University Press, 1986).

2   Kenneth Clarke, *Dark Ghetto: The Dilemmas of Social Power* (New York: Harper TorchBooks, 1965), 178.

3   C. Eric Lincoln and Lawrence Mamiya, *The Black Church in the African-American Experience* (Durham: Duke University Press, 1990), 213.

4   Ida Johnson [pseud.], interviewed by author, taped recording, Ebenezer Missionary Baptist Church, New York City, 15 June 1999.

5   James A. Christenson, Kim Fendley, and Jerry W. Robinson Jr., "Community Development," in *Community Development in Perspective,* ed. James A. Christenson and Jerry W. Robinson Jr. (Ames: Iowa State University Press, 1989), 13–14.

6   See Avis C. Vidal, "CDCs as Agents of Neighborhood Change: The State of the Art," in *Revitalizing Urban Neighborhoods,* ed. W. Dennis Keating (Lawrence: University Press of Kansas, 1996); Xavier de Souza Briggs and Elizabeth J. Mueller, *From Neighborhood to Community: Evidence on the Social Effects of Community Development* (New York: Community Development Research Center, New School for Social Research, 1997); W. Dennis Keating and Norman Krumholz, eds., *Rebuilding Urban Neighborhoods: Achievements, Opportunities, and Limits* (Thousand Oaks: Sage Publications, 1999); Michael Leo Owens, "Renewal in a Working-Class Black Neighborhood," *Journal of Urban Affairs* 19 (1997):183–206; Sarah Stoutland, "Community Development Corporations," in *Urban Problems and Community Development,* ed. Ronald F. Ferguson and William T. Dickens (Washington, D.C.: Brookings Institution Press, 1999); and Robert Zdenek, "Community Development Corporations," in *Beyond the Market and the State: New Directions in Community Economic Development,* ed. Severyn T. Bruyn and James Meehan (Philadelphia: Temple University Press, 1987). Nationally, there are approximately 1,872 CDCs serving urban neighborhoods (National Congress for Community Economic Development, 1999). Typically operating with a small staff, annual budget, and project portfolio, their prime mission is to alter the socioeconomic conditions of specific neighborhoods: holistic — physical, economic, and human — development is their objective. They focus much of their energies on effecting redevelopment of the physical infrastructure of majority-minority and low-income neighborhoods through affordable housing production, along with expanding the ability of their residents to become upwardly mobile through a set of CDC-run programs. As of 1997, CDCs nationally had built or renovated 550,000 units of housing, both rental and owner-occupied; they had developed approximately 71 million square feet of commercial and industrial space; and they had created 247,000 jobs. In just five cities (Boston, Cleveland, Philadelphia, Pittsburgh, and Washington, D.C.), CDCs have leveraged $139.1 million to develop 3.1 million square feet of commercial, industrial, and retail space and create 10,719 jobs. See Ford Foundation, *Seizing Opportunities: The Role of CDCs in Urban Economic Development* (New York: Ford Foundation, n.d.).

7   Robert A. Clemetson and Roger Coates, *Restoring Broken Places and Rebuilding Communities: A Casebook on African-American Church Involvement in Community Economic Development* (Washington, D.C.: National Congress for Community Economic Development, 1992); Harold A. McDougall, *Black Baltimore: A New Theory of Community* (Philadelphia: Temple University Press, 1993); and Michael Leo Owens, "Black Church-Affiliated Community Development Corporations and the Coproduction of Affordable Housing in New York City," in *Nonprofits in Urban America,* ed. Richard Hula and Cynthia Jackson-Elmoore (Westport, Conn.: Quorum Books, 2000).

8   Basil Wilson and Charles Green, "The Black Church and the Struggle for Politi-

cal Empowerment in New York City," *Afro-Americans in New York Life and History* (January 1988): 64.

9 See, for example, Elijah Anderson, *Code of the Street: Decency, Violence, and the Moral Life of the Inner City* (New York: Norton, 2000); William Julius Wilson, *When Work Disappears: The World of the New Urban Poor* (New York: Vintage Books, 1997); and Adolph Reed Jr., *Without Justice for All: The New Liberalism and Our Retreat from Racial Equality* (Boulder: Westview Press, 1999).

10 Stephen V. Monsma, *When Sacred and Secular Mix: Religious Nonprofit Organizations and Public Money* (Lanham, Md: Rowman and Littlefield Publishers, 1996), 109.

11 Alvin Mares, "Housing and the Church," *Nonprofit and Voluntary Sector Quarterly* 23 (1994): 139–57.

12 Ibid.

13 June Manning Thomas and Reynard N. Blake Jr., "Faith-based Community Development and African-American Neighborhoods," in *Revitalizing Urban Neighborhoods,* ed. W. Dennis Keating, Norman Krumholz, and Philip Star (Lawrence: University Press of Kansas, 1996), 139.

14 Michael Leo Owens, "Pulpits and Policy: The Politics of Black Church-Based Community Development in New York City 1980–2000" (Ph.D. diss., State University of New York at Albany, 2001).

15 Henry G. Cisneros, *Higher Ground: Faith Communities and Community Building* (Washington, D.C.: United States Department of Housing and Urban Development, 1996).

16 John J. DiIulio Jr., "Living Faith: The Black Church Outreach Tradition" (New York: Manhattan Institute, 1998); Glen C. Loury and Linda Datcher Loury, "Not by Bread Alone: The Role of the African-American Church in Inner-City Development," *Brookings Review* 15 (1997): 10–13; Owens, "Renewal in a Working-Class Black Neighborhood"; Owens, "Pulpits and Policy"; and Thomas and Blake, "Faith-based Community Development and African-American Neighborhoods."

17 June Manning Thomas, "Rebuilding Inner Cities: Basic Principles," in *The Inner City: Urban Poverty and Economic Development in the Next Century,* ed. Thomas D. Boston and Catherine L. Ross (New Brunswick, N.J.: Transaction Publishers, 1997), 71.

18 The ten churches are Abyssinian Baptist Church; Allen African Methodist Episcopal Church; Bethany Baptist Church; Bethesda Missionary Baptist Church; Bridge Street African Wesleyan Methodist Episcopal Church; Canaan Baptist Church of Christ; Concord Baptist Church of Christ; Ebenezer Missionary Baptist Church; Memorial Baptist Church; and Saint Paul Community Baptist Church. For an extensive treatment of the research methodology and data, see Owens, "Pulpits and Policy."

19 Dennis R. Judd and Todd Swanstrom, *City Politics: Private Power and Public Policy* (New York: Longman, 1998), 238.

20 Richard L. Cole, Delbert A. Taebel, and Rodney V. Hissong, "America's Cities and the 1980s: The Legacy of the Reagan Years," *Journal of Urban Affairs* 12 (1990): 345–60.

21 R. Wood, "Cities in Trouble," *Domestic Affairs* 1 (1991): 230.

22 Cited in Pamela Ann Toussaint, "Concord Baptist Church: Taking Care of Business in Bed-Stuy," in *Signs of Hope in the City: Ministries of Community Renewal,* ed. Robert Carle and Louis A. DeCaro Jr. (Valley Forge, Pa: Judson Press, 1999), 64.

23 Marvin Holmes [pseud.], interviewed by author, taped recording, Manhattan, 24 June 1999. The Faith Center for Community Development, Inc. provides technical assistance to congregations interested in neighborhood revitalization and religious-associated nonprofits seeking to expand their service capacity. For more information, contact the Faith Center for Community Development, Inc., 120 Wall Street, 26th Floor, New York, New York 10005–4001.

24 Harvey K. Newman, "Black Clergy and Urban Regimes: The Role of Atlanta's Concerned Black Clergy," *Journal of Urban Affairs* 16 (1994): 23–33, and Michael Leo Owens, "Local Party Failure and Alternative, Black Church-Based Nonparty Organizations," *Western Journal of Black Studies* 21 (1997): 162–72.

25 Charles Green and Basil Wilson, *The Struggle for Black Empowerment in New York City: Beyond the Politics of Pigmentation* (New York: McGraw-Hill, 1992).

26 The term "alliance-based CDC" accurately describes these CDCs, for the intent of the clergy who chartered them ran counter to coalitions based on temporary unions or federations where individuals cede authority to a central institution. Rather, the clergy and the churches that united to incorporate CDCs among themselves did so to create enduring associations with common objectives.

27 Alan Watkins, *Faith-Based Community Development Corporations in Impoverished Communities* (New York: Chase Manhattan Community Foundation, 1998), 6.

28 Mark Weinheimer, *Faith in Our Neighborhoods* (Washington, D.C.: National Congress for Community Economic Development, 1996), 14.

29 The membership estimates of the churches in 1999, ranked from high to low in terms of congregation sizes reported by their pastors, are: Allen AME (11,000), Abyssinian Baptist (7,500), Bridge Street AMWE (4,700), Concord Baptist (3,800), and Canaan Baptist (2,300).

30 Mares, "Housing and the Church," 140. See also Priscilla A. La Barbera, "Commercial Ventures of Religious Nonprofits," *Nonprofit Management and Leadership* 1 (1991): 217–33.

31 Owens, "Black Church-Affiliated Community Development Corporations," 181.

32 National Congress for Community Economic Development, *Coming of Age: Trends and Achievements of Community-Based Development Organizations* (Washington,

D.C.: National Congress for Community Economic Development, 1999), and Avis C. Vidal, *Rebuilding Communities: A National Study of Urban Community Development Corporations* (New York: Community Development Research Center, New School for Social Research, 1992).

33 Katrina Scott [pseud.], interviewed by author, taped recording, Manhattan, 21 July 1999.

34 National Credit Union Administration, *Credit Union Directory* (Washington, D.C.: National Credit Union Administration, 2000).

35 Allen African Methodist Episcopal Church, *Annual Report of the Allen African Methodist Episcopal Church* (New York: Allen African Methodist Episcopal Church, 1998), 8.

36 Ibid., and Allen African Methodist Episcopal Church, *Annual Report of the Allen African Methodist Episcopal Church* (New York: Allen African Methodist Episcopal Church, 1992), 3.

37 Stoutland, "Community Development Corporations," 202.

38 Charles J. Orlebeke, *New Life at Ground Zero: New York, Homeownership, and the Future of American Cities* (Albany: Rockefeller Institute Press, 1997).

39 Terry Pristin, "A Supermarket as a Spur for Change: New Harlem Pathmark Promises Competition and Convenience," *New York Times,* 28 April 1999, B1.

40 The Local Initiatives Support Corporation and Deutsche Bank jointly administer the citywide Neighborhood Franchise Project, which introduces franchises into the city's minority neighborhoods. See http://www.liscnet.org/whatwedo/programs/nfp/index.shtml.

41 The Bridge Street Development Corporation (BSDC) also participates in the Neighborhood Franchise Project. As facilitator and limited-equity investor, BSDC is recruiting entrepreneurs to co-own an undetermined number and type of franchises with it in Bedford-Stuyvesant. In the interim, the BSDC plans to expand its business enterprise program to include financial literacy and wealth accumulation workshops for community residents, along with technical assistance workshops to assist neighborhood entrepreneurs to develop business plans, obtain capital, and enlarge their markets. As of 2000, BSDC was searching for private sponsors to develop an Individual Development Account program to provide community residents with matched savings accounts for homeownership, education, training, and small business capitalization. For more information, see http://bsdc.org.

42 Andy Geller, "Harlem to get $83M Complex," *New York Post Online,* n.d. Available at http://www.nypostonline.com/business/17521.htm.

43 Donald Littrell and Daryl Hobbs, "The Self-Help Approach," in *Community Development in Perspective,* ed. James A. Christenson and Jerry W. Robinson Jr. (Ames: Iowa State University Press, 1989), 48.

44 W. Franklyn Richardson, "Mission to Mandate: Self-Development Through the

Black Church," in *The State of Black America,* ed. Billy Tidwell (New York: National Urban League, 1994), 122.

45 James W. English, *Handyman for the Lord: The Life and Ministry of the Reverend William Holmes Borders* (New York: Meredith Press, 1967), 120–51.

46 Ainsley Jenkins [pseud.], interviewed by author, taped recording, Manhattan, 2 June 1999.

47 Monsma, *When Sacred and Secular Mix,* 42.

48 Reginald Earl Gilliam, *Black Political Development: An Advocacy Analysis* (Port Washington, N.Y.: Dunellen Publishing, 1975).

49 Richard P. Nathan, "The Nonprofitization Movement: An Examination of the Effects of Devolution on Nonprofit Organizations," paper presented at the 1996 University of Minnesota–Indiana University New Partnership Project Conference.

50 Owens, "Pulpits and Policy."

51 This definition of political development was informed by Ross and Margaret Wilder, "Community Development Corporations: Critical Factors That Influence Success," *Journal of Urban Affairs* 21, no. 3 (1999): 341–62, and Norman Glickman and Lisa Servon, "More Than Bricks and Sticks: Five Components of Community Development Corporation Capacity," *Housing Policy Debate* 9, no. 3 (1998): 497–540.

52 Green and Wilson, *The Struggle for Black Empowerment;* Owens, "Local Party Failure and Alternative, Black Church-based Nonparty Organizations"; and Clarence Taylor, *The Black Churches of Brooklyn* (New York: Columbia University Press, 1994).

53 Eloise Hightower [pseud.], interviewed by author, taped recording, Bronx, 25 January 2000.

54 Carson Sinclair [pseud.], interviewed by author, taped recording, Queens, 8 June 1999.

55 Reverend Flake prefers individual action on civic issues. In contrast to some other Afro-Christian religious leaders in New York City, like Al Sharpton (National Action Network) and Herbert Daughtry (United House of Prayer), Flake rarely participates in mass action or public agitation. For instance, with the exception of the killing of an unarmed African immigrant by the New York Police Department in 1999, Reverend Flake has joined few of the notable protest demonstrations in New York City. His absence from the frontlines of protest in New York City is not due to a lack of concern. Rather, social reform through boycotts and demonstrations is not his method. Therefore, he limits his participation in direct protest action. Perhaps as a result, public officials and corporate executives invite him to sit on influential boards, call on him to give them policy advice, and sometimes seek from him political cover for actions that have negative consequences. For more on the political actions of Reverend Flake, see Michael Leo Owens, "The Reverend Floyd Flake: African Methodist Episcopal Church Minister for School Choice," in *Religious*

Leaders and Faith-based Politics: Ten Profiles, ed. Jo Renee Formicola and Hubert Morken (Lanham, Md.: Rowman and Littlefield, 2001).

56 Remarks made by Reverend Calvin O. Butts on *Like It Is,* Show # 1108, 31 May 1998.

57 Philip Lentz, "Giuliani Blocks Harlem Project in Butts Feud," *CRAINS,* 1–7 February 1998: 1.

58 Alice Pendarvis [pseud.], interviewed by author, taped recording, Manhattan, 18 October 1999.

59 New York City Department of Housing Preservation and Development, "The Rebirth of Harlem Continues: Over $100 million in Public-Private Funds to be Invested in 116th Street," 14 July 1999 (#17-99) press release.

60 Gregory J. Dees, "Social Enterprise: Private Initiatives for the Common Good" (Cambridge: Harvard Business School, Note #9-395-116, 1994).

61 Fred Robinson [pseud.], interviewed by author, taped recording, Brooklyn, 30 June 1999.

62 Darryl Bluestone [pseud.], interviewed by author, taped recording, Manhattan, 23 November 1999.

63 Pamela Myers [pseud.], interviewed by author, taped recording, Queens, 8 June 1999.

10

FAITH-BASED INITIATIVES AND THE

CONSTITUTION: BLACK CHURCHES, GOVERNMENT,

AND SOCIAL SERVICES DELIVERY

David Ryden

In a meeting in Austin with black ministers from around the country, [President-elect] Bush will return to one of the first themes of his presidential campaign and the bedrock of his "compassionate conservative" message: the use of religious programs to deliver services such as drug treatment and welfare-to-work programs that typically have been handled by government. Bush is calculating that by reaching out to the African-American clergymen, he can find common ground with the black community on such issues as charity tax credits, lighter regulations for "faith-based" social service providers and school vouchers for disadvantaged students. — *Washington Post,* 19 December 2000

The session provoked complaints of exclusion from civil rights leaders and representatives of the nation's largest denominations of black churches. "I know the subplot: This is an attempt to play one group against the other," Jesse L. Jackson said in an interview. "Meeting with political leaders is one thing and meeting with ministers is another." — *Washington Post,* 21 December 2000

The provision of the 1996 welfare legislation known as Charitable Choice aimed to clarify church-state relations in the realm of social service delivery and to encourage government solicitation of faith-based organizations in administering social services. It did so by easing the restrictions and regulations that normally accompany such involvement. As a result, policymakers have become increasingly open to faith-based organizations' participation in adoption, day care and foster childcare, substance abuse rehabilitation, juvenile justice and corrections, and a host of other social programs.

Charitable Choice existed in relative obscurity, receiving little attention from academics, public officials, or social service practitioners. However, President George W. Bush's establishment of a White House Office of Faith-Based and Community Initiatives has catapulted Charitable Choice into the limelight, provoking a vigorous debate over the merits of governmental/religious sector partnerships.

Charitable Choice and the rise of governmental/religious sector partnerships are of particular relevance to black churches, given their long-standing involvement in the public square. Yet the positions of African American churches and clergy on Charitable Choice have varied widely. For some, black churches' rich history of political activism and social outreach uniquely positions them to apply governmental resources toward the betterment of their neighborhoods. For others, taking on the government as partner would inevitably come at the expense of the historically prophetic presence of black churches. The paucity of empirical evidence on the effectiveness of governmental/religious sector partnerships makes it difficult to offer firm conclusions as to their wisdom. Conclusive answers require significant additional empirical testing and rigorous analysis of Charitable Choice programs—to clarify their utility as a social service delivery mechanism and to determine any detrimental impact on churches and religious organizations that enter into a pact with the government.

Of particular importance to both advocates and opponents of Charitable Choice is the question of its constitutional viability. Charitable Choice presents a complicated constitutional picture, especially in light of the unsettledness of current Establishment Clause doctrine. The constitutionality of state/religious sector ventures is an open question, dependent largely on the details of the relationship between the government and the religious organization in any given case. It is incumbent upon public officials and religious organizations to exercise caution in crafting Charitable Choice programs and to do so with an eye to possible constitutional constraints.

*Charitable Choice and the Personal Responsibility
and Work Opportunity Act of 1996*

The demarcation between public and private in the social services arena has always been blurred and porous, a unique sharing of responsibility. Religious charities played a central role in establishing practices of private charity.[1] Even in the context of the modern welfare state, private faith-based social service organizations were the beneficiaries of substantial federal monies. In recent decades, those practices have existed in increasing tension with an evolving set of legal constraints imposed by the Establishment Clause of the First Amendment of the U.S. Constitution. Religious groups' inclusion in government-funded social service delivery survived in part due to public officials' willingness to gloss over First Amendment complications in instances where needed social services were being provided. First Amendment concerns did lead, however, to subtle and not-so-subtle pressures on organizations to mute their religious character, to alter their spiritual mission and strategies — in short, to submerge their religious character to avoid legal retribution.

The collective attitudes of policymakers toward church-state linkages in social services underwent a marked change with the advent of the Republican congressional majority in 1994 and the heightened presence of religious conservatives at all levels of government. Lawmakers were more willing to invite religious groups to actively take part in government programs; they also asserted a corollary need for explicit legal protection for those organizations that did. This paradigmatic shift culminated in the Charitable Choice provision of the Personal Responsibility and Work Opportunity Act of 1996. This hotly debated and highly controversial welfare bill brought to an end the six-decade-old federal entitlement for welfare.[2] It shifted primary responsibility and financial support for the poor to states via block grants that included strict time caps for receipt of benefits and mandated work requirements.

Meanwhile, the Charitable Choice provision of the bill provided legal "cover" for expanded interaction between government and faith-based organizations. The provision had two parts — it put religious groups on equal footing with other groups in the pursuit of public welfare funds, while insulating those receiving funds from governmental demands to compromise their religious identity and character. The statute required states to "contract with religious organizations, [and] to allow religious organizations to accept certificates, vouchers, or other forms of disbursement . . . *on the same basis as* any other nongovernmental provider *without impairing the religious character of such organizations.*"[3] In short, the government cannot discriminate against religious organizations. Religious providers of welfare-related services cannot be excluded from public programs that use the independent sector simply because they are religious. Moreover, participating religious groups retain their independence in (1) how they define, practice, and express their religious beliefs, (2) their form of internal governance, and (3) their right to display religious art, icons, scriptures, and other symbols and imagery.[4]

Charitable Choice contained several protections for the religious liberties of program beneficiaries. It moved to preempt constitutional objections by specifying that all programs are to be implemented consistent with the Establishment Clause. It also precluded faith-based providers from discriminating against welfare recipients on the basis of their religious belief or for refusing to take part in religious exercises.[5] Finally, the statute explicitly barred the use of any funds for "sectarian worship, instruction, or *proselytization.*"[6]

The Impact of Charitable Choice to Date

The tale of Charitable Choice's implementation is one with multiple story lines. One thread is that Charitable Choice has not produced a major shift of public monies to private religious charities or churches. While there has been little comprehensive analysis of Charitable Choice to date, those attempts to quantify its impact reveal modest success at best. Mark Chaves's National Congregations Study shows the extent to which Charitable Choice has yet to take hold. His survey of 1236 congregations found that while over half of them carried out social service projects, only 3 percent received government money to help fund those programs.[7] Amy Sherman of the Hudson Institute recently completed a partial cataloging of Charitable Choice collaborations within nine selected states. She found that, from fiscal 1997 to the end of the summer of fiscal 1999, a total of 125 programs represented Charitable Choice collaborations. Those programs totaled just over $6 million out of a total of $17 billion in Temporary Assistance to Needy Families.[8] Michael Leo Owens concludes from Sherman's study that Charitable Choice at the state level is being implemented only at the most primitive level.[9]

The level of awareness among churches and religious organizations is strikingly low. According to Chaves, among those individuals identified as holding key positions of authority in their congregations, eight in ten were unaware of Charitable Choice.[10] In a survey of four hundred leaders of sectarian institutions in the Philadelphia area, Ram Cnaan of the University of

Pennsylvania found that only 8 percent of responding clerics knew about Charitable Choice.[11] Moreover, the lack of familiarity with Charitable Choice is not limited to the faith-based sector. It is found in equal measure among public officials. Amy Sherman, who has closely monitored the implementation of Charitable Choice, characterized it as marred by "vast ignorance both in the government sector and the faith sector."[12] The Center for Public Justice, the most aggressive watchdog of Charitable Choice issues, recently issued a state-by-state report card grading efforts to implement Charitable Choice.[13] Only a dozen of the fifty states received passing grades. The report card found that most states had done little or nothing to further Charitable Choice, displaying either ignorance or mistaken understandings of its content.[14] The California Religious Community Capacity Study by the Center for Religion and Civic Culture found California's welfare agencies "slow to implement the Charitable Choice provisions" and failing to "systematically orient" county welfare agency directors to Charitable Choice.[15] A case study of the impact of Charitable Choice on the Salvation Army by the Center for Public Justice concurred, concluding that "few state agencies know about [Charitable Choice] much less have acted on [it]."[16]

But while these reports suggest that the impact of Charitable Choice has been limited thus far, it cannot be written off as an insignificant or irrelevant piece of legislation. A second story line is the significant potential for Charitable Choice to expand well beyond its currently modest proportions. This is reflected in relatively high numbers of clergy who have expressed interest in obtaining public funds for their churches' social outreach. Chaves's study found that 36 percent of the clergy interviewed, representing 45 percent of churchgoing Americans, would be open to applying for government money to support their human services programs.[17] A recent survey of several thousand voters, conducted by Brookings and the Pew Charitable Trusts, found that 64 percent supported the idea of allowing religious organizations to apply for public funding for social services.[18] Ram Cnaan's study of Philadelphia pastors likewise indicated that well over half (62 percent) expressed interest in their congregations' receiving public funds for their social service programs.[19] These numbers indicate that "the 'market' for charitable choice implementation in American religion apparently is fairly sizeable."[20] A concentrated effort to increase the awareness and knowledge of both public officials and private leaders might well lead to significant expansion of Charitable Choice.[21]

Moreover, the breadth of the reach of Charitable Choice has yet to be determined. We may have only scratched the surface regarding those federally funded programs to which Charitable Choice might be extended. In addition to welfare funds, Charitable Choice was included in the Community Services Block Grant of the Health and Human Services Reauthorization Act of 1998.[22] It was also extended to cover substance abuse treatment funds, as part of the reauthorization of the Children's Health Act of 2000. And there are ongoing efforts in Congress to dramatically expand Charitable Choice. At the close of the 106th congressional term in 2000 at least ten pending bills contained some variation on Charitable Choice. Those bills addressed such subjects as juvenile justice, family literacy, home ownership, youth drug and mental health services, adoption, and parental support.[23] The Charitable Choice Expansion Act (S. 1113) would apply Charitable Choice provisions to virtually every public health and social service program receiving federal funds.[24] Those efforts have continued with the introduction of additional Charitable Choice legislation.[25] Finally, and perhaps most significantly, the power of the presidency is now firmly behind the expansion of Charitable Choice and faith-based initiatives. As governor of Texas, George W. Bush led the most aggressive effort of any state to establish Charitable Choice ventures, and Texas received the highest marks in the Center for Public Justice's Charitable Choice Compliance report.[26] On taking office as president, he promptly created the White House Office of Faith-Based and Community Initiatives. His trumpeting of faith-based initiatives, while generating serious opposition, has also galvanized a level of support and enthusiasm for faith-based efforts that had heretofore been absent. In short, Charitable Choice in the welfare context may only be the tip of the iceberg; the issues it raises conceivably could extend to virtually all publicly sponsored social programs.

Charitable Choice and Black Churches

Among African Americans and black churches, a similar disjuncture exists between the actual and potential impact of Charitable Choice. Of 1531 urban black churches surveyed by Lincoln and Mamiya, only 8 percent acknowledged receiving public support for social service activities.[27] In Tobi Jennifer Printz's study of 266 mostly African American churches in the Washington, D.C., area, only eleven were receiving government funds, representing only 5 percent of the aggregate budgets of the churches surveyed.[28] At the same time, the interest in Charitable Choice among black churches, and among African Americans generally, is substantially higher than that of whites. The National Congregations Study found that 64 percent of black congregations, compared to only 28 percent of white ones, were interested in receiving public funds for their programs. When controlled for other variables, the study concluded, "predominantly black congregations are five times more likely than other congregations to seek public support for social service activities."[29] Chaves concluded that if Charitable Choice does in fact grow into a more successful policy initiative, it is likely "that large African-American congregations will be substantially over-represented among those who take advantage of these opportunities."[30]

The reality behind these numbers is more complicated, however. There is hardly consensus among African American churches and clergy regarding the wisdom of pursuing Charitable Choice. If anything, welfare reform and Charitable Choice have only amplified long-standing differences within the African American community regarding "the appropriate roles of government — the powerful but distant potential defender, and the church — the central communal institution."[31] These divisions can be traced to the multiple roles filled by churches in black communities.

Black churches are much more than simply spiritual centers or places of worship. They also provide political direction, leadership, and a forum for speech, and they generally serve as a catalyst for black cultural identity.[32] They represent a source of neighborhood stability and social structure and, as Ronald Walters notes, they provide a base for black empowerment and mobilization politically, socially, and economically.[33] Harold Dean Trulear has called churches the "centers of neighborhood and community life."[34] The strong social mission of black churches is evident in a host of studies. A 1990 nationwide survey of 2100 black churches found that 70 percent had one or more social outreach programs.[35] Two-thirds of black church leaders surveyed in the National Black Church Family Project testified to having at least one community outreach program, with over 40 percent having at least three such programs.[36] Another study of African American churches in the Atlanta area revealed that 85 percent engaged in some form of outreach beyond pastoral or educational programs.[37] Chaves and Higgins concluded from an empirical study in the early 1990s that black churches are significantly more involved than white churches in providing programs for the poor.[38]

Proponents of Charitable Choice contend that because black churches are such a noticeable presence in the community, they are especially suited to help build a sense of community. Charlene Turner Johnson, the director of Michigan Neighborhood Partnership in Detroit, describes churches as "ideally suited for neighborhood-based work . . . we're real, human, touching."[39] John DiIulio, who until recently led Bush's Office of Faith-Based and Community Initiatives, likewise asserts that this attentiveness to the political, economic, and social needs of African Americans gives churches a unique community-building power.[40] As the most permanent institutional presence in urban neighborhoods, black churches are thought to have a capacity to bind together individuals, groups, and society that the state cannot match.

The tensions between the social and political roles of churches have produced reactions to Charitable Choice that are often at odds. The political dimension—what Trulear calls the "prophetic presence" in the face of a society dismissive of the needs of black communities—generates a suspicion of and wariness toward the state as formal partner.[41] The social dimension—the active role churches play in meeting the social needs of their members—yields a willingness to consider Charitable Choice as a means of increasing their capacity for such services.

The Political—The Churches' "Prophetic Presence"

Black churches in their prophetic role have served as voices of opposition, "more confrontational than cooperative, more protest than partner."[42] The churches' protest voice was reflected in adamant opposition to the welfare reform of 1996, which was viewed as depriving urban minorities of badly needed public assistance. In this context, one would expect resistance to Charitable Choice among black churches. The law was the product of a conservative Republican majority in Congress, part of a welfare bill regarded as anathema by the black community. The Congressional Black Caucus was outspoken in its opposition to the passage of the welfare legislation, and the NAACP likewise opposed it. Strong opposition also came from liberal black church leaders accustomed to defending the federal government and its role in caring for and uplifting the black community.[43]

The "prophetic" voice of black religious leaders also generated skepticism toward Charitable Choice, due to its attachment to a law they saw as unjust. The study by the Center for Religion and Civic Culture found that, among politically liberal African American religious leaders, "Charitable Choice . . . evokes negative reactions." The study cites the irritation felt by urban African American "civil rights" congregations toward Charitable Choice. "Many specifically resist seeking public funds for welfare-to-work programs, because they do not like what welfare reform is doing in African-American communities."[44] Several pastors invoke the prophetic voice of justice in describing their dissatisfaction with Charitable Choice:

> James Lawson (Pastor Emeritus of Los Angeles's Holman United Methodist Church) often speaks about welfare reform as being a new form of indentured servitude, and he suggests that African-American churches should seriously question whether they ought to conspire with the makers of such a corrupt welfare-to-work system. William Campbell, an African-American pastor who currently administers Clergy and Laity United for Economic Justice, agrees. "Welfare reform is a disentitlement program," he says. "We need to do guerrilla work, not to cooperate with the dismantlers of our safety net."[45]

Charitable Choice and the larger welfare law were viewed as "cover" for shrinking the government's commitment to the urban poor under the rubric of devolution and privatization[46]; the state was seen as dumping its responsibility for care of the poor on an already overburdened faith community. For many clergy, black churches already overtaxed in their capacity to serve could not fill the gaps left by government's retreat. Earl Graves, editor of *Black Enterprise* magazine, spoke for black clergy and other leaders in stating that "black businesses and the black church are doing more than their fair share" in ministering to those affected by decreasing government assistance.[47] In her survey of churches in the Washington, D.C., area, Tobi Jennifer Printz found that "the majority of survey respondents believe they do not currently have the facilities, staff, or funds to satisfy an increase in demand" for services.[48] In the end, the political stance of black churches against an unpalatable welfare law made it difficult to embrace Charitable Choice.

The churches' political role created another basis for opposition to Charitable Choice—concern that collaboration with the government will undermine the churches' capacity to speak and act prophetically. William Campbell describes Charitable Choice as "a feeding frenzy, an unseemly hustle to get contracts. We should be promoting advocacy around economic issues and standards. It shouldn't be about who gets money."[49] The danger is that black churches and other religiously affiliated organizations, once they have enjoyed the fruits of government resources, will be timid in condemning ongoing injustices or policy shortcomings affecting black communities. Charitable Choice could represent a new form of political patronage, where acceptance of public funds dilutes the black church's function as moral conscience for government's treatment of society's dispossessed. Charitable Choice could mean the contracting out of social services to those clergy and congregations willing to endorse and politically support the administration. The muting of the voice of protest would be the cost of participation in governmentally sponsored programs. As Joan Walsh notes, lucrative "community development" contracts and generous government resources have turned more than one militant preacher into defender of a corrupt power structure.[50] The question is whether collaboration with government can be had without compromise of the church's moral voice.

Black Clergy and Charitable Choice—Opportunity or Opposition?

As a result of these dual roles, fault lines have appeared between liberal and conservative black clergy over the merits of Charitable Choice. Liberal "civil rights" congregations and black political leadership tend to oppose the bill.[51] Conservative religious leaders such as John Perkins, Tony Evans, and Gerald Austin castigated the old federal welfare system and are outspoken in their support for reforms, including Charitable Choice.[52] As an illustration of the differences among black clergy, Ron Walters cites the case of Reverend Floyd Flake, a former Democratic U.S. Congressman from New York. Flake directs a series of social service programs through his large AME church in Queens and is highly supportive of Charitable Choice. Once a member of the Congressional Black Caucus, Flake resigned over its opposition to Charitable Choice.[53] The California Religious Community Capacity Study likewise found conservative African American churches to be supportive of Charitable Choice; it cited the right-leaning Coalition on Urban Renewal and Education (CURE) as the most prominent example. CURE "regularly expresses support for Charitable Choice" and offers workshops to aid African American churches in competing for welfare-to-work contracts.[54] An informational Charitable Choice conference sponsored by the Coalition on Urban Renewal and Education in mid-1998 in Los Angeles drew some four hundred urban pastors representing over a quarter of a million members.[55]

The fissures among African American leaders were recently brought into focus when then President-elect George W. Bush hosted a meeting of ministers to discuss faith-based initiatives in his administration.[56] Although the group of pastors who met with Bush represented diverse faiths and ethnic backgrounds, the largest representation came from black clergy sympathetic to Charitable Choice.[57] Meanwhile, the meeting drew loud complaints from civil rights leaders and representatives of the Congress of National Black Churches.[58] Some viewed it as an effort to drive a wedge between black clergy and the political black leadership, calling it "an end run around the traditional civil rights groups and their leaders."[59]

Meanwhile, some black churches have moved away from their initial opposition to welfare reform and now collaborate in the implementation of the policy. A growing number of African American churches are courting public funds and embracing public/private social service ventures. In Indiana, for example, a major effort to reach out to churches has resulted in the establishment of an initiative called FaithWorks Indiana, which has received its most enthusiastic response from urban African American churches.[60] Additional examples are provided by Harold Dean Trulear, who documents black churches' collaborations with public officials in addressing high-risk urban youth;[61] and by a Center for Religion and Civic Culture study that focuses on the completion of a welfare-to-work contract by a prominent African Methodist Episcopal Church in Los Angeles.[62]

Despite such anecdotal evidence, the ultimate success of such partnerships is unknown.[63] Careful monitoring and in-depth analysis are needed to verify how Charitable Choice programs are performing and to determine their structural impact on churches and other faith-based organizations. Until then, Charitable Choice presents a difficult choice for black churches and religious organizations. Committed to ministering to the poorest and most alienated in society, they may view Charitable Choice as an appealing source of funds through which to provide expanded social service. At the same time, participation in Charitable Choice programs might be seen as condoning welfare reform or its primary political sponsors, thereby weakening the churches' voice of protest.[64] It remains for African American churches to decide whether their prophetic and social service roles can be reconciled.

The Constitutional Perils of Charitable Choice

The final set of concerns surrounding Charitable Choice programs is the legal and constitutional dimensions of state/religious sector partnerships. In stark contrast to the pitched debate over public funding of parochial schools, the constitutional implications of state/faith-based collaborations have largely been ignored to date.[65] Such complacency is ill-advised, as questions as to the constitutionality of Charitable Choice have shifted from the hypothetical to the actual. In July 2000, two civil rights organizations filed a legal action in Texas challenging a publicly funded job-training program; this marked the first formal test of a Charitable Choice program.[66] That suit has been followed by at least three other formal legal challenges to faith-based governmental programs.[67] Moreover, President Bush's support for faith-based programs has brought Charitable Choice out of the shadows, thereby elevating the constitutional stakes. Heightened legal scrutiny is inevitable.

Again, African American voices are found on both sides of the legal debate. On one hand, there has traditionally existed among black churches a lower barrier between church and state than with other religious communities.[68] As a result, there is a relative lack of concern over constitutional objections for large numbers of black clergy willing to consider Charitable Choice funding.[69] Harold Dean Trulear of Public/Private Ventures in Philadelphia and a strong supporter of Charitable Choice is representative of those who view Charitable Choice as having resolved church-state issues for religious groups partnering with government.[70]

On the other hand, the Congressional Black Caucus has maintained its opposition to Charitable Choice on legal grounds. The CBC's most recent annual legislative conference included a session titled "Charitable Choice — A New Threat to Civil Rights."[71] Representatives of the NAACP's Legal and Educational Fund also took part in the conference, opposing Charitable Choice on grounds that it impermissibly allows discrimination in hiring on the basis of religious belief.[72]

Among some black religious leaders, opposition to Charitable Choice stems in part from their strong Baptist affiliation. While Mark Chaves's National Congregations Study found that two-thirds of black congregations were interested in pursuing Charitable Choice funding, among black Baptist congregations, the level of support dropped to 40 percent.[73] Many black clergy are "appropriately wary of the strings that often come attached to public funding."[74] The Baptist Joint Committee on Public Affairs (BJCPA) officially opposes Charitable Choice, terming it "a frontal assault on the First Amendment's Establishment Clause."[75] By permitting the funding of "pervasively sectarian organizations," the BJCPA views Charitable Choice as condoning the unacceptable public funding of religious worship and education.[76]

Charitable Choice: Insulation or Illusion?

Who is right? For those collaborating with the government, how much cause for concern is there with respect to the legal soundness of Charitable Choice? Again, definitive answers are elusive, due both to contradictions within the Charitable Choice statute and the lack of clarity plaguing Establishment Clause doctrine.

The specter of constitutional impropriety in the past has enfeebled religious organizations' desire and ability to access government funds for social service outreach. Pressures, perceived and real, to mute or purge a contracting organization's religious character to avoid legal challenge eliminated the very dimension that, in the minds of many, ensured lasting success. Charitable Choice meant to remedy this by (1) enhancing policymakers' ability to tap the religious sector in administering social services, and (2) easing the First Amendment demands to secularize the services of participating faith-based organizations. Charitable Choice sought to bring faith-based service providers to the table, while insulating their spiritual character and autonomy.

But does Charitable Choice achieve the desired results? An honest reading of the law and a sense of its underlying spirit suggest intrinsic tensions, if not outright contradictions. First, the law requires programs to be implemented in compliance with the Establishment Clause. But it also explicitly permits religious organizations receiving grants to hire based on religion and to maintain overt religious displays in the workplace. The permissibility of these practices under the Establishment Clause is by no means clear. Second, Charitable Choice ensures the rights of participating religious organizations to fully practice or express their religious beliefs. Yet no government funds "shall be expended for sectarian worship, instruction, or proselytization." The potential problems are self-evident; for some evangelical religious organizations, witnessing and proselytizing are essential components of their religious practice.

Finally, the statutory language is arguably at odds with the very spirit of the Establishment Clause. Charitable Choice expressly prohibits the use of funds for religious dissemination. But the subsidizing of religious groups in social welfare programs is based on a tacit acknowledgment of the transformative power of religion. As one pair of scholars notes, "the obvious difficulty in limiting government assistance to religious social activism lies in the most important reason why church-based institutions achieve good results: They convert people."[77] The assertion that religious groups have a special capacity to effectively address destructive behavior warrants their involvement in social service delivery only if the underlying religious belief is shared with the program beneficiary. Contrary to its specific language, Charitable Choice arguably presumes that religious values will at some point be conveyed in the service delivery. At the very least, Charitable Choice "pushes the envelope of existing judicial interpretations of the establishment of religion clause of the First Amendment."[78] Given these questions, it is unlikely that Charitable Choice merely codifies existing First Amendment law, as some have argued.[79]

Constitutional Arguments Surrounding Charitable Choice Programs

Charitable Choice has not resolved the constitutional uncertainties surrounding state/religious sector collaborations. At the same time, ambiguities in current Establishment Clause guidelines prevent a more definitive answer.[80] It remains unclear whether the Constitution allows public funding of a secular purpose via religious organizations that might also incidentally advance or involve religion in the process. The only certainty in the realm of Establishment Clause jurisprudence is its uncertainty—the bounds of constitutional propriety are murky at best. There exists no single, settled line of jurisprudential analysis governing establishment disputes. While members of the Supreme Court are openly dissatisfied with the controlling *Lemon* test, they have been unable either to completely jettison it or to settle on a suitable substitute standard. Nor is the Court's current alignment on church-state issues by any means secure, given the election of George W. Bush and multiple appointments possible in the near future. In short, any predictions of how the Court might rule on Charitable Choice are highly suspect.[81]

THE TRADITIONAL LEMON TEST

The infamous three-part *Lemon* test provides the general constitutional framework for evaluating Establishment Clause queries.[82] The first prong, the presence of a legitimate secular purpose, is almost always easily satisfied. In the case of Charitable Choice partnerships, the aim might be to boost a welfare recipient to self-sufficiency, revitalize the economic viability of a neighborhood, or promote health and physical well-being. The constitutional rub comes with the tension between the second and third prongs; they simultaneously require that the primary effect of a program be neither to advance nor to inhibit religion, and that it not foster excessive entanglement between government and religion. Each prong is difficult to satisfy without breaching the other. By minimizing regulatory oversight to avoid excessive entanglement, the state may allow an organization to freely mix the spiritual and secular dimensions of its ministry. Greater oversight is necessary to guard against programs that might integrate the spiritual into the services. With that, of course, comes the danger of excessive entanglement.

Under the *Lemon* analysis, that which makes church-state partnerships attractive as policy may be their constitutional Achilles' heel. Religious nonprofits are appealing precisely because they are free to fashion alternative means of program delivery that fit local communities and individual clients. Yet constitutional constraints in the form of government regulation dampen nonprofit autonomy and innovation. But a hands-off approach to avoid micromanaging FBO activities raises theoretical and practical legal questions. Inattentiveness by the state may enable the organization to laxly interpret Charitable Choice and permit overt sharing of faith or more coercive evangelizing, contrary to the Establishment Clause. From the state's perspective, the ambiguities in Establishment Clause doctrine mandate closer supervi-

sion of Charitable Choice programs, not less. But can this be accomplished
without compromising programmatic effectiveness?

BOWEN V. KENDRICK AND THE "PERVASIVELY SECTARIAN" STANDARD
The general prohibition against public money for the advancement of religion is hardly definitive. Countless layers have been added to the *Lemon*
analysis, particularly when considering the constitutionality of programs
that permit public funds to go to private religious institutions. Perhaps the
most significant addition was the "pervasively sectarian" standard, compli-
ments of the Court's 1989 ruling in *Bowen v. Kendrick*.[83] That more specific principle permits public subsidies of religious organizations, provided
they are applied only to the secular activities of those institutions. Funds
received by a sectarian organization must be earmarked and used only for
segregated secular activities. "Pervasively sectarian" organizations — those so
thoroughly religious that their secular and religious activities cannot be separated — are disqualified from receipt of government funds. For such institutions, public funding inevitably would advance religion.

The Supreme Court's decision in *Bowen v. Kendrick* is most analogous
factually to Charitable Choice programs. That case involved the Adolescent
Family Life Act (AFLA).[84] The act sought to reduce teenage pregnancy among
unwed mothers by authorizing funds for private organizations, religious and
otherwise, to provide counseling and education. It furnished grants for nonprofits to provide counseling to women on premarital sex, contraceptives,
pregnancy, and child rearing. Services included pregnancy testing, mater-
nity counseling, adoption counseling and referral, pre- and postnatal care,
and childcare. The statute stressed the need for "the provision of support by
other family members, religious and charitable organizations, voluntary associations, and other groups."[85] It explicitly included religious charities as
qualified to compete for and receive grants.

When the law was challenged under the Establishment Clause, the Supreme Court upheld its constitutionality but drew the line against federal
funds flowing to institutions that were "pervasively sectarian." Applying the
Lemon test, the majority found a legitimate secular purpose in the statute's
desire to reduce the socioeconomic fallout from teenage pregnancy. With respect to the second prong, the Court concluded that the statute's "primary
effect" was not to advance religion, since there was no actual intent to endorse

religion. The statute did not require religious grantees, nor did it require that programs or services be inherently religious. It was considered facially neutral toward religion, since religious organizations were only one among a list of nonprofits and private sector actors who qualified. The majority found no precedent to bar Congress from giving religious organizations a hand in addressing certain secular problems.

In addressing the third prong and the threat of excessive entanglement, the Court addressed the "pervasively sectarian" threshold. The standard to be applied was whether a grantee's secular purposes and religious mission were inextricably intertwined. The question was whether the service provider was so pervasively religious that a substantial portion of its functions was subsumed under its religious mission. The majority found that, on its face, AFLA did not disseminate funds to organizations so pervasively sectarian that funds could not be earmarked for secular purposes alone within the organization. Instead, the case was remanded to determine whether funds were in fact flowing to pervasively sectarian religious institutions.

Challenges to Charitable Choice may well depend on the continuing validity of the "pervasively sectarian" standard. If that standard remains good law, it presents serious problems for the future of Charitable Choice.[86] The statute explicitly allows several practices that previously had been thought to constitute evidence that an organization was pervasively sectarian and therefore disqualified from receiving federal funds. The *Bowen* majority identified possible signs of a "pervasively sectarian" organization — proximity of the organization to a sponsoring church, the presence of religious symbols and paintings on the premises, formal church or denominational control over the organization, application of religious criteria to hiring decisions, whether the organization engages in religious services or other religious activities. Each of these is permissible under the explicit language of Charitable Choice.[87]

Charitable Choice would appear to facilitate the transmission of public dollars to "pervasively sectarian" organizations. A study by John Orr and Cleveland Stevens suggests that, since Charitable Choice's passage, groups taking public funds are less careful to keep their secular and sacred parts distinct. Their examination of a handful of Los Angeles–area FBOs that rely in part on public monies found that their "human services and religious activities are usually intertwined to greater or lesser degrees." Publicly funded human services were housed and scheduled side by side with religious activities. They shared staff and personnel. Funds supported religious and social services activities simultaneously. Even technically independent nonprofits remained infused with the religious culture and identity of the parent institution. There was an "obvious intermingling of religious, moral, and therapeutic language" among the human services.[88]

The Orr study suggests that organizations partnering with government have been emboldened by the support at the public policy level; they are more willing to openly link their participation in government programs with their religious identity and purpose. For such groups, involvement in government programs is as much about the transmission of faith as it is about service. Their ministries are premised on the notion that effective social service necessitates a spiritual component. The secular and sacred components cannot be partitioned but are intertwined and integrated; they cannot be unraveled without undermining the core of the services. This inevitable coupling of service with faith is difficult to reconcile with a constitutional prohibition against funding of "pervasively sectarian" groups by the government.[89]

DOES "PERVASIVELY SECTARIAN" STILL APPLY? — THE ALTERNATE STANDARD OF "NEUTRALITY"

Proponents of Charitable Choice argue in response that, in the face of the statute, the "pervasively sectarian" standard is no longer applicable. The Center for Public Justice bluntly concludes that Charitable Choice directly excludes public officials from withholding funds from "pervasively sectarian" groups.[90] Trulear of Public/Private Ventures similarly asserts that "we can now move beyond social services provided by 'religiously affiliated' organizations to services provided by what we may call 'pervasively religious' institutions."[91] Instead, backers of Charitable Choice have argued for a standard of neutrality. This would allow the state to enact policies in which benefits flow to religion, provided governmental assistance to religious groups is offered neutrally and without distinction or discrimination between different religious groups or between religious and nonsectarian groups. Charitable Choice, its supporters contend, would easily survive a neutrality statute, since it does not favor a particular denomination or faith.[92]

The Court's most recent decision confirms the conflict over the applicable standard. *Mitchell v. Helms*[93] failed to resolve the question but revealed that neither the "neutrality" nor the "pervasively sectarian" standard has a majority of the Court on board. In *Mitchell,* the Supreme Court upheld by a 6–3 vote a federal program that provided educational equipment and materials, such as library books and computer software, to public and private schools. A four-justice plurality embraced "neutrality" as the applicable standard. They would allow public aid to religious organizations, provided it is "allocated on the basis of neutral, secular criteria that neither favor nor disfavor religion, and is made available to both religious and secular beneficiaries on a nondiscriminatory basis." The plurality also explicitly rejected the pervasively sectarian standard, concluding that "nothing in the Establishment Clause requires the exclusion of pervasively sectarian schools from otherwise permissible aid programs."

Yet neither of these facets of the plurality opinion was able to garner a fifth and decisive vote on the Court. In fact, the likely fifth vote, Justice O'Connor, objected in her occurrence to the potential breadth and application of such a "neutrality" standard. As a result, it is clear only that the pervasively sectarian standard is of questionable viability. Whether "neutrality" is an acceptable substitute is open to debate and will depend on the circumstances at hand and the potential breadth of its application. Scholars as well as interested advocacy groups have been lining up on both sides of the conflict.[94] On one side, organizations like the Christian Legal Society and the Center for Public Justice seek the death knell of the pervasively sectarian standard.[95] The American Civil Liberties Union, Jewish organizations, and Americans United for Separation of Church and State continue to invoke the standard, maintaining that "the constitutional prohibition against direct funding of pervasively sectarian institutions, especially where the funds will be used for religious purposes, remains intact."[96]

Conclusion

The fractures on the Supreme Court preclude any authoritative interpretation of the Establishment Clause in the context of aid to religious organizations. The interminable debate over the parameters and implications of the Establishment Clause is not close to resolution. Competing accommodationist and separationist positions reflect fundamental differences of opinion and interpretation, neither side of which is without merit. Consequently, the unsettledness of Establishment Clause doctrine presents a peril for those who plunge into Charitable Choice programs unaware of its vagaries or the issues upon which constitutionality hinges. Religious nonprofits receiving government funds occupy a legally vulnerable position. Legal challenges could have serious ramifications for governmental actors, the religious nonprofits doing business with them, and program recipients themselves. The lack of constitutional clarity in Establishment Clause doctrine compels FBOS and their governmental allies to proceed with caution.

Some conclusions are possible. The constitutional viability of any program will depend heavily on the details of individual programs and their implementation. In the spirit of *Bowen,* Charitable Choice might be found to be neutral on its face, in which case questions of constitutionality will proceed case by case and depend on the details of particular programs. It is important, then, that FBOS or churches contracting with the government take precautions to minimize the risks of unconstitutionality. Traits that might palliate the constitutional threats include (1) delivering services through a separately incorporated organization rather than directly out of a church, (2) ensuring a real and accessible array of nonreligious alternative service providers, (3) evenhandedness in dispensing contracts between faiths, denominations, and between secular and religious organizations, (4) explicit training for FBOS to avoid evangelizing and proselytizing, and (5) the use of vouchers.[97]

The constitutional issues as they apply to African-American churches are especially nuanced. First, black churches are less disposed to treat the Establishment Clause as some pristine wall separating church business from politics. Many black clergy are accustomed to spicing worship and preaching with the political. They may be more inclined to consider potential partnerships with the government, constitutional objections notwithstanding.

Moreover, the case for allowing black churches to participate in government-sponsored social programs is arguably more compelling than it is for their white counterparts. The rationale for funneling government services to recipients through faith-based organizations is especially apt for black churches, given their integral place in poorer, urban communities. If black churches indeed occupy a more central role in the community than do white churches—and if they are in fact more active in social outreach to the communities they serve—then they are uniquely situated to get government benefits into the hands of those who need them. This is especially true given the higher levels of distrust and skepticism that exist among young black men toward the government. Government programs that rely on churches to serve poor or at-risk populations may be looked on with greater favor by judges called on to weigh the constitutional merits of such programs.

In the end, Charitable Choice is an opportunity for black churches to influence the public sector through engagement. This means adding to, not abandoning, past practices — infusing confrontation with collaboration, supplementing petition with participation, not just appealing to government for justice for the community but also working proactively with government to implement policy, in the process effecting justice. It is more than legal/political change through advocacy; it is the pursuit of change in society through service made possible by government.

The perils of partnering with government are multifold, from losing the clarity of one's prophetic voice and primary mission, to the undermining of the religious or spiritual component of service, to excessive dependence on public funds. Before churches wholeheartedly embrace Charitable Choice, they must be cognizant of the constitutional restraints and implications, and how programs might be structured to minimize legal objections. Affiliation with government holds out promise for black religious groups hoping to positively influence their communities; such partnerships, however, are fraught with dangers, legally and organizationally. It is incumbent upon churches to apprise themselves of all considerations before embracing a pact with the government.

Notes

1 See generally Walter I. Trattner, *From Poor Law to Welfare State: A History of Social Welfare in America,* 5th ed. (New York: Free Press, 1994).

2 Public Law 104–193, Title I, sec. 104 (22 August 1996); 110 stat. 2161; 42 U.S.C.A. 604a.

3 Sec. 104(b) (emphasis added).

4 Sec. 104(d).

5 Sec. 104(g).

6 Sec. 104(j) (emphasis added).

7 Mark Chaves, *Religious Congregations and Welfare Reform: Who Will Take Advantage of Charitable Choice?* (Washington, D.C.: Aspen Institute Nonprofit Sector Research Fund, Working Paper Series, spring 1999), 7.

8 See generally Amy L. Sherman, *The Growing Impact of Charitable Choice: A Catalogue of New Collaborations Between Government and Faith-Based Organizations in Nine States* (Washington, D.C.: Center for Public Justice, 2000).

9 See generally Michael Leo Owens, *Sectarian Institutions in State Welfare Reforms: An Analysis of Charitable Choice* (New York: Nelson A. Rockefeller Institute of Government, 2000).

10 Chaves, *Religious Congregations and Welfare Reform*, 7.

11 Ram A. Cnaan, *Keeping the Faith in the City: How 401 Urban Religious Congregations Serve Their Neediest Neighbors* (Philadelphia: Center for Research on Religion and Urban Civil Society, 2000).

12 Amy L. Sherman, *The Growing Impact of Charitable Choice.*

13 See generally Center for Public Justice, *Charitable Choice Compliance: A National Report Card* (Washington, D.C.: Center for Public Justice, 2000), 19 November 2000, http://cpjustice.org/stories/StoryReader$296.

14 States were guilty of a variety of misinterpretations. Some claimed that Charitable Choice was optional and they were free to ignore it. Others wrongly believed that their state constitution exempted them from Charitable Choice. Still others simply ignored Charitable Choice and made no effort to consider its requirements. See Center for Public Justice, *Charitable Choice Compliance.*

15 Center for Religion and Civic Culture, *California Religious Community Capacity Study: Faith-Based Organizations and Welfare Reform*, 30 November 2000, http://www.usc.edu/dept/LAS/religiononline/WelfareReform/capacity/summary.htm.

16 Diane Winston, *Soup, Soap, and Salvation: The Impact of Charitable Choice on the Salvation Army* (Washington, D.C.: The Center for Public Justice, May 2000), 11.

17 Chaves, *Religious Congregations and Welfare Reform*, 8.

18 See generally Brookings Institution, "God-Fearing Voters, God-Fearing Candidates: How Important Will Religion Really Be in the 2000 Election?" press briefing, 29 November 2000, http://brook.edu/comm/transcripts/20000920.htm.

19 Ram A. Cnaan, *Keeping the Faith in the City.*

20 Chaves, *Religious Congregations and Welfare Reform*, 8.

21 A recent survey by Pew Research Center and the Pew Forum on Religion and Public Life revealed strong levels of support generally for faith-based initiatives. Seventy-five percent of survey respondents endorsed allowing churches and houses of worship to compete for government grants and contracts in the social services arena. That survey did reveal reservations about the details of such plans, however. Hanna Rosin and Thomas B. Edsall, "Survey Exposes 'Faith-Based' Plan Hurdles," *Washington Post*, 11 April 2001, A4.

22 Public Law 105–285, Title II, sec. 201 (27 October 1998), 112 Stat. 2749; 42 U.S.C.A. 9920.

23 See generally Center for Public Justice, "Growing Momentum: Legislation to Fur-

ther Expand Charitable Choice," 19 November 2000, http://cpjustice.org/stories/
StoryReader$277.

24   Congress has made other, mostly unsuccessful, efforts in recent years to facilitate
such partnerships. The Project for American Renewal was a legislative effort sponsored by Senator Coats and Congressman Kasich to make available demonstration
grants for programs to match communities of faith with welfare families and non-
violent offenders for mentoring and other assistance to program recipients. Congressman J. C. Watts also proposed removing barriers for faith-based neighborhood
groups to qualify as drug abuse treatment providers. The defeated Religious Freedom amendment also attempted to loosen constraints on federal funds for religious
nonprofits.

25   The Community Solutions Act of 2001 (H.R. 7), introduced by Congressman J. C.
Watts in March 2001, would substantially expand the reach of Charitable Choice.

26   See generally Center for Public Justice, *Charitable Choice Compliance*.

27   Eric Lincoln and Lawrence H. Mamiya, *The Black Church in the African-American
Experience* (Durham, N.C.: Duke University Press, 1990).

28   Tobi Jennifer Printz, *Faith-Based Service Providers in the Nation's Capital: Can They
Do More?* (Urban Institute, no. 2 in "Charting Civil Society" 1999), 11 August 1999,
http://www.urban.org/periodcl/cnp/cnp_2.html. An earlier study by Mark Chaves
reached similar results: Mark Chaves and Lynn M. Higgins, "Comparing the Community Involvement of Black and White Congregations," *Journal for the Scientific
Study of Religion* 31 (1992): 425–40.

29   Chaves, *Religious Congregations and Welfare Reform,* 13. A September 2000 survey
of 1999 voters conducted by the Brookings Institution and the Pew Charitable Trusts
found that 74 percent of blacks endorse direct funding by the government of church-
run social programs, compared to only 51 percent of whites. See Brookings Institution, "God-Fearing Voters." When the question was phrased to allow organizations
to apply for government funding, the support among African Americans rose to 86
percent.

30   Chaves, *Religious Congregations and Welfare Reform,* 836–46. Chaves asserts that
interest among black clergy in Charitable Choice is also more likely to yield concrete programmatic action than among white clergy. He attributes this to a "lower
barrier — both culturally and institutionally — between church and state in African-
American religion," as well as greater power enjoyed by clergy of black churches to
initiate and implement programs of their choosing.

31   Stanley W. Carlson-Thies, "'Don't Look To Us': The Negative Responses of the
Churches to Welfare Reform," *Notre Dame Journal of Law, Ethics, and Public Policy*
11 (1997): 684.

32   Patricia M. Y. Chang, David R. Williams, Ezra E. H. Griffith, and John Young,

"Church-Agency Relationships in the Black Community," *Nonprofit and Voluntary Sector Quarterly* 23 (1994): 93.

33 Brookings Institution, "God-Fearing Voters," 14.

34 Harold Dean Trulear, *Faith-Based Institutions and High-Risk Youth* (Philadelphia: Public/Private Ventures Field Report Series, spring 2000), 10.

35 See generally C. Eric Lincoln and Lawrence H. Mamiya, *The Black Church in the African-American Experience.*

36 Owens, *Sectarian Institutions in State Welfare Reforms,* 9.

37 John J. DiIulio Jr., "Spiritual Capital Can Save Inner-City Youth," 11 December 1997, http://www.intellectualcapital.com/issues/97/1211/icpro.asp. See also Edmund McGarrell, Greg Brinker, and Diana Etundi, "The Role of Faith-Based Organizations in Crime Prevention and Justice," 11 August 1999, http://www.welfarereformer.org/articles/faith_crime.html.

38 Mark Chaves and Lynn M. Higgins, "Comparing the Community Involvement of Black and White Congregations," *Journal for the Scientific Study of Religion* 31 (1992): 425–40.

39 Charlene Turner Johnson, personal interview, 19 October 1999.

40 DiIulio, "Spiritual Capital Can Save Inner-City Youth"; see also McGarrell, Brinker, and Etundi, "The Role of Faith-Based Organizations in Crime Prevention and Justice," 6.

41 Harold Dean Trulear, *The African-American Church and Welfare Reform: Toward a New Prophetic Perspective* (Washington, D.C.: The Center for Public Justice, 1999).

42 Ibid., 2.

43 Stanley W. Carlson-Thies, " 'Don't Look To Us'," 684.

44 Center for Religion and Civic Culture, *California Religious Community Capacity Study.*

45 Ibid.

46 E. J. Dionne, "Faith, Hope, Politics," *Washington Post,* 22 December 2000, A33.

47 *American Baptist Churches USA,* 1997, http://abc-usa.org/news/022097.htm.

48 Tobi Jennifer Printz, *Faith-Based Service Providers in the Nation's Capital.*

49 Center for Religion and Civic Culture, *California Religious Community Capacity Study* Findings, 7.

50 Joan Walsh, "Churches Convert — From Opponents to Collaborators in Welfare Reform," 1998, 4 August 1999, http://www.pacificnews.org/jinn/stories/4.16/980804-welfare.html.

51 Dana Milbank, "Bush to Host Black Ministers," *Washington Post,* 19 December 2000, A1. See also Bruce Nolan, "Baptist Leader Blasts Bush Plan," *Times-Picayune,* 7 September 2001, 11.

52 Amy L. Sherman, *Restorers of Hope: Reaching the Poor in Your Community with*

Church-based Ministries That Work (Wheaton, Ill.: Crossway Books, 1997), 6. The Bush initiative suffered a setback with the departure of John DiIulio from the White House Office of Faith-Based and Community Initiatives in August 2001. DiIulio had long been committed to the plight of poorer, urban minority neighborhoods and was a key link to black clergy serving those communities. Samuel K. Atchison, "The Wrong Signal to Black Churches," *The Christian Century,* 29 August 2001: 8.

53 See generally Brookings Institution, "God-Fearing Voters."

54 Center for Religion and Civic Culture, Findings, 2.

55 Coalition on Urban Renewal and Education, "400 Urban Community Leaders Discuss Public Policy," 2000, 1 December 2000, http://www.urbancure.org/archives/pro1.htm.

56 Dana Milbank, "Bush to Host Black Ministers."

57 Republican Congressional leaders employed a similar outreach to African Americans when introducing their latest Charitable Choice legislation. Black religious leaders comprised a sizable majority of those attending a GOP-sponsored Summit on Faith-Based Initiatives, held in April 2001 on Capitol Hill.

58 Milbank, "Bush to Host Black Ministers."

59 I have examined several case studies in the state of Michigan, which has been among the more aggressive states pursuing Charitable Choice implementation. See generally David K. Ryden, *Governmental Relations with the Religious Non-Profit Sector in Michigan: A Survey of Opinions and Attitudes from the Front* (Washington, D.C.: Aspen Institute Non-Profit Sector Research Fund Working Paper Series, 2000). In Grand Rapids, urban black churches are part of a larger welfare-to-work initiative that provides mentors from local churches for welfare recipients. Some 300 participating area congregations include Protestant, Catholic, and evangelical faiths, but also non-Christian faiths, including Jewish and Baha'i faiths. In Detroit, the Michigan Neighborhood Partnership (MNP) is a predominantly African American coalition of nine member churches and several hundred affiliated organizations, most of them faith-based. It has used public funding to pursue its mission of assisting "neighborhood organizations in Detroit to strengthen individuals, families, and communities through social and economic development." Working in conjunction with federal, state, and local agencies, and with the benefit of a state contract, MNP provides funding, technical assistance, and training to churches to facilitate Charitable Choice partnerships between local faith-based organizations and state departments. Among the efforts are health care services and child immunization, job fairs and training, an African American male health initiative, a youth development initiative, housing development, a charter elementary school, and a nationally funded gang violence prevention and intervention project. MNP also plays a significant educational role, informing churches and religious organizations about Chari-

table Choice opportunities and participating in several national conferences on "faith-based community development." For case studies of black churches working with public officials to address criminal justice and prevention issues, see McGarrell et al., "The Role of Faith-Based Organizations," 7–10. Joan Walsh also has documented the movement of California's urban black churches from protest to participation. See Walsh, "Churches Convert—From Opponents to Collaborators in Welfare Reform." In California, the Council of Churches has been the primary galvanizing force behind the local welfare initiatives. Another observer opines that "black churches . . . are becoming more sophisticated in their fundraising appeals and long-term investment strategies. . . . Churches are also increasing their ties with grant making foundations." See Foundation Center, http://www.foundationcenter.org/. In Mississippi, a controversial plan titled "Faith and Families Project" coupled welfare restrictions with the matching of local churches with families in a "de facto social worker" arrangement. While the state chapter of the NAACP opposed the measure, the National Baptist Convention endorsed it. An example of a black congregation making use of it is the Stronger Hope Church, a small middle-class church in depressed Jackson, Mississippi, that adopted seventeen poor black families. See Joe Loconte, "Delta Force," *Policy Review* 75 (January–February 1996), http://policyreview.com/jan96/faith.html.

60 Laurie Goodstein, "Many Churches Slow to Accept Government Money to Help Poor," *New York Times*, 17 October 2000, A1.

61 Trulear, *Faith-Based Institutions and High Risk Youth*.

62 Center for Religion and Civic Culture, California Religious Community Capacity Study Findings, 4.

63 Beyond the scope of this essay is a broader debate over privatization generally and its application to FBOs. Proponents of state/religious sector partnerships cite a host of benefits—programmatic flexibility, personalized and relational service delivery, civic renewal and community development. It is argued by some that religious service providers in particular are more effective for a number of reasons—from a supposed deeper commitment to service when motivated by faith, to the benefits that come with programs offered within a moral and spiritual framework. For a detailed statement of the case for Charitable Choice, see generally Charles L. Glenn, *The Ambiguous Embrace: Government and Faith-Based Schools and Social Agencies* (Princeton: Princeton University Press, 2000). Opponents cite a host of complications that FBOs are likely to face when stepping into a formal relationship with the government—the loss of organizational autonomy, professionalization, standardization, loss of creativity and responsiveness, undue bureaucratic demands, organizational drift and mission creep, and inevitable pressures to compromise or mute one's religious orientation or identity. For a thorough discussion of these dangers, see Steven

Rathgeb Smith and Michael Lipsky, *Nonprofits for Hire: The Welfare State in the Age of Contracting* (Cambridge: Harvard University Press, 1994); James Castelli and John D. McCarthy, "Religious-Sponsored Social Services: The Not-So-Independent Sector," 1998, 11 August 1999, http://members.aol.com/jimcast/recent.htm.

64 Ellen Sorokin, "Church Sees 'Strings' in Bush's Aid," *Washington Times*, 1 August 2001: C1.

65 Most take away a sense of security from Charitable Choice, and from the blind eye that for decades has been turned to the constitutionality of public aid to religious nonprofits. See Amy L. Sherman, *Restorers of Hope*. Several isolated voices have warned that religious nonprofits receiving government funds or contracts occupy a legally vulnerable, uncertain position. See Stephen V. Monsma, *When Sacred and Secular Mix: Religious Nonprofit Organizations and Public Money* (Lanham, Md: Rowman and Littlefield, 1996), and Sherman, *Restorers of Hope*.

66 The suit was filed by the American Jewish Congress and the Texas Civil Rights Project against the Texas Department of Human Services (DHS). The plaintiffs complained that a Jobs Partnership Program funded by the DHS included proselytizing and used funds to purchase Bibles for participants, in violation of the First Amendment. See Texas Civil Rights Project, "American Jewish Congress and Texas Civil Rights Project File Suit Against Job Program," press release of 24 July 2000, 21 November 2000, http://www.igc.org/tcrp/press/brenham.html.

67 Evan P. Schultz, "Justices Sure to Face Faith-Based Initiative Cases," *Legal Times*, 6 February 2001.

68 Chaves, *Religious Congregations and Welfare Reform*, 6.

69 Ibid.

70 Trulear, *The African-American Church and Welfare Reform*, 17.

71 Among the concerns voiced at the conference were (1) the jeopardizing of the religious liberty rights of program participants, (2) the undesirability of asking the state to determine which of some several thousand sects and denominations in the country to fund, (3) the threats to the autonomy and vitality of churches and FBOs taking public funds, and (4) the provision of Charitable Choice that allows publicly funded FBOs to discriminate in hiring decisions on the basis of religious beliefs and affiliation of the applicant. National Association of Community Action Agencies, "Washington News: Issues Forum on Charitable Choice Highlights Problems, Suggestions, Solutions," 2000, 1 December 2000, http://www.nacaa.org/newsarchives.htm.

72 OMB Watcher Online, "Charitable Choice Included in Multiple Appropriations Bills," 25 September 2000, http://www.ombwatch.org/ombwatcher/ombw20000925.html.

73 See generally Chaves, *Religious Congregations and Welfare Reform*.

74 Trulear, *Faith-Based Institutions and High Risk Youth*.

75 Baptist Joint Committee on Public Affairs, "Our Stances: Resolution on the Chari-

table Choice Provision in the New Welfare Act," 1996, 1 December 2000, http://users. erols.com/bjcpa/timely/charchc.html.

76 Melissa Rogers, "Charitable Choice: Threat to Religion," *Sojourners Magazine* (July-August 1998), 6 February 2000, http://www.sojourners.com/soj9807/980722bhtml.

77 Isaac Kramnick and R. Laurence Moore, "Can the Churches Save the Cities? Faith-Based Services and the Constitution," *The American Prospect* (November-December 1997): 47–53.

78 David M. Ackerman, *Charitable Choice: Background and Selected Legal Studies* (Washington, D.C.: Congressional Research Service, 15 December 1999).

79 For the specific statutory text, see P. L. 104–193, Title I, section 104 (August 22, 1996); 110 stat. 2161; 42 U.S.C.A. 604a et seq.

80 Space constraints do not allow for a full-blown analysis of the constitutional issues. Professor Carl Esbeck, the primary author of Charitable Choice, has written extensively in favor of its constitutionality: Carl H. Esbeck, "A Constitutional Case for Governmental Cooperation with Faith-Based Social Service Providers," *Emory Law Journal* 46 (1997): 1. See also Douglas Laycock, "The Underlying Unity of Separation and Neutrality," *Emory Law Journal* 46 (1997): 43. For an explanation of the argument that Charitable Choice is unconstitutional, see Alan E. Brownstein, "Interpreting the Religion Clauses in Terms of Liberty, Equality, and Free Speech Values — A Critical Analysis of 'Neutrality Theory' and Charitable Choice," *Notre Dame Journal of Law, Ethics, and Public Policy* 11 (1997): 667; Alan E. Brownstein, "Constitutional Questions about Charitable Choice," in *Welfare Reform and Faith Based Organizations,* ed. Derek Davis and Barry Hawkins (Waco, Texas: J. M. Dawson Institute of Church-State Studies, 1999); Derek Davis, "Right Motive, Wrong Method: Thoughts on the Constitutionality of Charitable Choice," *Welfare Reform and Faith Based Organizations,* ed. Derek Davis and Barry Hawkins; Joel Weaver, "Charitable Choice: Will This Provision of Welfare Reform Survive Constitutional Scrutiny?" *Perspectives* (spring 1997), 2 February 2000, http://www.urich.edu/~perpec/issue3/ weaver.htm.

81 As if to reinforce this point, the current Court's most recent church-state decisions have both been by a narrow 5–4 margin, but in opposite directions. In *Santa Fe Independent School District v. Doe,* No. 99-62, 19 June 2000, the Court struck down as violative of the Establishment Clause a school policy that allowed for student-led, student-initiated prayer at high school football games. A week later, in *Mitchell v. Helms,* No. 98-1648, 28 June 2000, the Court upheld a federal program that allowed for funding of school equipment for both private and public schools.

82 The three-part test originated in *Lemon v. Kurtzman* (1971) and required that government funds or support (1) be intended for a legitimate secular purpose, (2) have a primary effect that neither advances nor inhibits religion, and (3) not result in an excessive entanglement between religion and government.

83   489 U.S. 589 (1988).

84   42 U.S.C. sec. 300z et seq. (1981).

85   Sec. 300z(a)(10)(C).

86   In signing Charitable Choice, President Clinton contended that it still forbade "funding of pervasively sectarian organizations" and that governments could consider the structure of the grant applicant in its decision making. For an impartial analysis of the constitutional arguments, see Ackerman, *Charitable Choice.*

87   See Ackerman, *Charitable Choice,* for an articulation of this view.

88   John B. Orr and Cleveland W. Stevens, "Church-State Relations in Los Angeles' Religiously Based Community Development Programs" 1996, 1 February 2000, http://www.usc.edu/dept/LAS/religionandpublicpolicy/9609churchstate.html.

89   Thomas H. Jeavons, *When the Bottom Line Is Faithfulness: Management of Christian Service Organizations* (Bloomington: Indiana University Press, 1994), 49.

90   See generally Center for Public Justice, *Charitable Choice Compliance.*

91   Trulear, *The African-American Church and Welfare Reform,* 17.

92   Carl H. Esbeck, "A Constitutional Case," 1; Monsma, *When Sacred and Secular Mix.*

93   *Mitchell v. Helms,* No. 98-1648, 28 June 2000.

94   Justice Kennedy has argued for the displacement of *Lemon* with a neutrality standard (*Rosenberg v. Rector,* 1995). A number of scholars have lined up behind the neutrality standard. See Esbeck, "A Constitutional Case"; Laycock, "The Underlying Unity of Separation and Neutrality"; Monsma, *When Secular and Sacred Mix;* Monsma, *Positive Neutrality: Letting Freedom Ring* (Westport: Greenwood Press, 1995). For critics of neutrality, see Brownstein, "Interpreting the Religious Clauses"; Martha Minow, "Choice or Commonality: Welfare and Schooling after the End of Welfare as We Knew It," *Duke Law Journal* 49 (1999): 493.

95   The Christian Legal Society asserts that FBOS are free under the statute to inculcate program recipients with religious principles that directly pertain to the need for changes in behavior and attitudes contributing to dependency. In its Charitable Choice guide, CLS contends that as long as a "public purpose is served by the [religious] principles being taught, . . . a faith-based organization may use principles rooted in its belief system." *Christian Legal Society,* home page, 9 June 1998, http://www.clsnet.com/ccqanda.html#qanda.

96   Americans United for Separation of Church and State, "Analysis of *Mitchell v. Helms* and Its Significance for Charitable Choice and Private School Vouchers," 29 November 2000, http://www.au.org/helmsanal.htm.

97   Stanley W. Carlson-Thies, *Charitable Choice: Top Ten Tips* (Washington, D.C.: The Center for Public Justice, 1999) 9 November 2000, http://cpjustice.org/charitablechoice/tipspo.

Cases Cited

Bowen v. Kendrick, 489 U.S. 589 (1988).

Lemon v. Kurtzman, 403 U.S. 602 (1971).

Lynch v. Donnelly, 465 U.S. 668 (1984).

Mitchell v. Helms, No. 98-1648, 28 June 2000.

Rosenberger v. Rector and Visitors of University of Virginia, 515 U.S. 819 (1995).

Santa Fe Independent School District v. Doe, No. 99-62 (June 19, 2000)

11

ON SEDUCING THE SAMARITAN:

THE PROBLEMATIC OF GOVERNMENT AID

TO FAITH-BASED GROUPS

Samuel K. Roberts

President George W. Bush's call for governmental support of faith-based social programs revives a historic vision within American culture in which religion and the secular powers cooperate ostensibly for the common good. He seeks to marshal the enormous potential of these "armies of compassion"[1] to help solve many of America's pressing social ills. This tradition goes back as far as the seventeenth century in America, when the General Court of the Massachusetts Bay Colony voted to provide the sum of 400 pounds "towards a schoale or colledge," thus founding Harvard College.[2] Another tradition, however, is equally revered in the American experience. This tradition, ensconced in the First Amendment to the Constitution, has looked askance at direct governmental aid to religion. In Thomas Jefferson's vivid image, a "wall of separation" exists between the governmental powers and the personal affirmation of religious beliefs. Thus Bush's call also revives historic fears that a collaboration of government and faith-based groups will violate this time-honored "wall" between church and state in America. We face a real dilemma.

In the wake of the Bush initiative, many African American churches have sensed an opportunity to augment and sharpen their social outreach efforts while securing desperately needed funds from what was for many of them an improbable source — the federal government. Much has been made of the seeming racial divide that has characterized how many American churches have reacted to President Bush's initiative. The 24 March 2001 issue of the *New York Times* carried a story noting the anecdotal evidence that seems to suggest that while affluent and conservative white churches have rejected the initiative on the grounds that government intrusion would compromise the integrity of religious positions, less-well-off black churches, intent on doing social ministry, were more likely to embrace Bush's initiative.[3] One suburban white pastor was heard to say, "When there's work to be done, I would rather see my church come up with the money and the people do it. If we rely on the government, it compromises our witness." His counterpart, a black minister, struggling to meet the perceived needs of an inner-city context, said, "Now, I'm a minister, but if I have to remove the Bible, remove the cross from the wall, remove the Ten Commandments to get that government money, I'll do it. If God is in me, that's good enough."

We have no reason to doubt the sincerity of this black minister and the countless others who seek to meet overwhelming social problems in their neighborhoods with woefully meager resources. Yet we dare not be too sanguine about the ultimate prospects that the ideals of prophetic religion and liberal democratic theory can be squared with the well-intentioned aims of the White House initiative of government aid to faith-based organizations. In this essay, at the very least, I will urge caution to African American churches as they contemplate these initiatives from the government.[4] At a maximal level I will argue that government support of faith-based social action programs cannot enjoy consistency with either the prophetic or liberal democratic traditions, traditions affirmed by the vast majority of mainline religious denominations in America. Moreover, the prophetic tradition has had particular import within African American religious consciousness since it informed those churches' leadership in the struggle for equal rights and social justice. Accordingly, if the ideals of prophetic religion and liberal democracy are understood to be operative in the American context, then the embrace of some African American churches of government aid to faith-based organizations is rendered highly problematic. This essay affirms that government aid to faith-based groups, particularly African American churches, compromises the autonomy of such groups and, secondly, renders tenuous the wall of separation between church and state implicitly affirmed in the First Amendment.

The Thrust of the Prophetic Tradition

African American churches, to the extent that their genesis was occasioned by a demand for social justice for black people, have perforce exemplified the essence of prophetic religion. Prophetic religion is fundamentally at variance with the values of any culture when those values, in the judgment of the adherents of that religion, do not foster ideals considered normative by that religion. And to the extent that cultural values of any society tend to become codified in the legal structures of government, prophetic religion invariably finds itself at critical points at odds with governing political structures. Given the social opprobrium with which African Americans have been held by the general American society historically, and given the unfortunate history of state-sponsored and sanctioned discrimination, the black churches have perforce had to exercise a prophetic sensibility as they sought to give spiritual shelter to their adherents. This sensibility came to maturity in the rise of the African American independent church movement with the formation of the Free African Society in Philadelphia in 1787. This Society ultimately became the progenitor of the African Methodist Episcopal Church, officially organized in 1816. Early independent black communions of Baptists and Presbyterian churches were founded in the early years of the nineteenth century, communions that affirmed as well that the call for social justice was consistent with theological tenets of Christian faith.[5]

The model for the African American prophetic tradition can be traced to the Judaic tradition, which itself formed the backdrop for one strand of Christian theology and indeed a Christian understanding of the relationship between faith and the political order and the relationship between religion and the state. Statecraft and the specific ways in which human beings are to be governed has been a perennial issue in human societies, and ancient Israel was no exception. Ancient Israel began as a loose confederation of clans imbued with an unshakable belief that Yahweh, their God, had effectuated their release from Egyptian bondage. Freed from Egyptian bondage, and still self-identifying as a confederation of tribal clans, early Israel gave rise to a distinct political consciousness, the assumption that God ruled the people through the human agency of the judges. The early judges were men — and one notable woman, Deborah — who, by virtue of their acknowledged wisdom, character, and prowess in war, became the acknowledged rulers of Israel. This confluence of rulers with integrity who were guided by the perceived will of God constituted the basis for a "state," if you will. But we see the dissolution of this formula with the end of Samuel's reign as judge and the recognition of the people that Samuel's sons did not possess his integrity, character, and ability to rule wisely. It was at this point that the people clamored for a king, a model of statecraft evidenced by the then-great powers surrounding them, notably Assyria and the still powerful Egypt. This demand from the people is preserved in 1 Samuel, chapter 8. But Samuel rebukes the people, and assuming the role of a prophet himself, warns them against the notion of a political state ruled by a king. Samuel's warning is ideologically based, but it is grounded in disarming practicality. Samuel prophesied that the king would conscript the people's sons for his army and their daughters for his palace. He would tax them unmercifully, rendering them his virtual slaves (1 Samuel 8: 11–18, *Revised Standard Version;* hereafter RSV).

Clearly, Samuel is describing a kind of absolutism, the very bane of an early political consciousness in Israel that was suspicious of centralized human authority lodged in a political state. The prophetic tradition affirmed that, at best, the state was a flawed institution and at worst could be guilty of moral transgressions, prominent among them being the oppression of the people. Thus there is in early Israel's halting embrace of kingship and a political state a distinct ambiguity. Even when Saul is affirmed as the political leader of Israel, according to one tradition he is given the title of *nagid* (ruler or commander) as opposed to *malek* (king), thus suggesting that in the beginning "kingship in Israel was of a limited variety."[6] Government is affirmed as long as it maintains the tradition of liberation of the people from bondage; if the reverse should occur, that is, if government were ever to institute policies of oppression of the people, then divine justification of government is withdrawn. This explains why throughout the prophetic tradition whenever there is opposition from the prophets it is because of the oppressive policies of the king and his government. It is precisely when Israel becomes unfaithful to this admonition to govern with equity, justice, and compassion that the prophets rise up against the governing powers. Hosea could lament, "There is no faithfulness or kindness, and no knowledge of God in the land" (4:1b, RSV). Isaiah could declare: "For they have transgressed the laws, violated the statutes, broken the everlasting covenant" (24:5b, RSV). Against the established religion, Amos railed. Said Yahweh, through the mouth of Amos, "I hate, I despise your feasts, and I take no delight in your solemn assemblies. Even though you offer me your burnt offerings and cereal offerings, I will not accept them, and the peace offerings of your fatted beasts I will not look upon. Take away from me the noise of your songs; to the melody of your harps I will not listen. But let justice roll down like waters, and righteousness like an ever-flowing stream" (Amos 5:21–24, RSV). It should be remembered at this point that a latter-day prophet, Martin Luther King Jr., was fond of quoting Amos, since King himself regarded the cause for which he gave his life consistent with the urgency and critical focus of prophetic religion. The black church's gift to twentieth-century America may be its insistence on recovering the vibrancy of the prophetic tradition, a tradition that indicts government if it does not fulfill its moral expectations.

We are left, therefore, with three insights derived from the prophetic tradition that may be helpful to us. One, prophetic religion presumes the autonomy of religion from government. Two, government has a useful value but it is a conditional value, that is to say, government is legitimate only to the extent that it performs positive functions for the human good and not policies that eventuate in human oppression. Three, prophetic religion, to the extent that it is autonomous from government, always maintains the ability to critique government, always reminding government of its conditional value.

The Thrust of the First Amendment to the Constitution of the United States

Now I turn to a brief assessment of the import of the First Amendment to the issue at hand. While there are two clauses in this amendment, one prohibiting governmental favor or the "establishment" of any religious tradition, and the other guaranteeing the "free exercise" of religion, Justice Arthur Goldberg has wisely advised us to understand the two clauses as a composite affirmation of religious freedom. Wrote Goldberg in 1963:

> The First Amendment's guarantees . . . foreclose not only laws "respecting an establishment of religion" but also those "prohibiting the free exercise thereof." These two proscriptions are to be read together, and in light of the single end which they are designed to serve. The basic purpose of the religion clause of the First Amendment is to promote and assure the fullest

possible scope of religious liberty and tolerance for all and to nurture the conditions which secure the best hope of attainment of that end.[7]

Just as we saw an aversion to a facile confluence of religion and the political order from the standpoint of prophetic religion, there has been an equally adamant aversion of a facile confluence between the two from the standpoint of liberal democratic theory. Liberal contract theory, the progenitor of modern democratic theory, arose as a rebuke to the absolutist regimes of Europe, many of which were veritable theocracies. They were theocracies to this extent: almost without exception the absolutist regimes of Europe in the seventeenth and eighteenth centuries were state churches, arrangements in which the state recognized only one religious tradition and in return that tradition blessed uncritically the affairs of the state.

The Framers of the Constitution felt that there were many justifiable reasons for ensuring that either no one religious tradition or that religion in general be "established" or favored by the federal governmental system. Rather, as Goldberg pointed out, the end was *freedom* for religion, and, one might construe, freedom *from* religion. Europe, with its state-supported churches, was a model that the Framers did not want to emulate in this new nation. In many of the European countries monopolistic religious establishments fomented religious intolerance, which in turn led to persecution and a general level of social strife. Rejection of the European model did not mean that the Framers were irreligious people. They sought a balance between the laudatory goals of a "largely secular state and a society shaped by religion."[8] Most saw the value in religion, although the religion they espoused was of the more rationally oriented stripe, Deism being a significant mode of religious orientation. They could affirm the presence of a providential guiding hand in the destiny of the new nation but they did not want religion to be a governmental enterprise.

Three Models

After having assessed the import of the prophetic tradition and the liberal democratic tradition with respect to religion as suggested in the First Amendment, we may consider possible models for interaction between government and religion as suggested by the recent initiatives from the White House.

There are essentially three formulas or models available to us as we contemplate relations between government and religion. The first model, let us
call it the *Establishment Model,* would countenance government supporting
the religious activities of religious organizations; in this case government
supports religion, its work, and its activities. But even the proponents of
government aid to faith-based programs reject this model. Such proponents
tacitly acknowledge the "wall of separation" between government and religion that disavows outright governmental support of specifically religious
activities. They reject the notion of government paying for the salary of a
chaplain in a drug treatment center, for example, or paying for utility bills to
keep the lights on during prayer meetings while in the same building hungry people are being fed. (Presumably, clever tax accountants will ferret out
these fine distinctions.) For his own part, President Bush is insistent that religious liberty be preserved in the implementation of the programs and that
participating agencies would "ensure the religious liberty of recipients of services, forbidding any religious discrimination against them."[9] The focus of
the proponents of government aid to faith-based groups seems to be on the
practical ends of such programs, the work that is being done by them, the
presumption being that one can neatly separate the guiding principles of an
organization from the practical work it is accomplishing.

Now, if we reject the Establishment Model and leave aside programs that
directly and unabashedly fund religious activities of faith-based organizations, we are left with only two other models or reasons why government
would fund social programs run by faith-based organizations.

Another model would affirm that worthwhile, laudatory, and even humanitarian programs need to be accomplished by the government, but because government resources are limited, government depends on the already-
existing resources of faith-based groups. Let us call this the *Contractor Model.*
Thus, for example, if the State Department, as part of its strategy in a war-
torn country, contracts with an American faith-based group to do relief work
among refugees, government gives financial support to a religious group.
Government contracts out its work to a willing subcontractor. That group is
doing the government's work — laudable to be sure, but it is the government's
work nevertheless.

Yet a third model for government supporting faith-based organizations
would be based on the assumption that there is a shared concern between

government and religious groups relative to some social problem. Let us call this the *Alliance Model*. Reasoning, for example, that it is well within the public good to decrease the number of persons addicted to drugs, government would then enter into alliances with faith-based programs geared toward substance abuse treatment. If the development of affordable housing is a government policy, then governmental agencies might work with faith-based groups whose aim also is to build adequate housing in their neighborhoods. Reducing hunger by feeding those in need also comes to mind. Inherent in this reason is the presumption that government and religion are viable partners in the solving of such social problems; there is a common understanding with respect to the nature of the problems, their treatment, and their solution.

With each of these attendant arrangements between government and faith-based organizations there are serious ethical problems, particularly from the standpoint of prophetic religion. The problem with the Contractor Model is that it puts religion in the lamentable position of being a tool of government. Good and humanitarian work is being done, to be sure, consistent in many respects with the values of the religious body, perhaps for certain, but religion is nevertheless a paid functionary of the state. This is untenable for religion that is truly prophetic in nature.[10] The problem with the Alliance Model is that we run the risk of compromising the integrity and singularity of religious and faith-based reasons for ameliorating social problems. The flaw with this model is that it presumes that the coalition of government and religion can be constructed rather facilely. But such a coalition has the potential to effectively obscure the presuppositions each entity would bring to the solving of a problem. For example, while government sociologists might have their own presuppositions as to how communities become fractured and thus how social problems arise, social theorists who have distinct *theological* presuppositions in place will bring a different point of view and perhaps a different prescription for the amelioration of such problems. Perspective makes all the difference. An alliance between government and religion may in fact be *too* facile; it can obscure the significant differences in the worldviews between government and religion and, in the process, diminish the integrity of the religious vision.

Practical Problems with Administering Government Aid
to Faith-Based Groups

Aside from the theoretical problems that are occasioned when government funds faith-based programs, many practical problems are engendered as well. And it is precisely because of the theological and political confusion at the theoretical level that nettlesome issues at the practical level are bound to occur. When we keep in mind the import of the prophetic tradition and the expectations inherent in the First Amendment, the problematic of government aid to faith-based groups becomes all too troublesome. First, there is the real possibility of discrimination against persons who might desire employment in such programs. Discrimination may eventuate because in the judgment of the leaders of such programs some would-be employees do not evidence either a lifestyle or belief patterns consistent with that religion; such persons are then either denied employment through being eliminated from the possible pool of applicants or fired outright. We must always keep in mind that religious groups are inherently discriminatory, not in an immoral sense but in an inherently essentialist way. By this I mean that religious groups must recognize a line of demarcation between those within the normative structures of beliefs and behaviors and those outside of such structures. This line must be real or else the religious tradition that generates normative beliefs and behaviors makes no sense. Religious groups cannot be indifferent about the importance of beliefs or tenets. Thus, for example, if a religious group earnestly believed that practicing homosexuals evidence a behavior pattern that is antithetical to the group's belief system, then that group would have no choice but to deny employment to homosexuals.

The adjudication of a case underway in the state court of Kentucky may have some effect in determining the constitutional destiny of the governmental financing of faith-based programs. Alicia Pedreira worked as a therapist at the Kentucky Baptist Homes for Children for six months until a photograph of her and her female partner was circulated at the agency, whereupon she was immediately fired. In her suit she claims that her firing was unrelated to her performance but because she violated a demand explicitly spelled out in the agency's employment forms that employees "exhibit values in their professional conduct and personal lifestyles that are consistent with the Christian mission and purpose of the institution."[11] When the case comes to trial,

Pedreira's lawyers will ask why, if hiring discrimination is illegal in government jobs, why is it not in jobs paid for by the government? The issues joined in the Pedreira case will inevitably surface among African American religious groups as well, to the extent they choose to participate in the government's faith-based initiatives.

Bishop T. D. Jakes, a high-profile African American cleric and supporter of the Bush initiative, has affirmed the right of faith-based organizations to discriminate in hiring and firing based on the values of the group. As leader of a 26,000-member church in Dallas, the Potter's House, Jakes has publicly declared his intention to hire only people "who reflect our views and concerns," and this does not include homosexuals.[12] Liberal democratic government, however, as it has evolved recently in the American experience, would judge such an action by the group as unfair, unconstitutional, and, according to some case law, illegal. Thus we have a conflict between two normative systems. But the only reason we have this imbroglio — this conflict between two normative systems — is that we would have unwisely comingled the two belief systems in the first place through government offering financial inducements to religion.

A second practical question concerns whether the government will be able to withstand the temptation to regard some religious traditions as being inside the mainstream of American culture as opposed to some that may be regarded as peripheral to our culture. For example, early on Reverend Jerry Falwell protested the suggestion that the Hare Krishna movement or the Church of Scientology could be included among those faith-based groups eligible for government grants. To his credit, President Bush has established an open door, welcoming all faiths among the "armies of compassion," whether "Methodists, Muslims, Mormons, or good people of no faith at all."[13] But let us assume for the moment that the government will be able to withstand any temptation to discriminate against some religious groups and thus allow *all* groups to compete for and receive government grants. Such a policy would therefore make grants available to members of the Wiccan tradition, those who believe earnestly in the efficacy of witchcraft. It might even include a group that approves the use of severe corporal punishment of its young, a case that made the court docket in Atlanta during the last week in March 2001. Now, if government uses its funds, which are actually funds derived from tax revenues, to subsidize even the presumed nonreligious work of such groups, it runs the risk of offending the consciousness of many Americans who would find the views of such religious groups offensive, detestable, and, ironically, irreligious. Such a policy may force Americans to support — *against their will* — the work, even the relatively benign work, of groups they might otherwise not support. Again, we are brought into such a conflict if government insists on drawing religion into its orbit of financial support.

There is a third problem in government funding activities of religious groups. Anecdotal evidence has reminded us of the burdensome requirements that are oftentimes occasioned by the receipt of government grants and funds. In the 4 February 2001 issue of the *New York Times,* a reporter noted how the Reverend Herbert B. Chambers, who seeks to help poor people surrounding his church, the Young Memorial Church of Christ Holiness, has said he will continue his work and will not apply for government funds. Reverend Chambers has said, "I've got enough partners helping me now. When you invite Big Brother into your life you can spend your day filling out papers." But the prospects for some churches, Reverend Chambers believes, might be even more troublesome than the hassle incurred in filling out forms. "If you make money available to some of the small churches you have to help them manage it or they're going to get into trouble. Some of these ministers have never seen $10,000 and if they don't spend it right, Big Brother will put them in jail."[14] But even if we call Reverend Chambers an alarmist and discount his dire predictions, there is no doubt that many earnest but naive pastors and churches will be drawn inexorably into the orbit of governmental funding, only to be mired in paperwork, inadvertent fraud, and possible incarceration.

Conclusion

This essay has argued that the import of prophetic religion and that of liberal democratic theory raise serious problems with respect to the current initiative of government support for faith-based social programs, with particular reference to African American churches. The worthwhile nature of these programs notwithstanding, serious ethical and practical issues are raised when one attempts to square governmental aid with the presumed autonomy of prophetic religion and the freedom from state-supported religion that the First Amendment protects. Well-meaning African American churches, when confronted with the enormity of the social ills at their doorsteps, may inadvertently become Samaritans seduced by equally well-meaning governmental initiatives. The challenge of doing good and at the same time maintaining integrity remains.

The implications for the ongoing integrity of black churches and their ability to fulfill vital roles they have played nationally and within their local communities are very much at stake as these churches consider entering into contracts with the federal government. Among other things, black churches risk losing the moral credibility they gained through their leadership in the civil rights struggle and through other pursuits of justice. Rewards of any kind, favorable treatment, financial allotments or considerations can, even if unwittingly, undermine and erode the integrity of that tradition.

There are at least two practical aspects of this problem. The first has to do with self-identity and the desired clarity with which the churches should be able to declare their mission and go about their work. Earlier on in this essay, I pointed out the identity problems inherent in the Contractor Model and the Alliance Model. Both models betoken a problem with respect to the clarity and focus of the mission of religious groups when they become involved in covenants with government. A presumption that is made all too easily, in many of these instances, is that government and faith-based groups share the same perspectives on social issues and on social strategies. Clearly, there are points of convergence, as both faith-based groups and government strive for the common good, but the significant differences in perspectives must always be remembered.

A second moral difficulty for African American churches stems, ironically, from adherence by black churches to religious tenets that may run counter to First Amendment protections against discrimination. For example, some black churches adhere to the belief that divorced persons should not expect promotion within a religious organization. This can lead to conflict when government funds are awarded to faith-based groups that insist, for religious reasons, that they can make discriminatory judgments within the realm of personnel matters. In such instances, African American churches, though once at the forefront of the struggle against racial discrimination, become perpetrators of discrimination of a different sort. To the extent that black churches insist on exercising such religious freedoms in the conduct of their personnel matters, they will necessarily violate the rights of persons whose lifestyles, beliefs, and values are different from those of the churches in question.

Finally, governmental contracts and obligations present the real possibility that an inordinate amount of staff time in African American churches will be spent complying with regulations and monitoring the progress of programs according to governmentally imposed standards and expectations. It is clear that black churches have functioned in an essential role as civic and social centers for communities — accomplished many times despite a shortage of paid personnel.[15] Even when factoring in provisions for clerical support that are generally available in government grants, the paucity of resident staff persons at the typical black church would preclude the ability to exercise vigorous oversight or to escape the tedium of completing the incessant governmental forms. Moreover, the requirement to attend daily to governmental regulations and expectations cannot help but exacerbate the problems of ambiguous self-identity and lack of clarity of mission that are was part and parcel of the Contractor and Alliance Models.

Well-meaning persons within government and within faith-based organizations realize the enormity of the social problems that must be addressed within American society. Certain of these persons are persuaded at times of a convergence between government and religion with respect to effecting partnerships that seek the common good. Nevertheless, caution is advised. Governmental aid may seem appealing to black churches, but the costs to black churches — as measured in loss of theological integrity and moral leadership — may prove to be extremely high.

Notes

1   President George W. Bush, "Rallying the Armies of Compassion," January 2001.
2   H. Shelton Smith, Robert T. Handy, and Lefferts A. Loetscher, *American Christianity: An Historical Interpretation with Representative Documents,* vol. 1 (New York: Charles Scribner's Sons, 1960), 123.
3   "A Clerical, and Racial, Gap Over Federal Help," *New York Times,* 24 March 2001.
4   The title for this essay was influenced in part by Joe Locante, *Seducing the Samaritan: How Government Contracts Are Reshaping Social Services* (Boston: Pioneer Institute, 1997).
5   For useful treatments of the independent movement among early African American

churches, see Edward D. Smith, *Climbing Jacob's Ladder: The Rise of Black Churches in Eastern American Cities, 1740–1877* (Washington, D.C.: Smithsonian Press, 1988); Gary B. Nash, *Forging Freedom: The Formation of Philadelphia's Black Community, 1720–1840* (Cambridge: Harvard University Press, 1988); Carol V. R. George, *Segregated Sabbaths: Richard Allen and the Emergence of Independent Black Churches, 1760–1840* (New York: Oxford University Press, 1973).

6 Bruce C. Birch, *Let Justice Roll Down: The Old Testament, Ethics, and Christian Life* (Louisville: Westminster/John Knox Press, 1991), 209.

7 From Justice Goldberg's concurring opinion in *Abington v. Schempp*, 374 U.S. at 305 (1963), in Stephen V. Monsma, *When Sacred and Secular Mix* (Lanham, Md.: Rowman and Littlefield Publishers, Inc., 1996), 176.

8 A. James Reichley, *Religion in American Public Life* (Washington, D.C.: The Brookings Institution, 1985), 114.

9 President George W. Bush, "Rallying the Armies of Compassion," 9.

10 Other possible models are suggested in Charles L. Glenn, *The Ambiguous Embrace: Government and Faith-Based Schools and Social Agencies* (Princeton: Princeton University Press, 2000), chapter 4.

11 Eyal Press, "Faith-Based Furor," *New York Times Magazine,* 1 April 2001, 64.

12 "Another Trouble Spot for Charitable Choice: Hiring Policies," *Dallas Morning News,* 7 May 2001.

13 President George W. Bush, "Rallying the Armies of Compassion," foreword.

14 "Practical Questions Greet Bush Plan to Aid Religious Groups," *New York Times,* 4 February 2001.

15 Over ten years ago, C. Eric Lincoln and Lawrence H. Mamiya's authoritative study, *The Black Church in the African-American Experience* (Durham, N.C.: Duke University Press, 1990), reported that over half (56 percent) of black churches had a staff that consisted of only two persons, generally the pastor and a secretary (45). There is little reason to believe that that percentage has significantly increased over the intervening years.

APPENDIX

OVERVIEW OF NATIONAL SAMPLE FOR THE 1999–2000

BLACK CHURCHES AND POLITICS SURVEY

Sampling Methodology

A list of approximately 11,000 black churches was drawn from nineteen cities, twenty-six predominantly black rural counties, and two predominantly black suburbs. Within each city and the two suburban counties, all churches located within census block tracts that were 90 percent or more black were identified as part of the sample. Keyword searches were done of yellow pages databases in the cities to identify other obviously black churches that were outside the 90 percent black census tracts. Keywords included "African," "Greater," and "COGIC" (Church of God in Christ). Yellow pages telephone books were then manually consulted to include other churches listed within categories of obviously black churches that were not discerned through prior steps. Categories included African Methodist Episcopal Churches, African Methodist Episcopal Zion Churches, Christian Methodist Episcopal Churches, Church of God in Christ Churches, and any Baptist churches listed according to one of the black Baptist conventions. Churches were similarly identified in largely black rural counties in six deep-South states (two counties per state). Census tracts that were 70 percent black (instead of the 90 percent black standard applied to urban census tracts) were selected. This slightly increased the chances that the churches selected might not be black churches; nevertheless, the smallness of these rural counties necessitated casting a wider net to increase the overall number of churches. (Surveys completed by churches that were not predominantly black were not included in the final database.)

Surveys were mailed to all the churches on the list; churches that did not respond to the first mailing of the survey received a second mailing. Those that did not respond to the second mailing received a third mailing. Churches that did not respond after the three mailings received telephone calls and were asked to complete the survey over the telephone. In addition, in order to supplement initially low numbers of Pentecostal respondents, surveys were administered at a national meeting of the Church of God in Christ (COGIC). Surveys completed at the COGIC meeting were included in the database only if they were from congregations in the cities, suburbs, or rural counties designated by the Project as research sites. This multiple-step survey process yielded 1,956 completed surveys over a twelve-month period. With the completion of the national survey, a follow-up survey was conducted among the survey respondents. A total of 324 respondents of the 1,956 church leaders who responded to the initial survey provided answers to the follow-up survey. The follow-up survey solicited additional information on public policy matters probed in the initial survey.

Sample Characteristics

1. METROPOLITAN AREAS COVERED IN SAMPLE

Atlanta (also suburban DeKalb County); Birmingham; Boston; Charlotte; Chicago; Columbus, Ohio; Dallas; Denver; Detroit; Jackson, Mississippi; Los Angeles; Memphis; New Orleans; New York; Newark; Oakland; Philadelphia; Trenton; Washington, D.C. (also Prince George's County, Maryland).

2. RURAL COUNTIES COVERED IN SAMPLE

Alabama: Bullock, Greene, Lowndes, Macon (including Tuskegee town)
Florida: Hamilton, Jefferson, Madison
Georgia: Hancock, Stewart, Talbot
Louisiana: East Carroll Parish, Madison Parish, West Feliciana Parish
Mississippi: Claiborne, Holmes, Jefferson
North Carolina: Herford, Northampton
South Carolina: Allendale, Lee, Williamsburg
Tennessee: Haywood, Hardeman, Lauderdale
Virginia: Greensville, Sussex

TABLE A.1 Black Population by Region in the U.S.

Northeast/Mid-Atlantic	6,556,909	(18.0%)
Midwest	6,838,669	(18.7%)
South	19,528,231	(53.6%)
West	3,495,625	(9.5%)
TOTAL	36,419,434	(99.8%)

Source: U.S. Census Bureau, Census 2000.

TABLE A.2 Geographic Profile of Church Sample

Regional distribution	Overall sample	Follow-up sub-sample
Northeast/Mid-Atlantic	15.7% (307)	10.4% (34)
Midwest	20.0% (393)	17.5% (57)
South	47.6% (932)	65.4% (212)
West	6.6% (130)	6.4% (21)
No Response	9.9% (194)	0.0% (0)

TABLE A.3 Church Sample by Denomination

	Overall sample		Follow-up sub-sample	
AME	5.88%	(115)	11.11%	(36)
AMEZ	2.10%	(41)	3.40%	(11)
CME	5.73%	(112)	1.23%	(4)
Nat'l Bapt. USA	18.46%	(361)	26.23%	(85)
Nat'l Bapt. of Amer.	1.74%	(34)	1.23%	(4)
Prog. Nat'l Bapt.	5.88%	(115)	4.63%	(15)
Other Baptist	6.29%	(123)	7.72%	(25)
COGIC	10.38%	(203)	1.85%	(6)
Church of God	2.35%	(46)	2.78%	(9)
Full Gospel	2.35%	(46)	0.62%	(2)
United Methodist	3.37%	(73)	5.25%	(17)
Nondenominational	7.67%	(150)	11.11%	(36)
Catholic	3.89%	(76)	2.16%	(7)
Episcopalian	1.64%	(32)	0.62%	(2)
Presbyterian	1.89%	(37)	1.23%	(4)
Lutheran	1.84%	(36)	1.85%	(6)
UCC/Congregational	0.82%	(16)	1.23%	(4)
Disciples of Christ	0.77%	(15)	0.93%	(3)
Other	15.34%	(300)	14.81%	(48)
No Response	1.28%	(25)	0.00%	(0)
TOTAL	100.00%	(1956)	100.00%	(324)

TABLE A.4 Demographic Characteristics of Sample

	Overall sample		Follow-up sub-sample	
Respondents, Clergy vs. Non-clergy				
Pastors	81.6%	(1597)	83.6%	(271)
Other ministers	5.4%	(106)	5.2%	(17)
Nonclergy	2.7%	(53)	0.3%	(1)
Unconfirmed	10.2%	(200)	10.8%	(35)
Tenure of Pastor				
Five years or less	27.5%	(440)	23.6%	(64)
Six to ten years	15.3%	(246)	19.5%	(53)
Eleven to twenty years	25.2%	(403)	31.3%	(85)
Twenty-one years or more	21.7%	(348)	22.5%	(61)
No response	10.0%	(160)	2.9%	(8)
Respondents by Gender				
Women	10.9%	(215)	10.8%	(35)
Men	87.0%	(1702)	86.7%	(281)
No response	1.9%	(39)	2.4%	(8)
Respondents by Age				
Age 45 or less	21.9%	(430)	18.8%	(61)
Age 46 or more	74.6%	(1461)	77.4%	(251)
No response	3.3%	(65)	3.7%	(12)
Median age	55		58	
Respondents by Race*				
Black	93.4%	(1827)	91.9%	(298)
White	3.6%	(72)	4.3%	(14)
Other	0.2%	(5)	0.3%	(1)
No response	2.6%	(52)	3.4%	(11)
Respondents by Educational Background				
Grammar (1–8 years)	0.7%	(15)	0.6%	(2)
High School (1–3 years)	4.7%	(92)	3.7%	(12)
High School (4 years)	20.1%	(395)	21.9%	(71)
College (1–3 years)	15.2%	(299)	17.5%	(57)
College (4 years)	20.0%	(393)	20.6%	(67)

TABLE A.4 *Continued*

	Overall sample		Follow-up sub-sample	
College (5-plus years)	32.9%	(645)	29.6%	(96)
No response	5.9%	(117)	5.8%	(19)
Congregations by Size of Membership				
Less than 100	23.6%	(463)	19.1%	(62)
100–499	45.7%	(895)	45.3%	(147)
500–999	15.7%	(308)	17.9%	(58)
1,000–1,999	8.3%	(164)	11.7%	(38)
2,000–2,999	4.7%	(93)	4.0%	(13)
3,000 or more	1.2%	(25)	0.9%	(3)
No response	0.4%	(8)	0.9%	(3)
Congregations by Annual Income				
$1–9,999	15.0%	(294)	13.8%	(45)
$10,000–49,999	20.4%	(400)	20.6%	(67)
$50,000–99,999	19.3%	(378)	20.0%	(65)
$100,000–249,999	20.4%	(399)	19.4%	(63)
$250,000–499,999	13.0%	(256)	13.5%	(44)
$500,000 and over	1.8%	(37)	1.8%	(6)
No response	9.8%	(192)	10.4%	(34)

*Congregations can be majority black with nonblack pastors or ministers.

TABLE A.5 Survey Question Distributions

Q: Black churches should be involved in politics?

Strongly agree	713	37.7%
Agree	790	41.8%
Don't know/No opinion	90	4.8%
Disagree	109	5.8%
Strongly disagree	190	10.0%
VALID CASES	1892	100.0%

Q: In the last two years, how often have political candidates or elected officials delivered speeches or remarks within your worship services?

More than ten times	104	5.4%
Five to ten times	205	10.6%
A few times	572	29.7%
Never	1046	54.3%
VALID CASES	1927	100.0%

Q: During the 1990s, how often have international, national, or local political issues been discussed as part of your regular worship service?

Frequently	554	29.0%
Sometimes	928	48.6%
Never	427	22.4%
VALID CASES	1909	100.0%

Q: During the 1980s, how often have international, national, or local political issues been discussed as part of your regular worship service?

Frequently	337	19.9%
Sometimes	934	55.1%
Never	423	25.0%
VALID CASES	1694	100.0%

Q: Is your congregation currently involved in the activities of any civic or political organization?

Yes	973	49.7%
No	983	50.3%
VALID CASES	1956	100.0%

TABLE A.5 *Continued*

Q: In what ways has your congregation been involved with these organizations?*

Given money	819	84.2%
Attended meetings	898	92.3%
Advocated issues with public officials	695	71.4%
Participated in programs or events	792	81.4%
Served on a board or committee	608	62.5%
Participated in protest rallies or marches	398	40.9%

Q: How regularly has your congregation had the following involvements with civic and political groups?†

Given money		
Frequently	45	13.9%
Sometimes	129	39.8%
Rarely	108	33.3%
Never	42	13.0%
TOTAL	324	100.0%
Attended meetings		
Frequently	8	2.5%
Sometimes	116	35.8%
Rarely	62	19.1%
Never	138	42.6%
TOTAL	324	100.0%
Advocated issues with officials		
Frequently	7	2.2%
Sometimes	89	27.5%
Rarely	59	18.2%
Never	169	52.2%
TOTAL	324	100.0%
Served on board or committee		
Frequently	2	0.6%
Sometimes	44	13.6%
Rarely	70	21.6%
Never	208	64.2%
TOTAL	324	100.0%

TABLE A.5 *Continued*

Q: *It is helpful that the government is now encouraging churches to apply for*
and use government funds to provide social services.†

Strongly agree	29	9.0%
Agree	121	37.3%
Don't know/No opinion	3	0.9%
Disagree	62	19.1%
Strongly disagree	108	33.3%
Blank	1	0.3%
TOTAL	324	100.0%

Q: *Does your congregation have any programs for which it receives*
governmental funding?

Yes	474	24.2%
No	1482	75.8%
TOTAL	1956	100.0%

Q: *Tax dollars for public education can be put to better use in the form of*
vouchers that parents can apply toward private school fees for their children.†

Strongly agree	34	10.5%
Agree	108	33.3%
Don't know/No opinion	4	1.2%
Disagree	62	19.1%
Strongly disagree	115	35.5%
Blank	1	0.3%
TOTAL	324	100.0%

Q: *During the last ten years has your congregation engaged in any of the*
following activities?

Helped in voter registration drive

Yes	1326	67.8%
No	255	13.0%
Blank	375	19.2%
TOTAL	1956	100.0%

TABLE A.5 *Continued*

Given rides to the election polls

Yes	1013	51.8%
No	582	29.8%
Blank	361	18.5%
TOTAL	1956	100.0%

Handed out campaign materials

Yes	487	24.9%
No	1081	55.3%
Blank	388	19.8%
TOTAL	1956	100.0%

Advocated on behalf of a ballot issue, proposition, or referendum

Yes	432	22.1%
No	1129	57.7%
Blank	398	20.3%
TOTAL	1956	100.0%

Participated in protest rallies

Yes	256	13.1%
No	1289	65.9%
Blank	411	21.0%
TOTAL	1956	100.0%

Q: During the last ten years, has your congregation been directly involved with any of the following as part of their congregational mission?

Public school policies

Yes	813	41.65%
No	346	17.7%
Blank	797	40.7%
TOTAL	1956	100.0%

Public welfare policies

Yes	533	27.2%
No	628	32.1%
Blank	795	40.6%
TOTAL	1956	100.0%

TABLE A.5 *Continued*

Affirmative action policies		
Yes	473	24.2%
No	678	34.7%
Blank	805	41.2%
TOTAL	1956	100.0%
Civil rights policies		
Yes	608	31.1%
No	553	28.3%
Blank	795	40.6%
TOTAL	1956	100.0%
Criminal justice policies		
Yes	452	23.1%
No	698	35.7%
Blank	806	41.2%
TOTAL	1956	100.0%
Government economic development policies		
Yes	388	19.8%
No	764	39.1%
Blank	804	41.1%
TOTAL	1956	100.0%
Social rights and empowerment of women		
Yes	343	17.5%
No	807	41.3%
Blank	806	41.2%
TOTAL	1956	100.0%
U.S. policies related to Africa		
Yes	264	13.5%
No	877	44.8%
Blank	815	41.7%
TOTAL	1956	100.0%

TABLE A.5 *Continued*

U.S. policies related to the Caribbean or Latin America		
Yes	108	5.5%
No	1030	52.7%
Blank	818	41.8%
TOTAL	1956	100.0%

*Respondents answering this question are from the 973 who indicated involvement with civic or political organizations.

†Follow-up question

CONTRIBUTORS

Lewis Baldwin is professor of religious studies at Vanderbilt University

Allison Calhoun-Brown is associate professor of political science at Georgia State University

David D. Daniels III is associate professor of church history at McCormick Theological Seminary

Walter Earl Fluker is executive director of the Leadership Center and Professor of Religious Studies at Morehouse College

C. R. D. Halisi is the chair of the pan-African studies program and professor of political science at California State University at Los Angeles

David Howard-Pitney is professor of history at De Anza College

Michael Leo Owens is assistant professor of political science at The Pennsylvania State University

Samuel Roberts is Evans Professor of Theology and Ethics at Union Theological Seminary-Presbyterian School of Christian Education

David Ryden is assistant professor of political science at Hope College

Corwin Smidt is executive director of the Paul B. Henry Institute for the Study of Christianity and Politics, and professor of political science at Calvin College

R. Drew Smith is director of the Public Influences of African-American Churches Project, and scholar-in-residence at the Leadership Center at Morehouse College.

INDEX

R. Drew Smith is the director and principal investigator for
the Public Influences of African-American Churches Project.
He is a scholar-in-residence at the Leadership Center
at Morehouse College.

Library of Congress Cataloging-in-Publication Data
New day begun: African American churches and civic culture
in post-civil rights America / R. Drew Smith, editor.
p. cm.
Includes index.
ISBN 0-8223-3131-4 (cloth: alk. paper)
1. African American churches—History—20th century.
2. Christianity and politics—United States—History—
20th century. I. Smith, R. Drew.
BR563.N4 P83 2003
277.3′0089′96073—dc21 2002152634

277.3008
S6571

LINCOLN CHRISTIAN COLLEGE AND SEMINARY   108199

3 4711 00191 0266